# REIMAGINE
# CHURCH

**CLARIFY THE WIN, ESCAPE BUSYNESS
AND FULFILL YOUR TRUE PURPOSE.**

The totally doable, nuts and bolts essentials of
reproducing leaders, disciples and community.

Nic Harding
© Copyright 2018 by Nic Harding

For more info or to find out about bulk discounts:
www.missiopublishing.com
©2018 Missio Publishing
published by Missio Publishing

ISBN 978-164370087-8

missiopublishing.com

## ACKNOWLEDGEMENTS

I'd like to thank Mike Breen, Paul Maconochie, Rich Robinson and Caesar Kalinowski for the significant impact they have all had on my thinking and practices over these last 10 years. Their ideas and encouragement have been highly formational on my journey around the areas of community, mission and discipleship.

Thanks to Frontline Church[1] who have continued to support me in many, many ways since I handed on the senior leadership role to John Harding in 2015.

Thanks to Paul Briers for the delightful arty diagrams

Thanks to Jennie Taylor my long suffering PA / Operations Manager for masterminding the whole project and keeping me sane in the process.

Thanks to the Kairos Connexion family and especially for the hub leaders and others who gave me specific input to the first draft.

Thanks to Caesar and Tina Kalinowski, and Missio Publishing for believing in this book.

My thanks of course also go to my wonderful wife Jenny, who continues to put up with, and encourage me in my quest to find the church that Jesus died for and is coming back for, and to my missional community who knowingly or unknowingly have been my test bed for many of my ideas and innovations.

## DEDICATION

I dedicate this book to all those leaders who are 'looking for a city whose architect and builder is God'. And in particular for those who are convinced that the church in its decentralised scattered form is critical to the hope of God filling the earth with His glory, and Jesus returning for his bride. Don't give up!

I also dedicate it to every 'ordinary' believer who wants to live a life of significance and influence as a missionary disciple in their world.

## ENDORSEMENTS

*"It is rare when a leader can effectively synthesize essential tools and practices from across years of experience. It takes a true practitioner and student of discipleship like Nic Harding to combine the value found in this book. His own life and knowledge have combined here to give us the "what", the "why" and the "how" of missional discipleship."*

**Caesar Kalinowski,** missional strategist and author of the Gospel Primer, Transformed, Small is Big Slow is Fast, and Bigger Gospel.

*"Reimagine church is a timely book for anyone who is dissatisfied with church life based solely around Sunday services and midweek programmes, and is looking for an authentic model of how to learn to imitate Jesus in a 21st century context. Nic writes from years of experience and knowledge of how to build authentic communities of missionary disciples who are able to share life together as well as to gather in larger numbers to worship corporately. He deals with both the inner journey of heart change that is necessary and the practical details of what to do to see breakthrough. I am sure that this book will be life changing for those who are hungry for more."*

**Paul Maconochie,** 3DM Team Leader: USA and Canada

*"Reimagine church is a great reminder of the purpose of the Church! Packed full of wisdom, this is a playbook for anyone who wants to raise up an army of people who can truly represent Jesus and extend his kingdom on earth"*

**Paul Harcourt,** National Leader of New Wine England. Vicar of All Saints Woodford Wells

*"As a leader of a local church seeking to develop missionary disciples in Missional Communities the wisdom and insight that Nic brings from his passion and experience is invaluable to me. He provides not just*

*encouragement but practical tools to help me keep intentional and focused so that I am now closer to reaching this goal."*

**Andy Glover,** Team Leader of Fresh Streams Network UK, and Team Leader of HBC Chester

*"Nic Harding is a disciple who leads, and a leader who multiplies. Having seen him up close, I would thoroughly recommend his life and ministry. In this book, he helps us take a systematic and structured look at both disciple-making and leadership development in a new light. Nic encourages us see that missional discipleship is not just an activity or job description, but a call to embody the message with your lifestyle, and apprentice others in the way of Jesus. It is a timely challenge for the moment that we find ourselves in as the church. I would encourage you not only to read the book, but take it on and live out the principles found in the pages."*

**Rich Robinson,** Founder of 3dm Europe. Director of Catalyse Change. Leader of 5QCollective

*"My experience of Nic's input is that he brings an invaluable blend of personal story and depth of Bible teaching combined with wisdom and practical action. I am delighted that what I've heard him teach at our church and received personally is now available to many more people in this book. Read and enjoy putting into practise what you learn as you follow Jesus."*

**Anne Maclaurin,** Vicar of St. Barnabas Church, Cambridge

# CONTENTS

# INTRODUCTION

## IT'S TIME TO REIMAGINE CHURCH

I truly believe the church is at a great kairos moment – a moment where the kingdom of God is breaking in, a moment of revelation about what it is called to be and do, a moment of hearing the voice of God for our generation, a moment of decision. What will we do? Will we continue to do 'business as usual', hoping that more of the same will give different results? This was Einstein's definition of insanity!

The dictionary definition of kairos is 'a propitious moment for decision or action'. If the church fails to make crucial decisions about who it wants to be or what it wants to do, and fails to take action according to a renewed identity and calling, it will continue on its road to irrelevance at best, or at worst, extinction. It's time to reimagine church!

Some may say that the argument for missional church has already been successfully made over the last twenty years, with a plethora of books and new organisations promoting it. However, missional practice is still a long way behind, and our understanding of what it means to be missional is probably still stuck in old models of church that urgently need reforming. It's time to reimagine church!

Most churches that consider themselves to be missional are still working on an attractional model that places the Sunday service, combined with social action projects, and Alpha or equivalent, squarely at the centre of their strategy. This is clearly a positive move away from churches simply existing for the sake of their members. However, I'd like to suggest that to truly fulfil Archbishop William Temple's famous quote, 'The church is the only organisation that exists for the sake of its non-members', we need a much greater rethink and change of practice than has been embraced thus far. It's time to reimagine church!

**Clarify the win.** We've been building church in much the same way for so many decades. We've run programmes, services, projects and missions. We've built buildings, run conferences, and released our preaching podcasts. But have we really clarified the win? Do we know what we are aiming for? Do we know how to align all the various aspects of church life with the win? Are our members and volunteers working towards the same goal? What would it look like if we really achieved the thing that is most on the heart of God? What if we realised that the win was not in getting people to behave in the way we thought Christians ought to behave, or in filling our churches on a Sunday, or in getting enough volunteers to run all our programmes?

What if we understood that the win is found in simply enjoying the rich, full life in community that God has won for us through Christ? What if we discovered that the win was in living compellingly attractive lives in the context of His family, inviting others to join us, and then watching them do the same for others? What if we found that the win was in reproducing disciples and disciple-makers simply by living like that? And what if, as a result, we began to see churches grow and multiply, towns and cities be saturated with the gospel, and God's glory fill the earth? It would be a massive win. The win we are after needs ultimately to produce the bride that Jesus is coming back for and the family that God intends to spend eternity with. I hope this book will release faith in your heart for that to happen, and impart some practical steps towards achieving it.

**Escape busyness.** This amazing life that we have been given should not lead to ever more busy lives, increasingly pulling us away from those who don't know Christ, from our family, or from our passions. It was Jesus who said 'my yoke is easy, my burden is light' (Matthew 11:30). For many of us caught up in the treadmill of Church activity, that burden is no lightweight matter. We've lost sight of the abundant life he offers us. Excessive stress-inducing busyness is a sure sign that we have got something badly wrong. It's a litmus test of our understanding of the win. Joy is a hallmark of getting this right.

**Fulfil your true purpose.** As we clarify the win, and in doing so escape busyness, we will surely begin to find our true north, the purpose for which we were made. We will discover how our unique blend of gifts, personality, calling, relationships, and experience will be used by God to fulfil his disciple-making purpose for our lives. It was the Psalmist David who said 'the Lord will fulfil his purpose for me' (Psalm 138:8 ESV). As we work this out together the result will be amazing. It will fulfil our deepest desires and longings. It will be the joy filled life.

## THE HOPE OF RENEWAL AND REVIVAL

A misguided hope is that the next wave of renewal will do the trick. In other words, with enough of the supernatural taking place in terms of healings and miracles, the world will come rushing to our doors to find out the source of our great experiences and power. Hear me right: I long for the supernatural to break in in greater measure as much as anyone, and, like you, I am aware of many individuals who have come to Christ because of just such a healing or miracle. Having lived through at least four waves of renewal – the charismatic wave of the '70s, the Wimber wave of the '80s, the Toronto wave of the '90s and now the Bethel version of those in the '00s and '10s – I can confidently say that they have not resulted in widespread turning of unsaved people to Christ, at least not in the numbers we are hoping and praying for.

So do we abandon having great 'presence of God' filled Sunday worship services, social action projects or using Alpha or Christianity Explored courses? No! Far from it. We need to continue to do the stuff that we know builds up the body of Christ and gives hope to those who are seeking him. We need to continue to pray for and practise those things that we know lead to an increase in the supernatural. **But we do need to change** our priorities and practices so that every person in our churches becomes a missionary disciple. We need this so that all of our scattered / decentralised structures foster a culture of discipleship that leads to disciples making disciples. We need it so that we have small and mid-sized groups that are capable of growth and multiplication. It's a radical shift in the way we deploy our leadership and staff time, in the way we spend our money, in the way we as leaders model the life we expect of our church members, and in the messages that we give from our communication platforms – real and virtual. We will unpack this through the book.

This will not be easy because our mindsets about church are deeply engrained through our past experience, by the models we see around us, and the churches that are feted as the success stories in our Western culture. But I believe we need to return to the principles and many of the practices that were at the heart of the explosive expansion of the early church in its first 300 years, and are at the heart of many of the amazing disciple-making movements in developing nations today.

More of the same won't deliver on our hopes and aspirations. **A fundamental re-engineering of our DNA is required.** It's time to reimagine church!

So, there is a need not only to review our way of being and doing church to fulfil this privileged missional call, but also to find practical ways of supporting churches, leaders and members to truly live the missional life – the most fulfilled and rewarding life imaginable! This book will encourage and equip you to discover this life.

The call to be missional church, or as some would say, to build an apostolic movement, is rooted in two key elements. Firstly, in our individual acceptance that we are each called to be missionaries in our daily lives. We are all sent ones. We are all his representatives, his ambassadors. We are all called to 'go and make disciples' (Matthew 28:19), whether that is across the road, across the office, across the city or across the world. And secondly, that as churches, we understand that our attempt to be missional through a myriad of programmes, projects and events will not get the job done. Rather we need to fundamentally re-imagine, re-create and rebuild church around its missionary call and priority.

We need a fundamental redesign of church, *such that integrated mission and discipleship becomes the defining paradigm,* a yardstick by which all use of human, financial and physical resources, and all proposals, activities, and plans are measured. In fact understanding the win will help us start to measure the right things. In practice, this will require reapportioning the balance of resource allocation that goes into maintaining our Sunday services, structures and programmes versus those which help to develop mission and discipleship as a church. Some radical reassessment will be needed!

In a recent issue of Premier Christianity Magasine[2] (May 2018), in an article about megachurches, Jeff Vines, pastor of Christ's Church of the Valley (8,000 strong) in San Dimas, California admits, "The reality is, we megachurches don't do discipleship well. And it's because of the time and energy we spend on the big event every weekend. And the money we spend, it's astronomical."

Since coming out of full time general practice and into church leadership in 1986, the rediscovery and recovery of missional church has been my pursuit. For over thirty years, I have consistently looked for places where God seems to be working in new ways. I have travelled to many parts of the world to witness first-hand the different expressions of churches that are growing. I have experimented with ways of being and doing church in an attempt to find the church leader's holy grail of multiplication. I know I am not at the end of that journey, but I have come to some conclusions about how the church is most likely to fulfil the great commission and prepare itself for Christ's return. I hope these observations and experiences will help you to grapple with the same issues.

Aesop, the Greek storyteller, said in his Fables 'When all is said and done, more is said than done'. And because I know that words are easy, but real change is hard won and often bloody, I pray that God will equip you and protect you in the quest to become the church that Jesus died for and is coming back for.

In order to help you apply the content of this book into your particular context (both personally and corporately), I've added a number of 'pause' moments in which I encourage you to 'try this'. The idea is that you can spend time reflecting on, praying into, journaling about, or discussing with a friend or colleague particular aspects of the book. There will be times when it is clear that you want to take some kind of action in response to your reflection. On those occasions, allow me to encourage you to find someone to be accountable to for seeing through what you believe God wants you to do. So …

## TRY THIS

Do a quick calculation in your head. Have a guess at how much of your church's staff time, budget and other resources are used to maintain your Sunday services and social action projects, compared with the amount that is used to equip, support and release your members to become missionary disciples, sent into the world in which they live, work and play, to make disciples who make disciples.

(The words *missionary* and *apostle* are the same word; both meaning *sent one*. One is from the Latin, and the other from the Greek. I may use either or both in the rest of this book, but will probably mainly use *missionary* or *missional*, as the word apostle or apostolic is widely misunderstood and carries too many assumptions and preconceptions.)

## BY WAY OF CONTEXT

Since 2008, I have been involved as a participating church leader in the missional 3DM movement in the UK, and latterly in leading the England and Wales expression of 3DM, Kairos Connexion (Kx)[3]. This has further developed my understanding and conviction of what it will take to truly build apostolic movement and missional church.

For any who are wondering about the name Kairos Connexion, it is pretty simple. As a movement we depend on the God who speaks. He speaks mainly by creating kairos moments (more of this later) and He works through the three key relationships (i.e. connections / connexions) or dimensions of Up, In and Out. The following picture should speak for itself.

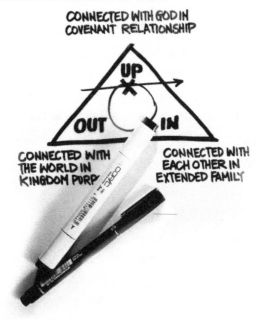

CONNECTED WITH GOD IN
COVENANT RELATIONSHIP

UP

OUT    IN

CONNECTED WITH
THE WORLD IN
KINGDOM PURP

CONNECTED WITH
EACH OTHER IN
EXTENDED FAMILY

So, Kairos Connexion at its heart embraces both the Learning Circle and the Triangle, (which I explore in chapter four). Both these tools (rooted in 3DM Lifeshapes[4]) are foundational to the way we work. They also connect us to the two strands of the Bible's DNA: Covenant and Kingdom[5]. All these provide a major undergirding to the missional movement we are part of. Kairos speaks of the breaking in of God's kingdom, and Connexion speaks of the covenant relationships through which we operate.

## TRY THIS

Take a moment with God and ask Him, 'What is the work you have given me to do? What would it look like to have completed that work?' Turn your answers into a prayer.

## AMBASSADORS

We are His ambassadors, the highest representatives of one nation or kingdom in another. The metaphor works well for us as His apostolic people, His sent ones, those sent as citizens of the kingdom of heaven (Philippians 3:20) to re-present the king of love to a lost and hurting world. Our true identity is as citizens of the kingdom of heaven; we are first and foremost 'born from above' (John 3:3 MSG), born of heavenly stuff. We happen to be living on earth but that is not our home. It's not our primary nationality or the basis of our identity.

Paul uses the term ambassador and specifically links it to our role in helping people to be reconciled to God).

> *We are therefore Christ's ambassadors, as though God were making his appeal through us. We implore you on Christ's behalf: Be reconciled to God.*
> *2 Corinthians 5:20*

In 1973, at the age of 19, I spent a summer with Youth with a Mission (YWAM), first in Paris and then in Amsterdam, building community, being discipled, and reaching out to unsuspecting people loitering on the streets of those cities. I can't say our methods of evangelism were particularly sophisticated, or even especially effective, but I can say that the experience changed me forever.

It was the first time I had seen and experienced church as a community of believers focused around the call to reach the last, the least and the lost. We were in many ways an extended family on mission.

What followed was an intense desire to see all church through that lens, the lens of living as a family on mission. Jenny, my now wife, had also had a life-changing encounter with YWAM that summer. Our first experience after that was of joining a small house church on a council estate on the edge of Bristol. We watched and participated in that church growing from twelve in a front room to 700 over the next eighteen years. I am forever grateful for the opportunities those in leadership gave me to grow into my own calling during that time, as I gradually left my medical general practice to take larger roles on the staff body of the church. One significant responsibility I took was in starting and running an evangelistic training team in the hope that that would infect the life of the church with missionary zeal.

Eventually the urge to plant a church completely shaped by the missional priority, led my wife and me, along with ten others and all our children, to move north to the Promised Land we know as Liverpool! We didn't have a name for the church initially so just referred to it as 'Church with a mission'. Once again, we started with twelve adults in our front room and watched the Lord grow the church, along with my wonderful co-pastor Dave Connolly, to about 1000 adults and kids over the next twenty years. These two church experiences have fundamentally shaped my convictions about church – both from the things that the Lord has blessed, and probably more so from the mistakes we have made.

Another conviction emerged from our time with both YWAM and the early house church movement. It was the conviction that the church Jesus is coming back for may not be the finished article, or the church triumphant, as some might call it, but it would be a church that was able to complete the great commission, bringing the gospel to every creature (Mark 16:15) and making disciples of all nations (Matthew 28:19).

As such, it would be an amazing church full of purity, zeal and wisdom; a bride fit for the returning bridegroom; a family of incredible inclusion in its mission; a temple full of the Spirit's power and presence; and a body in which every member played its part, with a fresh emergence of the fivefold gifts of Ephesians 4:11. It would be a church that would, as the apostle Paul describes it,

*come to such unity in our faith and knowledge of God's Son that we will
be mature in the Lord, measuring up to the full and complete standard
of Christ. Ephesians 4:13 NLT*

The church may never achieve structural unity this side of heaven, but it could be
'united in spirit and intent on one purpose' (Philippians 2:2 NASB), a sign to the
groaning creation that its release from bondage to decay is imminent (Romans
8:19-22), and a church therefore able to fulfil God's deepest longing for planet
earth.

This conviction has become my rallying cry as I speak to churches and leaders
around the UK, **'Let's be the church that Jesus died for and is coming back
for!'** I didn't sign up for any less. Did you?


## TRY THIS

Pause for a moment and reflect on your hopes and dreams for the church. Try
and separate yourself for a moment from the typical model of church you are part
of, or from the disappointments of recent years, to consider what Jesus might be
hoping for from His church.


## THE JOURNEY OF THIS BOOK

There are three phrases / three types fillings that have come to mind in describing
the journey of this book. While Section one is about Foundations, in section two
we'll start to look at the nuts and bolts of *Filling Our Churches With Missionary
Disciples*. Section three will draw this to a conclusion, looking at *'filling our places
with the gospel'*, and finally *'filling the nations with his glory'*. These three phrases
capture something of my excitement about this journey and have become the
emotional driver for writing the book.

Let's take these three fillings one at a time.

## 1. FILLING OUR CHURCHES WITH MISSIONARY DISCIPLES

There is in fact no other kind of disciple. If we do not see our discipleship as rooted in the call to be missionaries, then we are missing the key motivation to our discipleship. We are disciples called to make disciples (Matthew 28:20). We are not all evangelists, but we are all 'sent ones' – we are all witnesses (Acts 1:8). Jesus said, 'As the Father has sent me, I am sending you' (John 20:21).

We use the phrase 'missional discipleship', or 'missionary disciples', because we have to constantly remind ourselves that the call to 'come and follow' is also the call to 'go and make'. The missionary imperative is so easily lost. We quickly default to a pastoral or maturity mindset when we think about discipleship. That's why we have to add the adjective **missional** or **missionary** to remind us of the true nature of a disciple. Hopefully we will not have to do so forever.

As I have already mentioned, the family network of leaders and churches I direct is called Kairos Connexion, and its strapline is 'raising missionary disciples'. We need to commit ourselves to raising missionary disciples, as I like to say, **'because the world needs the church to be different'**. More of the same isn't going to make the difference. We know the local church is meant to change the world. I'm fully committed to the idea that the local church is the hope of the world. But how? It doesn't seem like it's going to happen any time soon. Perhaps it's because we don't see church, or practise church as Jesus and the early church saw it or practised it. Perhaps the consumer-based, convenience-orientated, Sunday-centric way of being church isn't how God intended His Son's bride to operate. Perhaps we are intended to be more like the first disciples and the early church! Perhaps we are called to be missionary disciples where we live, work and play, 24/7. What do you think?

## TRY THIS

When you think of the word disciple what is the first thought that comes into your head?

As we consider the journey of an emerging Christ-follower, we see the need for them to progress from **member**, one who is simply enjoying their connection to the body, to become a **missionary**. From those who are just delighted to find a place of belonging in a new family with a new identity, to those who see the need to build their own 'families on mission', their own missional households, with missional rhythms. The second section of this book will deal with some of the equipping process and key tools that enable this to happen.

We will also look at how those who have embraced the missionary lifestyle grow to become **multipliers**, i.e. those who help others to do the same. We will explore ways and tools that enable this to happen as well. This will reflect some of the key training that Kairos Connexion offers to churches and leaders.

## 2. FILLING OUR PLACES WITH THE GOSPEL

In the final section, we will explore how churches full of missionary disciples can work together to fill their neighbourhoods and workplaces with gospel-fluent, gospel-confident disciples. How churches can cooperate to flood whole towns and cities with the gospel. How this nation can be fully evangelised once again. How this generation can complete the work God gave them to do. How our places can see a mighty harvest and wonderful transformation take place.

Jesus said to the Father in the garden of Gethsemane, 'I have brought you glory on earth by finishing the work you gave me to do' (John 17:4). Imagine if we were able to say the same at the end of our lives. Paul said at the end of his life, 'From Jerusalem all the way around to Illyricum [Albania], I have fully proclaimed the gospel of Christ' (Romans 15:19). He too, it seems, had completed the work the Father gave him to do.

What would it look like for us collectively as the body of Christ in our towns and cities to 'complete the work the Father gave us to do'?

## TRY THIS

Just let your mind ponder the question above for a moment – what could that look like?

If you are part of a town or city-wide group of leaders, why not ask that question of each other and the Lord.

## 3. FILLING THE EARTH WITH HIS GLORY

In Numbers 14:21, after Moses has once again interceded for the rebellious Israelites, God agrees to pardon them and then says, 'as I live, all the earth will be filled with the glory of the Lord' (NASB). This promise is repeated by the prophet Habakkuk in Habakkuk 2:14.

What would Moses have understood by this statement? In Exodus 33:18, Moses asks to see God's glory. God's reply is interesting.

> 'I myself will make all my goodness pass before you and I will proclaim
> the name of the LORD before you. I will be gracious and will show
> compassion on whom I will show compassion.' Exodus 33:19 (NASB)

God's glory is His goodness, His grace, His compassion, and the proclamation of His name. As God's people, we are the agents of His goodness, grace, compassion and gospel proclamation in the world today. Maybe, just maybe, as we fill our churches with missionary disciples, fill our places with the gospel, we will also be filling the earth with His glory! How thrilling to be part of that filling of the earth with His glory, as the church begins to, 'measure up to the full and complete standard of Christ' (Ephesians 4:13 NLT).

And then Jesus returns. Hallelujah!

'Filling' is also a word key to understanding God's bigger purpose, not just filling the earth with His glory, but also filling the church with Christ. Much of the excitement around church in our day is focused on the big flashy **gathered, centralised** models. I love the big, the exciting, the spectacle, the crowds, the manifest presence of God, and the worship that can be experienced in big gathered church. However, I fear for us if that is all we have. Unless we have an equally, or perhaps more highly developed scattered church, where the body of Christ is mobilised to be the church in its **decentralised** expression, then we will fail to be the church that Jesus died for and is coming back for. We will fail to rediscover the dynamic of the church that for its first 300 years rocked the Roman Empire. It grew from 120 people in the upper room to 50% of the Empire by the time Constantine was so-say converted in AD 312[6].

Sadly, Christianity was then legalised, and eventually became the official religion of the Empire, which was the beginning of its decline. It changed from a radical, household-based, grass roots, multiplying movement, to one where priests, ornate buildings, state patronage, ritual and formality became the norm. In fact, it not only became highly centralised but consumerist and attractional (think about the money spent on beautifying their buildings). Are we in danger of the same as we pour money into our central facilities and, in the name of excellence, focus on the aesthetic experience of those who come?

Filling the earth with His glory is, I believe, a parallel journey to filling the church with Christ. Ephesians 4:11-13 says this:

> So Christ himself gave the apostles, the prophets, the evangelists, the pastors and teachers, to equip his people for works of service, so that the body of Christ may be built up until we all reach unity in the faith and in the knowledge of the Son of God and become mature, attaining to the whole measure of the fullness of Christ.

As we harness the power of the fivefold ministry gifts, graced to each one of us, (Ephesians 4:7) to equip the saints, filling the church with missionary disciples, then we will see the long-awaited maturing of the body. In doing so, we will see the church reflect and represent the fullness of Christ. Wow!

That little word, until, is also found in Acts 3:21: 'Christ, whom heaven must receive until the period of the restoration of all things'. It is also implied in Matthew 24:14:

> And this gospel of the kingdom will be preached in the whole world as a testimony to all nations, and then the end will come.

This is key to understanding the process we are in right now, preparing for and anticipating Christ's return. Ultimately, **it is our eschatology that defines our ecclesiology**. What we understand the Spirit of God to be doing today is a reflection of what we understand will happen before Christ returns, and upon what that return is conditional. We'll come back to this later on in section three.

So hopefully that explains where I am coming from with this book, and where I am trying to go.

Just a further note on the structure of the book. You will notice that at the beginning of each chapter or section, I will pose a couple of **questions**. These, I believe, are common questions that reflect some of our concerns, fears or frustrations about church. I will then go on to try and answer those questions in specific ways.

At the end of each chapter I will attempt to highlight key concepts, practices or tools which, I believe, fulfil the criteria of being simple, sticky, and reproducible. Simple enough for anyone to understand, sticky enough to be memorable, and easily passed on to others, i.e. reproducible.

## SIMPLE. STICKY. REPRODUCIBLE

- The Church is intended to be an extended family on mission

- The scattered, decentralised expressions of church need to be every bit as powerful as its centralised, Sunday based expressions

# SECTION 1

## Foundations:
## Building Something That Lasts

## INTRODUCTION

Foundations are important. Without them anything built above ground level is liable to subsidence and collapse. As we were watching the new Liverpool city centre shopping complex, Liverpool 1, being built during 2007, we were amazed how long was spent on creating really deep foundations. It seemed like they took forever! However once they were complete, the rest of the buildings seem to go up incredibly quickly. How important it is to get the foundations right. Time taken here will always be well spent.

I've highlighted three specific foundations; the foundation of identity – being before doing. The foundation of prayer - praying before doing. And the foundation of gospel demonstration – doing before speaking. The foundations of identity and prayer are so vital to success, yet often overlooked. The lack of either will tend to lead us to striving to make something happen in our own strength, and ultimately lead to burnout, or failure, or both. We will look at these in chapters 1 and 2. The foundation of gospel demonstration is key to credibility and compassion, but is on its own insufficient. We will look at how this works in chapter 3.

# 1

# BEING BEFORE DOING

**Questions:** Do we feel frustrated and exhausted by the work we do? Are we always feeling that we aren't quite meeting the mark in the missional journey?

## IDENTITY

Few of us would disagree that the call to be ambassadors, rooted in 2 Corinthians 5:20, is a core part of our identity. The scripture says 'we are..', 'not we do..'

> We are therefore Christ's ambassadors, as though God were making his appeal through us. We implore you on Christ's behalf: Be reconciled to God.

For many of us, however, taking on our identity as Christ's ambassadors isn't how we intuitively respond to this verse. When we read this Scripture, unless we are hard wired as a thick-skinned, card-carrying evangelist, we usually have a rather different response. It will probably look like one of the following:

> 'I know this is what I'm meant to be, but if I'm honest it feels like a heavy burden, one for which I feel pretty inadequate and ill-equipped.'

*'I must try harder to be His ambassador. My standing with God depends on being obedient to this call. If I don't act as His ambassador, many people will go to hell without having the chance to follow Jesus.'*

Or if you are that full-bloodied evangelist:

*'I'm actually doing pretty well at this ambassador stuff; it's a shame others are so fearful and disobedient.'*

So as church leaders we have a problem. How can we motivate and mobilise our members to act like ambassadors?

The answer to the question is in 2 Corinthians 5. The passage starts with the truth that we are new creations in Christ (v. 17), a verse that we often skip over through familiarity, but this is the key to everything. We are not what we were. We are new. We have a new identity in Christ as sons and daughters of our Heavenly Father, as those who have been forgiven and set free, as those who now have a new name, a new destiny, and a new nature.

Identity is one of the biggest issues of our day. 'Who am I?' 'What makes me who I am?' 'Who determines my identity?' 'Where do I belong?' 'Are there any solid points of reference to answer these questions?' Thankfully, the Bible does give us clear and solid ground on which to build our unique and precious identities.

So where does this new identity come from? From God himself. For the Bible tells us that we are created, re-created, and reborn **in His image**. So understanding who He is, the nature of the great iAm, is central to understanding how we get to live as this new family and operate in this new kingdom as ambassadors.

## AMBASSADORS

Indeed, as we understand God to be the great reconciler (v. 19) we understand ourselves also as reconcilers, because we are created in His image. We get to do this reconciling stuff. It's part of our new nature, not some great burden put on us by a God who wants to make our life miserable. Instead it's the greatest privilege to be representing Christ as the reconciling agent at work in the world.

**It's simply being who we have become** – from our original design, and through our rebirth into His family.

The word *ambassador* is originally from the Latin *ambactus* which means a slave or servant.

In contrast, take a look at the Chambers dictionary definition:

Ambassador

1.  A diplomat or the highest rank, sent by one sovereign or state to another as a permanent representative

2.  A messenger or agent

And here we have the tension of this great truth. We are of the highest rank. What else could we be as sons and daughters of The Most High God? We can stand in the marketplace with our heads held high, fearing no one, speaking boldly the words of entreaty and invitation to a lost humanity. However, as well as sons we are also servants.

In recognising the Lordship of Christ, we freely offer ourselves to Him, to serve Him unconditionally. Paul describes Himself as a bondslave, one who has voluntarily, out of love, surrendered all his rights to His master. We offer ourselves as His servants. We commit ourselves to His kingdom purpose.

## BEING BEFORE DOING

And so we are called to 'be' before we 'do'. All that we do for Christ comes out of our identity, our being. This discovery of 'being before doing' affects every area of life and service to God. Years ago I had a major encounter with God. For years I had been troubled by self-esteem issues to do with being 'vertically challenged' (short). It somehow made me feel less than others. I'm sure that some of my drive as a leader was to gain some self-esteem from my leadership role. Not very healthy. It's what the books describe as 'The Napoleon complex'! Then one day God spoke to me in the midst of worship and showed me the self-hatred that was at the heart of this. In a moment, as others simply prayed over me and declared truth over me, I was set free and have never looked back. I hardly ever even think about my height these days ... which is just as well, as with advancing years I'm actually shrinking!

Much has been taught on identity over the years, for example from the teaching of Neil Anderson and his books *Victory over the Darkness* and *Steps to Freedom in Christ*.[7] However, not a great deal has been taught about that teaching's specific relevance to the missional movement, in particular in tackling some of that 'drivenness' that often goes alongside it.

In any analysis of the missional church movement, it is impossible to avoid the impression that it is led by high-octane, often big personality, extrovert apostolic characters. As such, they are very much activists, and people who 'make things happen'. For those who may be more reflective or not gifted apostolically, this can be translated into pressure to perform, or the call to embark on a lifestyle that will 'take away your life as you know it', and ultimately lead to burnout. I confess to having contributed to that stress in others in our own church over the years, even though I don't fit that typical description of an apostle.

I'm grateful to Caesar Kalinowski for many of these ideas about identity, and want to ensure that any discussion of the missional movement is founded firmly on the sense of identity and 'being', not on the duty/obligation/guilt basis that is often preached either explicitly or by implication.

What do I mean? Simply that when we know who we are, and live out of that new identity, it creates a completely different motivation for the kind of actions and lifestyle that the great commission inspires. Even the word commission, rather than commandment, is imbued with privilege rather than pressure. 'Got to' becomes 'Get to'. What a difference a vowel makes.

## GOT TO → GET TO

Identity comes first, 'created in His image'. Family comes second; 'he created them male and female'. Authority comes third, the commission 'to be fruitful and multiply, and to rule over the earth', as His ambassadors (Genesis 1:27-28).

## MADE IN HIS IMAGE

Our identity is always a reflection of who God is, who Jesus reveals God to be. Because we are created in His image we can say that we are His sons and daughters, co-heirs with Christ. We are creative and generative, capable of great ideas and innovations. We are designed for community and to be members of His family. We are loving and patient just as God is. We are holy and righteous like our Father. We are passionate and compassionate. We are forgiving and gracious. And so the list goes on.

When we realize what is true about God, we start to understand what is now true about us, both in terms of what we are, but also in terms of what we are not. Tim Chester in his book *You Can Change*[8] summarizes many of God's attributes that directly affect our sense of identity in the simple "4G" statements below. Each one leads to a response that sets us free from wrong obligations and to be who we were created to be. He puts it like this:

- God is good – I don't need to look elsewhere (for comfort or satisfaction when things are stressful or sad).

- God is great – I don't need to be in control (leading to great freedom and peace in our calling).

- God is gracious – I don't need to prove myself (to God or others by my performance).

- God is glorious – I don't need to fear anyone (the awesome fear of The Lord, and desire to please Him totally preoccupies my thinking, leaving little room for concern about others' opinions).

These kinds of identity issues lead to a whole new way of viewing our calling and ourselves. Once we realize that our identity is that of an Ambassador, we start to see it as privilege not pressure. We see that we "get to" represent Him to the world. We haven't "got to"      anymore. It is liberating. And the only accountability is to live in the light of our new identity, not to live up to someone's idea of what we "should be" doing. It's time to abandon "should", "ought", and "must"' and embrace "identity", "privilege" and "authority". It's the divine "get to". I recommend Caesar Kalinowski's, Bigger Gospel, for further reading on this subject.[9]

## SATAN ATTACKS OUR IDENTITY

Satan knows just how important our identity is, which is why it was the very first thing he tried to deceive Adam and Eve about. The irony of the fall, of course, was that Satan was tempting Eve to consider eating the fruit of the tree so that she might become like God, the very thing that God had declared that she and Adam already were. No wonder that Satan is called the deceiver in Revelation 12:9 (ESV).

> The great dragon was hurled down – that ancient serpent called the devil,
> or Satan, who leads the whole world astray. He was hurled to the earth,
> and his angels with him.

Again, when he comes to Jesus in the desert, Satan challenges Jesus over the question of identity – "If you are the Son of God ..." (Luke 4:3). And so it is with us: Satan challenges our identity. He wants us to doubt who God has made us to be and what He calls us to do. Why? Because if he can dislodge our sense of who we are in the light of who God is, then he can push us into operating out of a false guilt, or false identity that is gained through the stuff we do, the things we are successful in, or the opinions and approval of others. This latter way of life is infinitely stressful and ultimately unsuccessful!

Jesus' temptation in the wilderness was specifically targeting His identity. But through that Satan was seeking to draw Jesus in to ungodly responses to the offer of food, power, and significance. By trying to undermine His identity, he hoped Jesus would become vulnerable to the temptations of appetite, ambition and approval (thanks to Mike Breen for this idea).[10]

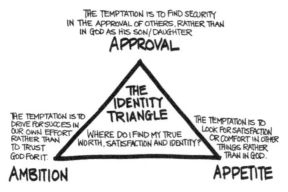

We find that most of us have points of vulnerability to one or more of the above. We may be tempted to find our satisfaction primarily in our physical appetites, be it food, alcohol, shopping, TV box sets, sex, or anything that takes the place of Jesus as our bread of life. We may be ambition-driven to succeed, leading to stress, burn out, and being pretty awful to live with (that's me). We may be tempted to look to others to give us our feelings of significance by seeking their approval. This may be in attention-seeking behavior, people pleasing (finding it very hard to say no), or even by staying in abusive relationships.

All of these temptations have little impact on us if we truly know who we are as sons and daughters of God – as those who are fulfilled by His provision and presence, given significance by our standing with God and our calling in His kingdom, and as those who, because of His love, are utterly secure in our knowledge of the Father's approval. Being sure of our identity is powerful and liberating.

When we map Tim Chester's 4Gs onto this identity triangle it looks a bit like this:

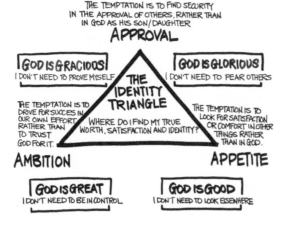

## TRY THIS

Look at the above triangle and think about which of the three As is your main area of weakness, your Achilles heel. Talk to a friend and figure out where in your identity or knowledge of God you need to grow.

All of this identity-based living is, of course, simply a reflection of God's amazing grace: unmerited favor, imputed righteousness, and the kindness of God. We are saved by grace. "For it is by grace you have been saved, through faith – and this is not from yourselves, it is the gift of God", (Ephesians 2:8). We are also exhorted by the Apostle Paul to continue as we have started, to live from this same grace and not revert to striving, to working from our own strength, or our own wisdom, "Therefore as you have received Christ Jesus the Lord, so walk in Him" (Colossians 2:6 ESV).

I love this translation of the verse in the Amplified Bible:

> Therefore as you have received Christ Jesus the Lord, walk in [union with] Him [reflecting His character in the things you do and say—living lives that lead others away from sin],

Notice that phrase, "reflecting his character". It's all about identity: who we are in the light of who He is.

## TRANSFORMED BY GRACE

Frontline Church (the church that started in our front room in 1991, and which I am now a very happy part of as a regular church member) has as its tag line "transformed by grace". It's the heart of all that we aspire to be. This grace sets us free from the hidden drivers of our brokenness. None of us starts out on the Christian life sorted and whole. We all bring our brokenness, our weakness and our human frailties to our roles in leadership, wherever they may be worked out. Whether we are leading a church, a missional community, an outreach project, or are leading in the workplace, we all find ourselves reacting in ways we don't like. We hear ourselves saying things that are inconsistent with the people we want to be. We know our hearts have dark areas that have yet to be ... transformed by grace.

REIMAGINE CHURCH | 33

And so we all continue to grow into the forgiveness, freedom and fulfillment that the gospel offers, as we truly understand who we are in the light of God's grace, and how we now get to live in the light of that new, reborn identity.

It was a Tuesday morning. I had been over-committing myself to a punishing work schedule, and unwittingly starting once again to operate out of pressure to perform (fear of failure) and a desire to please people (need for approval). I woke up as normal and had a breakfast meeting at home. On arriving at the office, I started to feel odd. I felt inwardly shaky. I had difficulty concentrating and remembering what I had said or written a few minutes earlier. I was experiencing feelings of depersonalization and anxiety. It was a horrible feeling. It continued all day.

I was due to speak at a church that night and doubted I could do it. My preparation for it was weak at best. In the end, I asked my wonderful wife, Jenny, to come with me and help me deliver this talk, which she did. And somehow I got through the event.

The next day I woke feeling completely normal. I couldn't understand it. But as I reflected on the experience and talked to others, it was clear that God was putting a warning shot across my bows. It was what we call a major kairos moment, a moment when the kingdom was trying to break into my life (Mark 1:15). I had to take some drastic action.

As I prayed about it and processed the massive light bulb moment, I felt God telling me to address a number of issues. Firstly, there was the practical issue of over-committing. I cleared about a third of my commitments from my calendar. I'd never done that before; it was pretty scary. I also committed to creating margin in my calendar by working towards keeping two half days clear from any commitments; this took a year to achieve. He then showed me that I needed to work "smarter". This was to involve doing much less preparation for a talk, and a lot more trusting God for what to say when the time came. In the past as a church pastor, I had usually taken at least ten hours to prepare for a sermon. He was now telling me to aim for one hour!

One of the delightful discoveries in creating margin in my calendar, in which I was free to do things that weren't scheduled, was that I was frequently having different kinds of unexpected God-connections, either with Christians or non-Christians. I discovered that it's a whole lot easier to have divine appointments if the calendar isn't full!

The more significant change was an internal one, a mindset one, and a review of my motivations not methods.

God began to show me that I had subtly and unwittingly started to look to my performance and what others thought of me for my sense of identity, more than what He thought of me. I had to once again get to grips with two of the 4Gs:

- God is great – I don't need to be in control.
- God is gracious – I don't need to prove myself.

These revelations were life changing and have been the bedrock of my leadership practice since. I have experienced little stress, better sleep, and much greater freedom from that time. It's almost certainly made me easier to work with too!

We must ensure that these identity issues are dealt with, or we will at best perform well below our potential, or, at worst, burn out and quit. This is especially true when it comes to the missional movement, which is high on aspiration, inspiration, and perspiration. We have to truly believe that because of who God is, the following is true of us:

- We get to live as family on mission - the most fun and fulfilling way to live

- We get to reach out to, and find people of peace, as they are all around us; and He wants to lead us to them. People of peace are those who are open to the gospel and leaning in to relationship with us, Luke 10:1-9 describes the disciples being sent out on mission to towns and villages in Galilee. When they entered a village and preached the gospel, they would look for a home that would welcome them. When they gave their greeting of peace, 'shalom', the man of peace would welcome them in and offer them hospitality.

- We get to share our story because it's who we are, and what we are excited about

- We get to be courageous in talking about Jesus because we are created in the image of a courageous, fearless God, who also lives in us and fills our hearts and minds on a moment-by-moment basis

- We get to spiritually procreate as spiritual parents, to make disciples, because it is our privilege to invest in the lives of others, raising other spiritual sons and daughters

- We get to lay our lives down for the King who laid down His life for us. There is nothing we would rather do. It is reward in itself

I hope you can begin to see the difference between "got to" (supposed to) and "get to", or, as Caesar Kalinowski says, the differences between "do to be" and "be to do."[11] Identity precedes function. Understanding who we are leads to freedom and fruitfulness in every area of our lives and calling. So let's press on to discover what this calling is all about.

## DO TO BE ⟶ BE TO DO

## TRY THIS

Go back over the 4Gs. Think about which you most often need to be reminded of. Start a conversation with God about it. Is there someone else you want to draw into that conversation?

## SIMPLE. STICKY. REPRODUCIBLE

- Get to vs Got to
- The 4Gs

# 2

# PRAYING BEFORE DOING

**Questions:** Are we confident that our plans have sufficient undergirding in prayer? Are we sure that what we do is birthed and sustained by heavenly power?

## FOUNDATION OF PRAYER

Too many apostolic initiatives fail to stand the test of time. We can build kingdom enterprises in our own strength and energy. We can get people on board with our great visions and plans. We can wow them with our charismatic personalities. We can persuade them to join in with the latest initiative. But how many are still bearing fruit ten, twenty or thirty years later? If not, it may just be that they were never birthed from, built on, or sustained by prayer.

In chapter one we explored the importance of securing our sense of identity as a first foundation, "get to" rather than "got to", being before doing. When it comes to outworking the missional call, we need to build on prayer as a second vital foundation. This undergirding is especially vital for activists who tend to "do now" and "pray later". Prayer is a crucial foundation in the missional movement.

It was Wesley who said, *"God does nothing except in answer to prayer"*. This is all the more significant coming from someone who almost single-handedly started a missional movement that paved the way not only for a spiritual revival but also for the transformation of the UK in the late 1700s and 1800s. If ever there was an activist, it was Wesley. Some of the statistics regarding his ministry are remarkable.

It is said that he traveled thousands of miles on horseback to serve the emerging movement in the UK and the USA. In his biography of Wesley, Stephen Tomkins writes that he *"rode 250,000 miles, gave away 30,000 pounds, and preached more than 40,000 sermons."* [12]

Definitely an activist!

Yet Wesley would rise up at 4 a.m. every day to seek God for the first four hours of the day. In his later years Wesley was known to spend up to eight hours in prayer. How did he manage it? Well clearly discipline played a big part, but at the root of it, in my opinion, was a man completely obsessed with how loved he was; and it was the knowledge of that love he experienced as a child of God that enabled him to find the grace to create a life of such discipline.

Why do I think that? Well we know that John Wesley preached and taught extensively about grace. He organized Methodism around what he called "means of grace". His brother, Charles Wesley, (who led the Methodist movement along with John), preached and taught about grace. He also wrote hymns about grace.

So even in the effort required in prayer, Wesley would have been digging into his grace-based identity to discover the privilege of the "get to", rather than the pressure of the 'got to'. He would have been responding to God's "Amazing Grace", as his contemporary John Newton wrote in the hymn of that name.

It was A. J. Gordon, the nineteenth-century American Baptist preacher, who said (probably quoting John Bunyan), *"You can do more than pray, after you have prayed, but you can never do more than pray until you have prayed."* Prayer precedes work - praying before doing; in fact, prayer is work. I have often said that prayer is where the heavy lifting is done.

## CONNECTING IN PRAYER

While this is not primarily a treatise on prayer, I want to share something that has become great joy to me in my prayer life in recent years. I was in a coaching group (a huddle) a few years ago when I felt God say to me, *"Nic, the problem with your prayer life is that you put transaction before connection"*. I knew exactly what He meant, that my prayer life was dominated by trying to pray the right kind of prayers, prayers that got the result I was hoping for. It was a kind of transaction – I do "x", and God will "y".

They weren't bad prayers, and in fact many were answered, but I never found real consistency in my prayer life. It would lurch from a season of high discipline to one of laxness and laziness, usually followed by a period of condemnation. The only grace in this cycle was that after a number of weeks, or sometimes months, of dryness, I would get sufficiently desperate to want to start to exercise some discipline again. And a new season of consistent prayer would begin again. Sound familiar?

What God said to me next was, *"I want you to put connection first"*. As I explored what this meant I realized God had me back at school, His school of prayer.

So for the next six months I re-learned to connect with God as my primary objective. On a normal day I'd spend thirty minutes in prayer, and initially, as I re-learned the art of connection, this was time spent in worship, singing in tongues, declaring his goodness, his names and attributes, rehearsing his promises, thanking him for many things, speaking out the truths of Scripture. But mainly it was spontaneous sung worship. All of this was done to a background of worship music in my headphones. Not that I would sing along to the songs I was playing, they just provided a worshipful context for me to try and connect with God.

I'm conscious that for all of us the way we connect with God is different, so I'm being descriptive, rather than prescriptive, in what I am saying here. The important thing is that we take connecting seriously and create intentional pathways appropriate to our wiring, to connect with God every day. His mercies are new every morning (Lamentations 3:22-23), and it's good to have a daily rhythm of time spent intentionally connecting with God.

And so I persisted in pursuing God in worship. I kept going until I felt some kind of visceral connection. I use the word visceral, as it seems best to describe something that was not solely emotional, nor intellectual, nor dutiful. It was a feeling, but more than that, it was a "knowing". It was a knowing in my spirit that I had connected with God, I was experiencing His presence, and I had faith that I was now in the throne room of God where I could approach him on any matter, and it was a place where all things were possible.

Initially this process could take twenty to twenty-five minutes. By the end of six months, it was like a well-worn track I could take with little effort. To switch metaphor, it was like setting off on a clearly marked out runway that would inevitably lead to a moment of "take-off". After six months this would take no more than a few minutes. And it continues to be my practice to this day. It is daily a great source of joy. I never have to psych myself up to go and pray, and I genuinely miss it if, for whatever reason, it doesn't happen.

Intimacy with God is the precursor and prerequisite to everything. We were made for this. It is very hard to sustain serving God, however well-intentioned, if we're not rooted in intimacy with God the Father, in friendship with the Lord Jesus, and in fellowship with the Spirit of God. And we will miss the whole purpose of God in creating us. As the shorter Westminster Catechism says, *"A man's chief end is to glorify God and enjoy Him forever."* Heaven really will be bliss, and earth is our training ground for heaven when it comes to intimacy with the Father!

Earth is also the training ground for our future heavenly kingdom assignments. As Paul E. Billheimer in his book *Destined For the Throne,* says, *"It's training for reigning".*[13] In fact, earth is our introduction to both covenant relationship and kingdom responsibility.

## CONTENDING IN PRAYER

Six months after starting this prayer journey, the Lord gave me a new assignment. Up until this time, I had done little in the way of intercession. It seemed the Father was determined to set a new foundation, to change deeply ingrained patterns in my prayer DNA before letting me move on.

What He said next was, *"Now you've learned about connecting, I want to teach you about contending."*

I had understood from the prayer Jesus taught His disciples (Matthew 6:9-13), that coming into the presence of the Father, *"Our Father in heaven"*, came before engaging with kingdom business, *"Your kingdom come, your will be done on earth as it is in heaven"*. This kingdom business included a number of things that Jesus' prayer went on to describe.

- It included getting the resources we needed to get the job done, "Give us today our daily bread".

- It involved breaking the chains of unforgiveness that the enemy would use to imprison us, "Forgive us our sins as we forgive those who sin against us". We know from Ephesians 4:26-27 (NLT) that the enemy uses unforgiveness to gain a foothold in our lives. "And don't sin by letting anger control you. Don't let the sun go down while you are still angry, for anger gives a foothold to the devil."

- We would need to be guided away from temptation, "Lead us not into temptation", in order to avoid the enemy's schemes. Satan's desire is to entangle us in worldly distractions, and especially the idolatry typical of our culture (like materialism, consumerism, and individualism).

- It included our liberation from the evil one; "Deliver us from the evil one".

But at its heart, His kingdom comes as we contend for people and territory, for God's will to be done, to believe for breakthrough in people's lives and in contested situations. So I started to practice contending.

We know from Colossians 1:13 that when we are saved we are "Rescued from the kingdom of darkness and transferred into the Kingdom of his dear Son" (NLT). It's not hard to see that this is a spiritual battle. Our enemy the devil doesn't give up easily. He contends for buildings, land, businesses, leadership positions, influence, cultural and moral change, and the heart of institutions. In fact, he contends for domination in all of the seven cultural mountains.[14]

Satan also works to bring miscommunication, misunderstanding, offense and disunity in the church. But above all he contends for the souls of men, women and children who have yet to meet Jesus. To do this he blinds the minds of unbelievers:

> "Satan, who is the god of this world, has blinded the minds of those who don't believe. They are unable to see the glorious light of the Good News. They don't understand this message about the glory of Christ, who is the exact likeness of God." ~2 Corinthians 4:4 NLT

In order to contend for kingdom territory and people, God brought me back to some of the lessons I had learned earlier in my Christian life in the area of spiritual warfare. I have documented these more fully in my book on spiritual warfare, *Living on the Frontline*.[15] I started to use the name of Jesus with more authority than ever before. He has been given "a name that is above every name, that at the name of Jesus every knee should bow" (Philippians 2:9-11). When we pray, we do so understanding the authority we have in His name.

I rediscovered the powerful combination of high praise and God's word in enforcing the judgements of God in any situation (Psalm 149:6). By high praise, I mean that kind of declaratory praise that releases the truth of who God the Father is, and what the Lord Jesus has done, into the spiritual atmosphere, and over the situation that I am contending for. God's word is a sword and it became my constant companion in the battles that lay ahead. That sword comprises his written Word, other prophetic words given to me, and also the simple whisperings of the Spirit that I received as I listen to His voice in the place of prayer and worship. I would use these words as powerful declarations into the situation I was contending for.

The apostle Paul, who endured many battles, helps us to understand the power of God's word as the sword of the Spirit. He culminates his teaching on warfare with great words about the power of prayer and preaching the gospel. The sword of His word is powerful in both prayer and gospel proclamation:

"Take the helmet of salvation and the sword of the Spirit, which is the word of God. And pray in the Spirit on all occasions with all kinds of prayers and requests.

With this in mind, be alert and always keep on praying for all the Lord's people. Pray also for me, that whenever I speak, words may be given me so that I will fearlessly make known the mystery of the gospel, for which I am an ambassador in chains. Pray that I may declare it fearlessly, as I should." ~Ephesians 6:17-20 [Emphasis mine]

Paul understood his role as an ambassador, and how to operate in both praying and doing.

## TRY THIS

Reflect on your prayer life and ask yourself the question: "Is this duty or delight? Is my prayer life foundational to everything I do?"

## TONGUES

I appreciate that not everyone speaks in tongues, and it's not my place here to try and persuade you that all can operate in this spiritual gift. Praying in tongues doesn't make you more of a Christian, or a more spiritual one. It is not a badge of membership of a special charismatic club. You may not be familiar or comfortable with the gifts of the Spirit as mentioned in 1 Corinthians 12 and 14. You may believe they are not for today. What I am going on to describe is not in any way meant to offend or sound superior or super-spiritual. I respect each person's experience and conviction.

However, the gift of tongues, and praying in tongues in particular, has been such a blessing to me that I will risk alienating some to describe how it works for me in prayer. For those who want to explore speaking in tongues further I recommend *The Hidden Power of Speaking in Tongues* by Mahesh Chavda[16].

Praying in tongues was, and is, a fantastic help. It seems that praying in an unknown language, the language of the Spirit, is a very versatile tool. When we read 1 Corinthians 14 we see speaking in tongues is not only used for personal edification, (v. 4), not only in bringing a message to a church gathering, (v. 5), not only in our sung worship, (v. 16), but also in our praying, (vv. 14-15). It may even, in some unknown way, lead to the Father activating angels to serve His kingdom purpose in the matter for which we are contending. I say this somewhat speculatively as there is only a hint of this, where Paul says in 1 Corinthians 13:1, *"If I speak in the tongues of men and of angels..."* I can only assume that the tongues of angels he is referring to is the gift of tongues mentioned three verses earlier in 1 Corinthians 12:30. It may just be that when we intercede in tongues that the Father who hears our prayers activates angelic hosts to act on our behalf

The beauty of interceding in tongues is that the Spirit prays through us prayers that we know are "according to his will". Romans 8:26-27 describes this kind of groaning in the Spirit, which I believe includes intercessory crying out in tongues.

> *"The Spirit helps us in our weakness. We do not know what we ought to pray for, but the Spirit himself intercedes for us through wordless groans. And he who searches our hearts knows the mind of the Spirit, because the Spirit intercedes for God's people in accordance with the will of God."*

We know that the Father always hears and answers such prayers that are according to His will (1 John 5:14-15).

> *"This is the confidence we have in approaching God: that if we ask anything according to his will, he hears us. And if we know that he hears us – whatever we ask – we know that we have what we asked of him."*

One of my favorite practices is what I call a "tongues / English sandwich". I pray for a while in tongues until I get a sense of what the Spirit is praying through me. As ideas, pictures or words come, I take those and start to pray in English, to the degree that I am able. Once I feel I have exhausted praying it through in English, I revert to praying in tongues again and so the cycle continues. When interspersed with worship (which sustains me like an airplane refuelling in mid-air), it makes quite long times of intercession possible without getting tired.

I have had to learn to persevere in prayer, as few battles are won overnight. I am continuing to learn how to wage war in prayer and see Satan's scheme's thwarted. I am still growing in my ability to see God's kingdom come and God's will done as I pray.

There was a period of time when several of the leaders and their churches in or around Kairos Connexion seemed to come under attack at the same time. As well as the more common assaults on finances, health and relationships, there was a specific strategy of false accusation against key leaders. The warfare around this was intense for many months.

During this time, the Lord spoke to me about the state of the church generally through this Scripture in Judges:

> *"These are the nations that the LORD left in the land to test those Israelites who had not experienced the wars of Canaan (he did this only to teach warfare to the descendants of the Israelites who had not had previous battle experience)." Judges 3:1-2*

I felt God say that many of the younger generation of leaders were not experienced in the ways of warfare and in particular, contending in prayer. I spent some months producing video blogs helping people to understand the principles of spiritual warfare and this led to the revising and re-publishing of *Living on the Frontline.*[17]

Satan had his schemes, but God had greater plans, He used what the enemy meant for evil, for his good purposes, as with Joseph in Egypt.

> *"But Joseph said to them, "Don't be afraid. Am I in the place of God? You intended to harm me, but God intended it for good to accomplish what is now being done, the saving of many lives." ~ Genesis 50:19-20*

God used the situation to help us get re-equipped for battle, to be ready and able to deal with warfare, to take more kingdom ground. Eventually after much concerted, persistent and united prayer, the enemy's schemes started to crumble, the false accusations were thrown out, and God's kingdom came. God's will was done. And the breakthroughs were much celebrated!

In other areas, particularly praying for our unsaved friends and family, where a person's free will is as much an obstacle as any scheme of the enemy, we will need to be prepared to contend for years. I remember well the wonderful day I was able to pray with my father, six months before he died, to receive Christ. It was a glorious moment in my life. But I had probably been praying for him for about thirty years before that point!

## CONTINUING IN PRAYER

After about a year of re-learning the practice of "contending" in prayer, the Spirit said that he simply wanted me to learn to "continue" in prayer. I understood this to mean not only persevering for however long it took to get breakthrough, but also to continue in prayer through the day. This usually takes the form of worship, fellowship, speaking in tongues, and at times specific moments of prayer, depending on what else is going on around me at the time. It also involves taking every opportunity to pray with those I'm meeting with. It's always good to weave prayer into our conversations with those we are with.

I still feel like a novice in so many ways, but I'm also grateful that God took me back into the school of prayer over the last few years. I have illustrated my 3Cs journey in prayer like this:

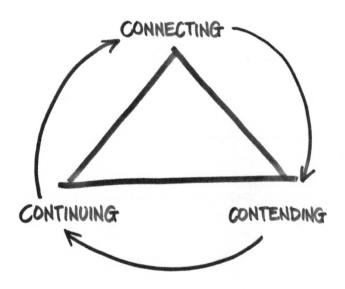

If we are going to be effective and fruitful as ambassadors, then we are going to have to learn to pray powerfully and effectively.

James describes the way that Elijah prayed:[18]

> "The prayer of a righteous person is powerful and effective. Elijah was a human being, even as we are. He prayed earnestly that it would not rain, and it did not rain on the land for three and a half years. Again he prayed, and the heavens gave rain, and the earth produced its crops." ~James 5:16b-18

The Amplified Bible (Classic edition) puts v. 16b like this:

> "The earnest heartfelt continued prayer of the righteous person makes tremendous power available, dynamic in its working."

We need that kind of prayer if we are to see breakthrough in our missional endeavors.

## TRY THIS

As you read this chapter, which "C" is getting your attention (Connecting, Contending or Continuing)? Let God speak to you about this more. Re-read that section and talk to a friend or two about it. As you do this, let a simple plan emerge of what you might do in response. Follow that plan until you feel God saying something new about your prayer life.

## SIMPLE. STICKY. REPRODUCIBLE.

- Prayer is where the heavy lifting is done.

- Connection before transaction.

# 3

# DOING BEFORE SPEAKING

**Questions:** Does our gospel have credibility? Does our gospel have power to change lives?

St. Francis of Assisi, the founder of the Franciscan Order is reputed to have said, *"Preach the Gospel at all times, and if necessary use words."* It may be apocryphal but it serves to illustrate that the gospel is communicated in two main ways – by what we do and by what we say. It's important to say that it's not two gospels, one a gospel of social justice, and the other of personal salvation. It is one gospel communicated in two different ways.

The *doing* of the gospel is massively important, as our third foundation, and it's to the shame of the broader evangelical church that we have only started to realize and enact this in the last thirty to forty years. While the more liberal wing of the church has taken the lead in this area for a long time, the evangelicals are catching up fast.

All over the world the church is serving its communities, reaching out to the poor and disadvantaged through the likes of food banks, CAP debt advice, street pastors, parent and toddler groups, groups for those in addictions, teams serving street sex workers and the homeless, schools work, youth clubs and so many others.

This love is typically unconditional and sacrificial. It blesses, it serves, it supports, it meets needs, and it gives dignity to those who feel they are at the bottom of the pile.

There are also those who are targeting the causes of injustice, like human trafficking, child poverty, worker exploitation, and homelessness. These are equally vibrant expressions of the gospel, bringing God's kingdom to bear not just on the individuals caught in oppression, addiction and injustice, but to the systems that helped create the situation in the first place. These are much longer-term commitments and are battling much bigger demons (take that figuratively or literally). I applaud and affirm all such amazing endeavors.

So, what's your point, Nic?

If I have one beef with these expressions of the gospel, it's that they are rarely combined with an opportunity for those caught in the traps laid by the oppressors to find personal freedom and forgiveness through the power of encounter with Christ and His saving grace.

There is often a fear that if we combine the gospel in deed with the gospel in word, that we are somehow making our love in actions conditional, or excluding people who don't accept our spoken offer of Christ's forgiveness and eternal life. This is understandable. The last thing we want is the situation that emerged in some of the early missionary endeavors in the Far East where receiving food was, or seemed to be, conditional on accepting the gospel of salvation, the so-called "rice Christians".

But this need not impair our efforts to bring both a gospel *demonstration* as well as a *gospel proclamation*. Our offer of the message of salvation can be brought with kindness, and without pressure. We can continue to show the same unconditional love whether those we serve respond positively or negatively to our efforts to explain that God's love for them motivates us to want to bless them; that this wonderful God in Christ died for their forgiveness, freedom and fulfillment; that He now offers them a new heart, a new start and new master.

So why do we so often separate the two dimensions of the gospel?

I believe it is, in part, due to wrong theology: a belief that somehow the gospel just *demonstrated* is complete in its own right. A hope that those who receive material blessings will be drawn to their Father in heaven without the aid of words or explanation (and of course this does occasionally happen).

It's also sadly, in part, a consequence of fear, compromise, and a desire for convenience on the part of those who serve. It's much more comfortable to be thought well of through giving goods, services and advocacy freely, rather than risk the feelings of rejection when we try to explain and make God's offer of salvation to them. None of us, even the most hard-core evangelists, enjoy being rejected, being made to feel stupid or ignorant.[19]

And finally, there are those who would like to make a gospel offer to those they serve but feel inadequate, untrained, or unprepared. They shy away from opportunities even when they are staring them in the face.

I see many churches doing great work with their projects to serve those in need. It is a very small proportion that sees the relationships built through these ministries as opportunities to truly love people by opening a door to eternal life as well as an improved material life. If those who staff these projects and the Christians who also use the services, like Christian parents at parent and toddler groups, were trained to be confident to share their faith as well as their goods, we might see a huge number of people coming to faith in Christ. We'd certainly discover a whole lot more people of peace who were leaning into our faith.

And it's fine to say, "Well if they ask about my faith..." that we will then talk about it. But there are many ways to engage with people that provoke questions, and many ways to share our lives with others that invite them to look further. It's called *intentionality*. Doing something because we believe it is the right thing to do. Doing something that we believe is in the other person's best interests. Doing something because we believe the gospel is both deeds and words. Doing something that has the intention of revealing Christ more fully. Doing something because we realize we are made in the image of a God who both acts and speaks.

I understand that there are sometimes restrictions on the use of funding we have received for our social action projects. There are sometimes limits on our freedom placed on us by partner organizations. I understand that we must be careful not to abuse positions of trust that others have given us through our connection with them in those social action ministries. But having said all that I believe we could be ten times more intentional in sharing the gospel in words than we are.

And yes, we must demonstrate the gospel by our unconditional love and commitment to those most in need. We must establish a platform of credibility with the communities around us. We must earn the right to be trusted to speak words of life.

This attitude of blessing others is applicable in all our relationships with those who don't know Christ. One of the best ways of finding people of peace, those who are leaning into the gospel, is to practically bless and serve as many people as possible (more on the "few to many" in chapter six). When we do this we give opportunity for people to reveal their true colors. I recently offered a bar of chocolate to a man who I was getting to know. Because the bar had The4Points[20] on it and came with an invite to an Easter service, he didn't want a bar of it (sorry about the pun). He showed where his heart was.

Another woman whose daughter had been really helped by our debt advice service was clearly moved by what she had experienced. She brought herself to church, eagerly checked into the Alpha course Jenny and I were about to start in our home (I think we even started it in response to the woman's eagerness), and both her and her husband got saved. She has since become a fabulously unthreatening evangelist volunteering in our food bank. She just loves people and can't help telling them about the love of God that she has discovered. She has never caused any offense as far as I know. She is very natural in the way she speaks to people and prays with them.

We must do before we speak.
And then we must speak.

The Apostle Paul said, *"Woe to me if I do not preach the gospel!"* (1 Corinthians 9:16). There is a fire in our bones that is almost extinguished in many of us. It's the fire of the gospel. Wesley said, *"I set myself on fire and people come to watch me burn."*

What would it take to set ourselves on fire so that others were deeply attracted to what they saw, and at the same time deeply challenged by the gospel? Is it time to take courage in both hands and commit to *both* expressions of the same gospel? What would it look like if we offered training in gospel confidence to those who are staff, and Christians who engage with the services we provide as churches? I think it would open up a massive mission field that the enemy has cunningly shut off from us.

It would be good to remind ourselves that at this point, this all comes out of our identity, not a pressure to perform or please. As I said earlier, when we are convinced of and secure in our identity:

- We get to share our story because it's who we are, and what we are excited about.

- We get to be courageous in talking about Jesus because we are created in the image of a courageous fearless God, who also lives in us and fills our hearts and minds on a moment-by-moment basis.

- We get to spiritually procreate as spiritual parents, to make disciples, because it is our privilege to invest in the lives of others, raising other spiritual sons and daughters.

## TRY THIS

What opportunities do you have to demonstrate the gospel to those around you through service and blessing? Spend some time reflecting on how you could add some gospel intentionality to your actions. Remember to discuss this with one or two trusted friends and let them know how it goes when you act on the plan that emerges.

In this section we have looked at the importance of recognising our God-given identity in our response to the missional call on us as ambassadors. We have understood the foundational and imperative nature of prayer as we seek to see His kingdom come. We have also looked at the two aspects of the gospel, both of which are vital if we are to see others come to faith.

## SIMPLE. STICKY. REPRODUCIBLE.

- The gospel is only fully communicated when we combine demonstration with declaration.

# SECTION 2

## Fit For The Purpose: Equipping Members, Missionaries and Multipliers

## INTRODUCTION

Is the church fit and prepared for her purpose? We will unpack that purpose as we continue. If the church is meant to be salt and light in our society, if it is meant to be an unstoppable force revealing the gospel in word and deed, if the church is meant to be the most inclusive family on the face of the earth, if the church is meant to be a place of God's unconditional love and acceptance, if the church is meant to be a bright light shining in the darkness – then it's probably true to say that we are not currently what we could and should be, and that we are not fit for purpose. Let's begin to think about what becoming fit for purpose might look like and involve.

When people are first drawn to Christ, whether they know it or not, they are on a journey. I will look at that journey in this section using the staging posts of *members, missionaries and multipliers.* Each stage overlaps with the last and builds on it. They are difficult to completely distinguish, and by the time you arrive at multipliers you are using all the tools and vehicles that members and missionaries have become familiar with and are using.

There is a natural progression from member to missionary to multiplier. The equipping requirements are different at each stage, and I will try and identify the key areas of equipping that are most relevant to each level. These three levels are similar to what we've called the leadership pathway in the past.

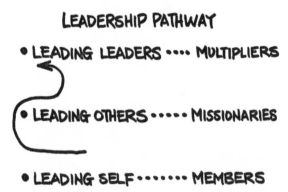

A member is one who is coming to Christ and learning to lead themselves. The missionary is one who is now learning to lead, or influence, others. The multiplier is the one who is growing in leading leaders.

## SIMPLE. STICKY. REPRODUCIBLE.

- The journey of the disciple is from member, to missionary, to multiplier.

# 4

# TRAINING JESUS STYLE

**Questions:** Are we making disciples or collecting converts? Do we have any simple, transferable tools that can be passed on from disciple to disciple?

## THE CURRENT SITUATION

As I talk to many church leaders I hear a similar heart cry from many. They know how to lead services and preach, they know how to do pastoral care and they are competent at least in some basic administration. But when it comes to making disciples most leaders are left scratching their heads.

They know deep down that they are called to "go and make disciples", but lack any coherent way of thinking about it. They lack any simple processes or tools to get the job done. They almost certainly don't know how to make disciples who go on to make disciples. They are very unlikely to have any serious budget or staff time dedicated to it.

At best, they are running some kind of maturity course, and the lucky few may get some one-on-one mentoring. Most leaders are relying on the impact of their preaching and teaching, along with optional small group Bible study to produce disciples. Most leaders know this isn't working.

It would be true to say that the depth of spirituality, biblical knowledge and God-honoring lifestyle of most people in most churches is pretty shallow. The consumer mindset tends to make it very difficult to inspire our members to engage in a discipleship journey and to connect with resources that will help them grow. The vast majority do not even have a daily pattern of Bible reading and prayer,[21] and that is in some of the most outwardly successful churches.

## CREATING A DISCIPLESHIP CULTURE

So how do we create a discipleship environment or culture? Sam Chand defines culture as "how we do things around here".[22] How do we create a context where it is the norm for every new member to look around them and think, *"Oh, this is what members do, they get involved in developing themselves in the context of communities of believers?"* They see that members are vulnerable and honest so that they can deal with things that hold them back and embrace things that may be challenging but will help them grow; they are receptive to others speaking loving truth into their lives. Wouldn't it be great to have a culture where that was "how we do things around here"?

So, what can we do to address these issues for members?

## MANY MEMBERS, ONE BODY

Before we go on to respond to this, let's first consider what it means to be a member of God's church. By members, I mean those who are connected to the body of Christ, those who are growing in their understanding of what it means to be a Christ-follower. Members in this sense are not people who have joined an organization and signed on some administrative dotted line. They are those who are joined to a body, a "body part", that kind of "member". In medicine, we talk about the arm or the leg being members of our bodies. It is in this sense that I am referring to members.

Paul puts it this way in 1 Corinthians:

*"For even as the body is one and yet has many members, and all the*

REIMAGINE CHURCH | 61

*members of the body, though they are many, are one body, so also is
Christ." ~1 Corinthians 12:12 NASB*

The picture in Ezekiel 37:1-10 is that of a valley of dry bones where a body
forms, bone to bone, ligament by ligament, limb after limb. It is eventually filled
with God's Spirit and rises as "an exceedingly great army". It is a great picture of
the body of Christ forming as each member is added, each one filled with God's
Spirit, collectively becoming a place which hosts His presence (like the temple
referred to in Ephesians 2:21-22), waging war on the domain of darkness,
rescuing lost souls and seeing them "transferred to the kingdom of his beloved
Son" (Colossians 1:13 ESV).

This great army we see in our imagination is a long way from the disparate
collection of misfits, failures and broken people that generally make up the body
of Christ. As Paul says:

> *"Brothers and sisters, think of what you were when you were called. Not
> many of you were wise by human standards; not many were influential;
> not many were of noble birth. But God chose the foolish things of the
> world to shame the wise; God chose the weak things of the world to
> shame the strong." ~1 Corinthians 1:26-27*

God does something remarkable with us as we get connected. He takes the
broken, the rejects of society and calls us His own. We become His sons
and daughters, citizens of the kingdom of heaven. He starts to heal us of our
brokenness. Courage and confidence replace fears and phobias. A soft, tender
forgiving heart replaces anger and bitterness. We discover a beautiful, if still
imperfect, family. We matter. We start to change. We discover we are of value and
have something to offer the King of Kings, and our fellow man. This connecting,
this joining, this becoming a member is a wonderful thing.

## GROWING IN MATURITY

We start as spiritual babies and begin on the path to maturity, even to the point
of starting our own spiritual families. I'll talk more about this later.

The path to maturity begins with an encounter with Christ, but interestingly there is a pre-Christ journey for many. As people watch the lives of other believers they realize there is another way to live. They observe new ways of handling conflict and pressure, of dealing with money and material possessions, coping with disappointment and failure, of engaging with work and play, and of husbands, wives and children relating to each other.

They see the kingdom of God being lived out by those who are on that same journey with the king, but a few steps further on than themselves. It's the process we call discipleship, becoming and growing as a follower of Christ.

The journey usually begins well before a person bows the knee to Christ. This process is often slow and sometimes involves three steps forward and two backwards. Unbelievers connect as they see something attractive. If they are true people of peace they will often end up belonging before believing, and certainly before behaving as a Christ follower.

The whole process of conversion is usually much more of a process than an event, though there may be specific events or moments along the way that prove to be very significant. Understanding this process is crucial to disciple making.

## JESUS' WAY OF DISCIPLE MAKING

The question is: *"Does this happen by chance, by force of will, by attending church services and programs, or does it happen as we understand and follow Jesus' way of making disciples?"* I suggest the latter is a healthier and more effective approach. We often talk about wanting to imitate Jesus' words, works and wonders but we rarely talk about His ways. He did say, *"I am the way."* It's time we took note of His ways and learned from them.

Jesus' way of disciple making is quite different from how we go about it in twenty-first-century Western culture.

We tend to operate:

- by formal teaching or preaching in Sunday services

- by tailored midweek or Sunday School programs

- by small group information-based midweek Bible study

- by one-on-one mentoring (if you are lucky)

We hope that these things will grow us to become mature disciples. And, of course, God can and does use all of the above in His grace to help us grow.

But Jesus' way of training his disciples was distinctly different. It was done:

- As a part of everyday life, not in specialised programs

- In the context of extended family, not one-on-one (this is often missed in our individualistic reading of the gospels; Jesus rarely did anything one-on-one, let alone mentoring)

- With a mixture of invitation to relationship and challenge to responsibility, not simply by giving out more and more information

- In the context of His mission, helping Him to reach out to the world around Him, getting their hands dirty

- By regularly getting rid of the crowds, not by seeing them as a measure of His success

- Through letting the disciples watch him work and then getting them to imitate Him, a kind of apprenticeship

We refer to the *Training Triangle* to describe this process.[23]

All of these three elements are needed. We have to give sufficient *information* to help those we are training as disciples to understand what the key principles are in the situation.

*Imitation* is usually the missing piece in our normal training culture. Imitation is the process of coming along side another person to observe what they do, and then trying to do the same thing under their watchful eye. Imagine a teenage lad watching his dad use a power drill, and then being given the opportunity to drill the next hole. This rarely happens in a normal church's program of discipleship. Most churches are very information orientated.

And then *innovation* is vitally important so that disciples can learn by doing, and in particular, learn by making mistakes. Innovation takes place when we give our new disciple the chance to "have a go". We give them the space and opportunity to implement what they have learned in a relatively low risk environment, but one where they can still get it wrong. I know that I have learned far more from my mistakes than I have from my successes!

As well as reflecting Jesus' method of training, we see that these three elements of information, imitation and innovation, potentially create three different learning styles at work – auditory (hearing the information), visual (watching how it's done), and kinesthetic (having a go ourselves). It's a powerful combination. There is often a dialling back from imitation to information, a recapping of what has been learned; or from innovation to imitation, perfecting the technique. It's not always a straightforward linear process.

The heart of a disciple is that of a learner. The Greek word for disciples is *mathetes*, which simply means a learner. It upsets me when I see people who have been Christians for a while but no longer have an appetite to learn. Don't they want to be disciples any more?

Jenny and I often have people for a meal at our house. We usually want to bless them, encourage them, and make them feel good. As with most of you, I expect, Jenny and I often have a post-mortem on the evening when they have gone home. One of the things we often comment on is whether or not they have asked us any questions. I am always asking questions of others - always wanting to learn from them, whether they have been a Christian for a short or long period of time. In fact I'm just as likely to do the same with not-yet-Christians. So it really surprises me when those who come for a meal ask nothing. I feel sad, that whether they lack confidence to ask, or just don't know what to ask, they miss opportunities to benefit from our experience or input.

## TRY THIS

Next time you hang out with someone, try spending at least the first ten minutes finding out about them, their views, things they have learned in life. You may be surprised what you learn.

## LEARNING FROM LIFE

It's often been said that leaders are readers (because they want to learn). I'd like to add that disciples are observers and questioners.

So, what tools and vehicles do we have that try and replicate the kind of discipleship process we see Jesus employ?

A simple tool called *The Learning Circle* undergirds discipleship dynamics. It's about learning from life. The Learning Circle is foundational in that it helps us answer the two discipleship questions.

- What is God saying?

- What am I going to do about it?

These two simple questions are dynamite. Jesus gave His disciples a dramatic picture of what this looked like in the story of the wise and foolish man. You will remember the two men in Matthew 7:24-27. One built his house on the rock and the other built his house on the sand. When the rain and floods came, the one stood firm and the other was washed away.

I've been amazed as I have taught this simple principle to many groups of leaders, just how many do not understand the point of the story. Most people talk about the need to build our lives on strong foundations. When questioned what that foundation is, they usually refer to the foundation of Christ, or the Bible, or good personal values. The passage is crystal clear. Matthew 7:24 says:

*"Therefore everyone who hears these words of mine and puts them into practice is like a wise man who built his house on the rock."*

Hear His voice and do what He says. It's pretty clear what those strong foundations are. How simple, yet how profound. Answering the two discipleship questions is fundamental to the life of the disciple.

## THE LEARNING CIRCLE HAS TWO FORMS

The first is the more established one from 3DM,[24] which has served us very well for many years. It has brought life and personal transformation to me over the last eight years.

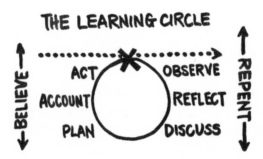

Jesus said in Mark 1:15, *"The time has come. The kingdom of God has come near. Repent and believe the good news!"* The word for *time* here is the Greek word *kairos*. It means a significant moment in time, not the passing of time, which is the Greek word *chronos*. A kairos moment is a moment when the kingdom is breaking in. Will we recognise it? Will we pause to respond to what God is saying through it?

Another way of thinking about this is that a kairos moment is a moment when God is trying to get our attention. He wants to change our thinking. The Greek word for repentance, *metanoia*, means a change of mind and direction. This should lead to believing. Believing (in Greek pisteo) is not a passive mental exercise. It is rooted in the same word for faith, *pistis*. This is a robust response to God's word. It involves action based on a new perspective. The heroes of faith in Hebrews 11 all took action as expressions of their faith.

So to unpack the two discipleship questions, when we find ourselves in a kairos moment, we could ask this question of ourselves and each other: *"In response to what God is saying to you and your new perspective on the situation, what faith-based action will be your response?"*

Once this is understood, the process of moving round the learning circle is fairly simple. We *observe* the kairos moment; we identify exactly what has happened. This may be an unexpected difficulty or trauma of some sort. It often takes this kind of situation to get our attention. It may equally be an unexpected good thing, a success perhaps. Often it is a word from Scripture or even simply a comment in a conversation, or something in a book, film or sermon, where we sense God is trying to get our attention.

Having identified the kairos, we then need to process it. Firstly, by personally *reflecting* on it (easier if you are an introvert), asking the questions, "What does this mean? What is its significance?" We will always gain a great deal more insight and confidence in our understanding as we start to *discuss* what has happened with others who we trust to help us discern the voice of the Father in the situation.

Once we feel sure we have an answer to the question, *"What is God saying?"* we move on to the second half of the circle, the action side, to answer the question, *"What am I going to do about it?"*

Making a plan is the starting point. *In the light of what God is saying to me, I'm going to...* However, the road to hell, as they say, is paved with good intentions! How many of us have made good resolutions, never to see them through, or to fall at the first hurdle, to stop when we encounter the first obstacle.

This is where the power of accountability kicks in. The second step is *account*. Who will we make ourselves accountable to for what we believe God is asking us to do? The power of accountability makes all the difference. In fact I would be as bold as to say that accountability is the hidden power behind discipleship. Without it we are likely to fail, to fall, to miss the moment.

I recently wanted to lose some weight to get back to a healthy BMI (body mass index). I tried repeatedly over the course of a year. Not a single pound was shed. Within three weeks of making myself accountable to a good friend who would regularly ask how it was going, I had lost seven pounds, and in a further month had reached my desired weight. The power of accountability!

This is no heavy, controlling, cult-like, authoritarian accountability. It is the most releasing and empowering experience because it is based purely on what we believe God is saying to us, on what we have discerned God wants us to do about it, and whom we have asked to hold us accountable. That's why we refer to this kind of discipleship culture as low control with high accountability.

It's important to note that there is no shame in failure. The occasions when we have not done what we said we were going to do simply become opportunities for encouragement from our accountability friends or coaching group, or they become new kairos moments when we ask the question, *"Why didn't I do what I said I'd do?"* Sometimes we need to dig a bit deeper into what is going on under the surface.

In fact, the "why" question is usually the most powerful question we can ask ourselves because it digs into the seat of our motivation, exposing stuff the Lord has been trying to put His finger of grace and healing on for years. Accountability is never to be feared, always embraced. Even if we experience the discipline of the Lord in the process, we know it's only the Father's love manifested in a different way.

*"No discipline seems pleasant at the time, but painful. Later on, however, it produces a harvest of righteousness and peace for those who have been trained by it." ~Hebrews 12:11*

One of my biggest kairos moments of the last twenty years happened in January 2008. I had persuaded Jenny, somewhat against her better judgement (and thereby hangs another massive kairos – listen to your wife!), to enter into a venture with me to try and boost our rather pathetic pension savings. As any in full time ministry will know, it's easy to put off the pension issue, believing that somehow it lacks faith to save for the future. Actually it's a very godly and wise thing to do from the beginning of our working life. (I once heard some good advice that I wish I had had at the beginning of my adult life – tithe 10%, save 10%, and live on 80%)

Along with many others (we later discovered) we invested in some Spanish properties in 2005 when the Spanish property market was booming. The aim was to sell them on before they had been completed. There was money to be made with some simple investments. The offer of re-mortgaging our house to pay for deposits seemed to be very low risk.

Then the Spanish property bubble burst in 2007, and the world economy dramatically collapsed shortly afterwards in 2008. We ended up unexpectedly having to find the money to complete on up to four properties. Thankfully only two had actually been completed, but even this pushed us to the limit financially. We ended up with four mortgages and one personal loan to fund the nearly £500,000 that was needed to complete on the properties. To say it was traumatic would be a massive understatement. If we had had to complete on the other two properties we would almost certainly have gone bankrupt. Thankfully, they were never completed and miraculously we were able to retrieve the 40% deposits that we had paid on those two.

The story of our financial recovery was slow and painful, but God gave us some promises early on in the process that we hung on to. One was a simple word that I felt God gave me. I felt God say that the process to recovery, to God restoring our fortunes, would be a ten-year journey. Not the most encouraging word, but nevertheless it kept us going. I'm pleased to say that as those ten years came to an end in January 2018 we became debt free. Thank you Jesus! To fully tell the story would probably take a book in itself.

However, the point of the story is that the crisis led to a massive kairos moment, as you can imagine. The questions, "What are you saying?" and, "What am I going to do about it?" were very much uppermost in my mind. Though I didn't have the language or understanding of the Learning Circle at the time, it was clearly what we were experiencing.

Processing "What are you saying?" led to a number of clear words from God. Some were more encouraging, like the ten-year journey, and the promise to restore our fortunes. Others were more to do with His loving discipline. He showed me that I had looked to man to provide instead of Him just as Abraham produced Ishmael instead of waiting for Isaac. In fact, He showed me there was some element of greed at the root of it. It was a painful time of receiving His discipline. But as Hebrews 12:11 says, His loving discipline is ultimately meant to bear righteous fruit in our lives. Pruning for greater fruitfulness!

When I considered "What am I going to do about it?" one of the things God asked me to do in response to His word to me about greed was to go on a journey of growing in generosity. I'd never have thought of myself as a mean person, but sometimes "good stewardship" can block the impulse to generosity. Some of you will no doubt identify with what I'm saying.

He asked me to carry on my person a £50 note and just be ready to give it away whenever he prompted me to. The fact that it was a single note made it a lot of fun. Over the years I've been in the bank and asked for £50 notes on dozens and dozens of occasions. I'm not sure what the bank staff makes of it!

Having the money in my wallet and it being solely for the purpose of giving away makes it very easy to do so. Once it's out of the bank, it has no other purpose. I have had so much fun over the years giving that thing away. It usually causes a great reaction as many have never seen a £50 note, let alone been given one. In the overall scheme of things £50 is not a huge amount of money, but it definitely has impact. The greatest impact, however, has been on me. I've experienced more of the joy of hilarious giving (2 Corinthians 9:7) than ever before. It's also broken something of the power of mammon in my life that I didn't even know was there. It's been incredibly liberating... and I'm still enjoying that act of hilarious giving today.

There have been times of giving away much larger amounts, but this is my bread and butter on the journey of generosity. I'm so thankful to God for His loving discipline. I'm quite sure one of the reasons we are debt free is that I've been obedient to His word and responded to the question, "What am I going to do about it?"

Sometimes the kairos can be provoked and prompted by a simple set of accountability questions. There are many different versions of this, but the basic idea of asking such questions probably stems back to John Wesley's discipleship meetings in which the disciples were asked each week to give an account of themselves. In the Holy Club in Oxford the list was extensive:

1.  Am I consciously or unconsciously creating the impression that I am better than I am? In other words, am I a hypocrite?

2.  Am I honest in all my acts and words, or do I exaggerate?

3.  Do I confidentially pass onto another what was told me in confidence?

4.  Am I a slave to dress, friends, work, or habits?

5.  Am I self-conscious, self-pitying, or self-justifying?

6.  Did the Bible live in me today?

7.  Do I give it time to speak to me every day?

8.  Am I enjoying prayer?

9.  When did I last speak to someone about my faith?

10. Do I pray about the money I spend?

11. Do I get to bed on time and get up on time?

12. Do I disobey God in anything?

13. Do I insist upon doing something about which my conscience is uneasy?

14. Am I defeated in any part of my life?

15. Am I jealous, impure, critical, irritable, touchy or distrustful?

16. How do I spend my spare time?

17. Am I proud?

18. Do I thank God that I am not as other people, especially as the Pharisee who despised the publican?

19. Is there anyone whom I fear, dislike, disown, criticize, hold resentment toward or disregard? If so, what am I going to do about it?

20. Do I grumble and complain constantly?

21. Is Christ real to me?

As Methodist "Band" and "Class" meetings developed later to serve the expanding movement, the questions were simplified to the following:

1. What known sins have you committed since our last meeting?

2. What temptations have you met with?

3. How were you delivered?

4. What have you thought, said, or done, of which you doubt whether it be sin or not?

5.  Have you nothing you desire to keep secret?

Don't you just love the last question!

## THE TRIANGLE

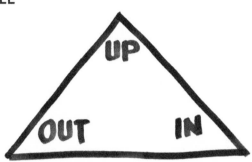

These kinds of kairos-provoking questions have been developed by 3DM to reflect the three relational priorities of the disciple, depicted in the Triangle, around the Up, In and Out dimensions of life – relationship with God (Up), relationship with our brothers and sisters (In), and relationship with the world (Out). See Chapter five for more on this. These three relational priorities in turn can be applied to character alone, or to both character and skills, i.e. in areas of character development, and also around a list of skills an emerging leader will want to be developing. One set of questions that we used in Frontline in the early days was as follows. We called them Personal Development Questions or PDQs. (See Appendix 2)

In recent years, we have created a new simpler version based around the 4 Frontline values of:

Authentic devotion (Up),

Extended Family (In)

Confident Witness (Out)

Kingdom Impact (Out)

These have been produced in a credit sized folding card for easy access and use. (See Appendix 2)

These are simple tools to help provoke kairos' (technically kairoi in the Greek!) that can be used in discipleship and accountability relationships. In a group context, each person can look through the list of questions, or perhaps one of the sections, and try to identify which area or areas the Holy Spirit is highlighting. Often the Spirit highlights similar ones in different members of the group. As with any kairos, the questions around the Learning Circle help to process it, and the two discipleship questions can be answered and used for personal growth.

The second version of the Learning Circle is from Caesar Kalinowski.[25] It's a further development of the original one. As with many innovations, it has evolved to be more nuanced, and potentially even more fruitful.

# THE CIRCLE

The starting point is the same kairos moment but instead of going through a simple observe, reflect, discuss process, we use a different approach to answer the first discipleship question, "What's God saying?"

When the kairos is a negative experience or a challenge (as it commonly is) we start by asking the question, "In the light of this kairos, what is it about God's nature I'm failing to believe?" Or, "What lie about God am I believing?" So, for example, if the kairos had been about being too busy to attend to my family, I would have asked, "What am I not believing about you, Lord, that causes me to put myself under pressure to work so hard that it leads to neglecting my family?"

I can process this in the same way I would with the 3DM Circle, first on my own and then with others, but specifically to get answers to the questions about God and what was now true about me. Eventually, I'd have got to the revelation that I was failing to trust in the greatness of God and His being in control of my life; and because of that I had been trying to work to control all the variables to get the outcome I thought I needed at work. If I had truly believed God was in control and so powerful that He could help me get the outcomes he knew I needed without sacrificing my family, I would not have neglected them.

It's really important to answer the basic question about the nature of God because everything in life comes back to understanding the attributes, nature and character of God. In understanding Him, we understand who we are, as made in His image, and this leads to change (as explored in chapter one).

As I quoted before from Tim Chester's book, *You Can Change*:[26]

- God is Great; I don't need to be in control.

- God is Glorious; I don't need to fear anyone.

- God is Good; I don't need to look elsewhere.

- God is Gracious; I don't need to prove myself.

We call these the 4Gs of God's character. While there are many other aspects of his nature, a lack of faith in these four often seems to be at the root of our unbelief and sinful behavior.

Once I have answered the basic question of what it is about God's nature that I'm not believing, or need to believe, then I can progress to the next point on the Circle. "How has God demonstrated this aspect of His character?" We ask this because we want to be deeply convinced and convicted about the truth, not just giving intellectual ascent to it. We look first at the testimony of Scripture, then to the cross, and finally to our own experience to see how God has demonstrated the particular aspect of His nature that we are considering. This process of verifying the evidence for God's attributes builds faith for us as we move round the Circle.

So in the example above, I may have considered the greatness of God in creation, in delivering Israel from Egypt, in other miraculous acts in scripture. I would have thought about the greatness of God in overcoming Satan, sin and death on the cross. I would have reminded myself of the times that God had intervened in my life either in response to prayer, or at times without any seeming action on my part; like the time he directed me to apply to study medicine at University through a letter from my uncle, without any prompt or question from myself: a decision that led to major blessing in my life. Doing so would have built faith enabling me to trust God for the new situation, and to turn away from trying to control it all myself.

The next question is crucial and asks this, "In the light of this aspect of God's nature, what is now true about me?" This is vital because it is helping us to realize something of our God-given identity. That identity is rooted in our being created in his image (Genesis 1:27). As we rediscover something of the nature of God, it always has implications for our identity. So we ask this question in three ways. "What is true of me in the areas of *identity, privilege and authority?*"

In the light of God being great, I realize what is true about me is that in terms of my *identity* I am utterly secure in God's ability to work things together for good in my life. I am His child protected by His awesome power. I have no need to be anxious or fearful about the future. In terms of *privilege*, I get to live free from the pressure to make everything happen, I don't need to be in control. I can enjoy each day in a brand new way. In terms of *authority*, I get to pray about the situations from a heavenly perspective, one in which God is able to overcome all the perceived obstacles to me living an integrated whole and healthy life. I get to speak to fear in my life in the name of Jesus, banishing it from my consciousness.

Having established what is now true about me, in the light of who God is, I can then answer the question "How then do I get to live?" Note, it's not "*got* to live", it's "*get* to live". This is where identity-based discipleship is most powerful. We realize that when we truly understand who we are in the light of who He is, we can operate out of our identity, not a "to do" list. In fact, Caesar Kalinowski calls this transition of perspective and response, "be to do, *not* do to be". If we are always looking to our "doing" to give us a sense of affirmation or success, we will be mercilessly driven and stressed. If we are rooted in our "being" we can live free from those tyrannical pressures.

So as I respond to this revelation of what is now true about me in response to the revelation of God's greatness, I realize that I get to put my family first in the pecking order of life's priorities. My family certainly comes before my work. And I can do this without fear of failing at work, because I know God is great and in control.

Can you see how different this is? When it comes to accountability and action, I'm primarily being accountable not to a task, but more importantly, to living out of my new identity, from "get to", not "got to". This is the liberty that we have as children of God.

The original Learning Circle at its best is a source of great life and fruitfulness. It has been so to me for many years. Occasionally it can create a long "to do list" of things I'm meant to be working at. As such it has potential to generate a sense of pressure. It can lead to self-righteousness when we succeed in our tasks, or a sense of failure if we don't. For that reason I value this revised version as it avoids those dangers. As I say, identity-based discipleship is where liberating growth and life come from.

In the light of my kairos of 2008, and my need to grow in generosity, the process would have been slightly different if I'd have used the second version of the Learning Circle. I'd have understood that God is a gracious, generous God who has demonstrated that time and time again in Scripture, in my past experience and most importantly at the cross. I'd have realized that I was created in His image as a generous liberated giver. As I'd meditated on that truth, I'd have seen "generous" as who and what I was, rather than something I wasn't. It would have led me to realize that I "get to" live the generous life and live free from all worries about money. Subtly different, but perhaps more powerful. And it would have placed me in good stead for other discoveries from the same revelation around identity, privilege and authority.

## TRY THIS

Take either of the Learning Circles and practice going round it. Ask God to show you a recent and relevant kairos, and begin to process it in one of the two ways suggested. Make sure you involve someone in the discussion and accountability.

## THE BEST CONTEXTS IN WHICH TO USE THE LEARNING CIRCLE

The Learning Circle doesn't exist in a vacuum; it has to be used in a context. What kind of contexts can benefit from using the Learning Circle?

## MISSIONAL COMMUNITY

As we work with people on the journey of discipleship, they may be obvious "people of peace" who are leaning into our input into their lives, orbiting in and out of our missional household (extended family on mission – see chapter seven). Or they may be those who have made a clear commitment to Christ and want to grow deeper as disciples. All of these, as I explored earlier, I will consider as members.[27]

For those who are "leaning in", we will sometimes want to use the Learning Circle in a one-on-one structured conversation, but more often in more organic, spontaneous, wider community conversations. In this context, Caesar Kalinowski calls this use of the identity-based Circle "gospeling each other". It's applying the bigger gospel to every area of our lives. Colossians 3:16 says,

*"Let the message of Christ dwell among you richly as you teach and*

*admonish one another with all wisdom through psalms, hymns, and*
*songs from the Spirit, singing to God with gratitude in your hearts."*

As the message about Christ, this bigger gospel (who God is, who we are in the light of that, and how we now get to live), permeates every area of our life, we let this good news infiltrate our everyday conversations, such that we end up teaching and counselling each other with the gospel. It becomes a way of life that everybody gets to take part in. We grow in our understanding of the gospel, and just how good the good news really is.

For example, imagine we are chatting over the washing up after a meal together. Anne mentions the fact that she is struggling to meet her deadlines at work and is losing sleep over it. Robert, who is a trusted part of the spiritual family is listening closely to Anne and asks, *"So Anne, what is it that you are not believing about God that leaves you feeling like that?"*

After a while reflecting, she admits she's not sure. Mary who is also listening says, *"Are there any of the 4Gs that might be relevant?"* After a further period of reflection Anne begins to realize and express that it could be that she's not really believing in the greatness of God and therefore worrying unnecessarily about her work because she can't control it. She also says that she thinks she is not really convinced about God the Father's love for her and his approval. This, she explains, has led to her trying to get approval from her boss, instead of from God.

Robert chips in again, *"So if it's true that God loves and approves of you, how has He shown that to you in the past, and how has He shown it in Scripture?"* By this stage the washing up has all but ceased, as Anne is again deep in thought.

After a moment she recalls a time when she was worried about a broken relationship with a family member, until she had the revelation that God's opinion of her was the defining opinion. She was then able to pray with faith, rather than fear, about the relationship. The end result was that God brought a full and beautiful reconciliation. She also remembered how Jesus was called "a beloved son, in whom the Father was well pleased", long before He did any kingdom work that could have earned Him any spiritual brownie points with His heavenly Father.

As she reflects on this, Grace chips in with, *"So if God has demonstrated that to you in the past and from Scripture, what is it that is now true about you?"*

Anne replies, *"Well, that I'm his daughter, utterly unconditionally loved and accepted by her heavenly Father."*

*"Wow,"* Robert quickly says, *"So how do you now get to live in this situation, Anne?"*

With a big smile on her face as Anne realizes the truth, she says, *"That I can go into work and be free from any of the pressure, fear of disapproval, or negative comments my boss may make. I'll still do my best, but I know that because I'm looking to my Father for approval, I get to live happily and peacefully in that difficult work environment. And what's more I get to encourage others who are feeling similar pressures. Hey, I could even offer to pray for one or two of them who might trust me to do that."*

I love Caesar's definition of discipleship in the light of this way of life: *"Discipleship is moving from unbelief to belief in every area of life."* [28]We can help each other in our everyday conversations. It doesn't need to be a special counselling session or heavy discipleship time. How much discipleship could we embrace simply by directing our conversations in this way?

## SMALL GROUPS

A more organized small group is also a great context for using the Learning Circle. It is often an opportunity for more intentional discipleship conversations. It may be in a discussion about a passage of Scripture or just in a more general, honest "how are you doing?" conversation.

We should expect plenty of revelation about the nature of God in Scripture. The best type of study for provoking kairos moments is what has been called a Discovery, or Inductive, Bible study.

A *Discovery Bible Study* (DBS) is one in which we let the Spirit speak directly to our hearts and minds through the text. It is not a Bible study in the traditional sense of the word; where someone prepares the study, looking into the meaning, the context, and the application of the passage beforehand. In this traditional type of Bible study they may come across as the expert, and those who attend are simply passive recipients of the leader's interpretation and understanding of the passage.

In a DBS no one comes as the expert but all as learners (disciples). We come expecting God to speak to each one of us. We come expecting a kairos. We read and re-read the passage a couple of times for the text to sink in. It may help after taking it in turns and reading round the group, for one person to read while others listen, this helps to process the passage from an auditory perspective. If there is time, the group can also try and recall as much of the passage as possible without reference to their Bibles. This process of recounting the passage is a powerful way of reinforcing the content through each person sharing the bits they can remember.

Having read the passage a couple of times, we ask some simple questions, like:

1.   What does this passage tell us about God (Father, Son or Spirit)?

2.   Does it give us any promises, principles, commands or warnings?

3.   What is God saying to me through this, and what am I going to do about it? (The two discipleship questions.)

4.   Who can I tell what I have learned here in the course of the next week? (This question is starting to prepare the member for becoming someone who invests in others – a disciple-maker.)

There are many variants of these questions. But question three is the most important, as it leads to the accountability moment.

I've put together some helpful suggestions on how to run a Discovery Bible Study with both Christians and non-Christians. See appendix one for the DBS overview.

I was doing a version of this type of Bible study with some not-yet Christians. Joy (not her real name) was attending regularly. We were studying the passages in John's gospel that describe His miracles. These are sometimes called the "Seven signs of John's gospel". As we looked at the stories, Joy began to see herself in some of the stories. She imagined what it would be like to be at the wedding in Cana of Galilee when Jesus turned water into wine or to be in the crowd when He fed the five thousand. She started to see God as a Father who loved, who provided, and who cared. This was in stark contrast to her own experience of her natural father.

As she saw God for whom He was, she started to be drawn towards Him. Eventually she could see herself as someone of great value. Following an experience in a bigger gathering, she realized she could come as she was and would be accepted by Him. She sensed this loving Father calling her to Himself, and within a short period of time was able to give her life to Him. And now she gets to live the life of a "loved one", and has the privilege of sharing her experience with others.

In a DBS, the first question we ask, "What does this passage tell us about God?" may be relevant to our identity discoveries and the use of the identity-based Learning Circle. As we see who God is, we can work through the Learning Circle's first half, answering the identity questions, and then onto, "How do we then get to live?"

Having identified some important aspect of God's nature, we can ask, "What is now true of us, and are we all living in the good of that renewed God-given identity?" It may prompt the response, "No, we aren't, in certain specific areas of our life." This then becomes the kairos that we develop in the light of who we are discovering God to be in the Scriptures. So the identity based Learning Circle can work in different ways: forwards (from realizing who God is) or backwards (from discovering something that is not healthy or happy in our life).

## ACCOUNTABILITY GROUPS

The Learning Circle works equally well in any simple accountability triplet. We sometimes call these DNA groups (Discipleship, Nurture, and Accountability groups). Three is the ideal size, but four can work if needed.

In summary, there are four contexts where we are likely to use some version of the two discipleship questions. These are the typical contexts and the kind of resource that may work best in them:

1. Missional Community – Gospel conversations

2. Small groups – Discovery Bible Study

3. Accountability / DNA groups  - Personal Development Questions

4. Coaching huddles – more of this later

## CALIBRATING INVITATION AND CHALLENGE

There are the two fundamental dynamics of a discipling relationship; invitation and challenge.[29] We *invite people into covenant relationship* with us. This may start with friendship and family fun but sooner or later we want to offer them a deeper discipling relationship, and this may lead to giving them opportunities to follow our example and learn from us. As they feel the covenantal nature of our commitment to help them grow as disciples, we also begin to *challenge them to kingdom responsibility* as they start to respond to God's call on their life.

People need a good balance of both invitation and challenge to thrive in their growth as disciples. In fact we all need that, whether a disciple, or discipler. Initially our relationship with a disciple is going to be heavily biased towards invitation, as we will still be building trust and growing in credibility. As the relationship develops, we are able to introduce some challenge. This may take many forms, for example, asking them to complete a task that puts them out of their normal comfort zone, or bringing a challenge about an area of attitude or behavior that you think exposes something God wants to help them with. The purpose of challenge is often to provoke a kairos that enables them to hear from God and respond accordingly.

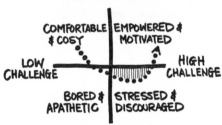

INVITATION AND CHALLENGE MATRIX

Where invitation and challenge are both low, there is no encouragement or being stretched in a healthy way, and people lose motivation, becoming bored and apathetic. Where there is too much challenge and not enough invitation and support, people become stressed and eventually discouraged. Where there is lots of invitation to relational support but little in the way of healthy challenge, then we leave people in the consumeristic mode of "cosy and comfortable". This is where most people in church life are. It's often the result of a very pastoral style of leadership and a consumer, convenience culture.

As you can see from the invitation and challenge matrix,[30] there are consequences to having too little invitation or not enough challenge. As with most matrices, the aim is to be in the top right quadrant where there is a healthy balance of both elements, and we produce empowered and motivated disciples. Most Christians find themselves in the cosy/comfortable quadrant. They find a way to get there and stay there! There is often resistance to moving out of that quadrant.

When we increase challenge to help people move out of their comfort zones they may complain that they feel stressed or distressed as they move out of the cosy/comfortable quadrant and towards an empowered life. This is the space we call the valley of the shadow of death! There is a dying to self that takes place here. It's not somewhere to avoid, but we must nurture and support those we've invited onto the journey through this space.

It's important that we continually calibrate invitation and challenge in all our relationships. Many will instinctively do this with friends and family who they know well. It's equally important to be deliberate with those we are getting to know as disciples.

A young couple that have recently become Christians in one of our communities come from very broken backgrounds. Their relationship is unstable and they repeatedly fall in and out of love with the church and the community. They have needed masses of invitation to friendship, to meals, and to being supported. They have needed lots of practical help, be it buying baby chairs or other items. Now that they have been around a while, their community leaders, who have become like spiritual parents to them are able to be more challenging, not only about their relationship, but also their engagement with church, and some of the more destructive behaviors they have been engaged in. Because they know they are loved, they are able to accept these challenges well. The combination of invitation and challenge has been key to helping them on their discipleship journey. It's important to realize that both invitation and challenge come from a place of love, because God is love. Love accepts you as you are, but doesn't leave you as you are!

For those in church leadership or small group leadership, this also needs to be the pattern of our input to the whole group or church. When we are preaching to the church, we mix invitation and challenge in how we preach. There will be seasons of invitation when we will be focused on preaching that reinforces our identity as children of God, the Father's love for us, the need for times of rest and restoration, and the grace of God which underpins all we are and all we do. There will be other seasons when we can be more challenging, for example, in calling us to sacrifice for the King who gave everything for us, in the call to radical discipleship, in the joy of extravagant generosity, and in the deployment of our gifts in serving the body.

For those in small group leadership, we need to ensure we are creating safe places for people to belong, to grow and to be healed, but we are also making space for members to be stretched and challenged, to get stuck into the mission of the community, and to care for others.

Invitation and challenge is a key tool for calibrating our leadership emphasis, the leading beat of our engagement with disciples.

## TRY THIS

Make a list of your relationships in which you have some discipling input. Consider how you might increase either invitation or challenge to develop your effectiveness in disciple making. Next to each relationship, write down which element you need to increase and what that might look like.

## SIMPLE. STICKY. REPRODUCIBLE.

- A disciple is a learner.

- The Learning Circles with the two discipleship questions.

- Low control and high accountability create the ideal culture for   discipleship.

- Invitation and challenge create the best dynamics for discipleship.

# 5

# THREE RELATIONAL PRIORITIES

**Questions:** How do we overcome our natural tendency to build church in our own image? How do we ensure each disciple grows in a balanced way?

Each of us as leaders has a preferred way of approaching life and church. We may be naturally pastoral, simply wanting to help create safe, secure places for disciples to grow. We may be deeply prophetic, constantly challenging folk to consider their lifestyles or levels of obedience to the Lord. We may love God's word and just want to continually expose people to its beautiful truths, increasing their biblical knowledge. We may be passionately apostolic, always wanting to take people out of their comfort zones and into mission contexts. We might be evangelistically motivated, constantly looking for ways to share the good news of Jesus with those who don't yet know him. Whatever our preference or gifting we need to be able to build balanced communities and healthy disciples.

The Triangle defines our three main priorities in life, our three key sets of relationships. This is a well-known 3DM tool[31] based around these three dimensions. It is the balanced life that Jesus demonstrated, with His three relational priorities:

- Up towards God (i.e. intimacy and intentionality in His relationship with the Father)

- In towards each other (i.e. friendship, family and community with His disciples)

- Out towards the world (i.e. mission and service, demonstrated in His preaching, healings and miracles)

Before we look at these, however, I'd like to come back to the idea of identity before function (being before doing, as we explored in chapter one). I'd like to use the Triangle to look at our created identity from Genesis 1:27-28, *the Creation Triangle.*

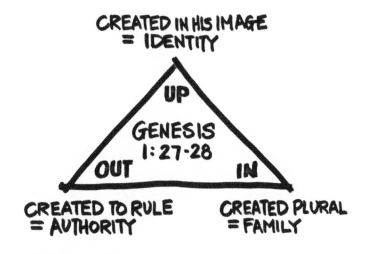

*"God created man in His own image, in the image of God He created him; male and female He created them. God blessed them; and God said to them, 'Be fruitful and multiply, and fill the earth, and subdue it; and rule over the fish of the sea and over the birds of the sky and over every living thing that moves on the earth.'"*

"The law of first mention"[32] says that the first time anything is mentioned in Scripture is often an unusually rich source of revelation on that topic.

Here we have the first mention of the creation of humankind. The passage clearly states that we are made in His image. This is the supreme source of our identity. We discover who we are in the light of who He is, as we have seen when using the Learning Circle.

Secondly, we are told that He made us male and female. We were created plural. He made us to be a family and community with complementary strengths, perspectives and gifts. This is not surprising considering that God Himself is plural. He is the trinity of Father, Son and Holy Spirit who live in perfect harmony, complementarity and community. They are a family. Even the choice of titles Father and Son defines their familial relationship.

Community is not an optional extra for humankind. It is essential to how God envisaged us to live. It is actually now quite countercultural to think of humankind in this way. In our twenty-first-century Western culture, we think of ourselves first as individuals and then see family and community as very secondary, even optional. The enlightenment and the gradual development of individual rights, while producing much of worth, has severely undermined our thinking and practice of what it means to be human in God's eyes, looking through the lens of "family".

It's not a question of whether we are single or married; it's a question of whether we see ourselves as part of a family first, or as an individual first. This is deeply challenging to our Western mindsets. It exposes our highly individualistic culture, and the idolatry of individualism. This revelation of family underpins much of the theology of our practices that we refer to later in the book.

Over time, this mindset has changed our perception of right and wrong to being what is right and wrong for *me*, rather than first what is right and wrong for the *family* and the community. It's not surprising then that, despite increasing levels of knowledge, education, wealth, technology, and opportunity, we continue to become a progressively more fragmented society comprising increasingly broken and dysfunctional families. We worship at the altar of "individual rights" while destroying the very fabric of what the world has known as "civilized society" for thousands of years.

As the famous Sister Sledge song says, "We are family!" But the reality of our culture is more like, "I did it my way". Thank you, Frank Sinatra, for that articulation of our current obsession with self and the idolatrous trinity of me, myself and I.

The third element in this Creation Triangle is the commission to be fruitful, multiply, fill the earth, subdue it and rule over it. This is the dimension of our authority: authority to be God's agents, His representatives, and His *ambassadors* in the world today. We are kingdom agents who fulfill the will of God on the earth.

We do so as we model a different way to live, as we pray, as we love those around us, as we include the last, least and the lost in our extended families, and as we teach them how to live as family themselves. As Caesar Kalinowski would say: *"We have become part of a family of missionary servants, sent as disciples who make disciples"*.[33]

We are rooted in the identity of who God is and the family nature of His essential being. We are sent with His authority flowing out of these realities. I can't over-emphasise the need for us to operate out of renewed identity, not out of task, function, or worse still the need for approval or success. In the same way that Jesus experienced the Father's approval at the Jordan river before He had done a single thing in His ministry, we also have the "you are my beloved child in whom I am well pleased" from our heavenly Father before we do anything for Him.

## DO TO BE ⟶ BE TO DO

So as we look at the Discipleship Triangle, with all its challenging implications let's bear in mind our creation covenant identity reality.

*The Discipleship Triangle of Up, In and Out* is one of the most basic tools for those who are connecting as members. It is vital that we help them prioritize these relational dynamics in which they will need to grow as followers of Christ. Jesus models these relational priorities. He spent time with the Father (up), time with the disciples (in), and time with the crowds (out), for example see Luke 6:12-19. This mix of up, in and out is a useful template for our personal development as disciples, it works for how we organize our life in communities or small groups, and it is a good health check for us as a whole church. Up in and out helps to inform our rhythms, patterns, priorities, activities and structures of church life. It's easy to create a set of values or even a vision / mission statement for our church that reflect these different priorities.

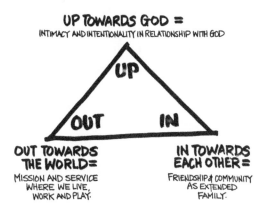

**UP TOWARDS GOD =**
INTIMACY AND INTENTIONALITY IN RELATIONSHIP WITH GOD

**OUT TOWARDS THE WORLD=**
MISSION AND SERVICE WHERE WE LIVE, WORK AND PLAY.

**IN TOWARDS EACH OTHER =**
FRIENDSHIP & COMMUNITY AS EXTENDED FAMILY.

Our efforts to help the new member grow in healthy balance needs to take each of these dimensions into account.

## UP

Helping them grow up in their relationship with God will include prayer practices, praise and worship, hearing God's voice, engaging with Scripture, using the two discipleship questions, and learning to do all of these as family as well as individuals.

The prayer and Scripture reading practices need to be developed to be part of a daily rhythm. Lamentations 3:23 (NLT) says *"Great is his faithfulness; his mercies begin afresh each morning"*, and Isaiah 50:4 (NASB) says of the Lord, *"He awakens me morning by morning, He awakens my ear to listen as a disciple"*. Daily rhythms reflect our need for daily spiritual bread. The daily supply of manna in the wilderness that the Israelites enjoyed was a picture of their need for spiritual bread that Moses reminded them about in Deuteronomy 8:3 when he said that, *"Man does not live by bread alone but by every word that comes from the mouth of the Lord"*. Scripture is clear about the importance of daily rhythms and hearing from God on a daily basis.

Ideally this should be both as an individual and as part of a household or community rhythm. The Moravian daily readings[34] are used by many in the missional movement and are a great tool. If a community uses this together, it allows for all its members to be interacting online around the daily reading. The aim of Scripture reading is to both understand more of who God is and how He works in the world today, and also to hear His voice at a personal level. Each time we read Scripture we can expect something to strike us by way of a kairos for the day. Those kairos moments in Scripture can then be turned into prayers for the day.

## PRAYER

Prayer of course can take many different forms. The disciples asked Jesus to teach them how to pray (Luke 11:1); I believe it was the only time they asked Jesus to teach then anything. In fact praying, *"Teach me how to pray"* is probably one of the most important prayers we can encourage the new member to pray. We all need to learn how to pray. My own example in chapter two (of connecting, contending and continuing) shows that we can keep learning, and keep asking Jesus to teach us.

Jesus response to the disciples' question was to teach them what is sometimes called "The Lord's Prayer" (Luke 11:1-4). While reciting it as a prayer as it is written is of benefit, most Bible teachers would agree that Jesus' intention was not for this prayer to be used as a prayer that is simply repeated day in day out. It is more of a condensation of key elements of prayer, and key lenses through which to pray. Jesus was giving His disciples the headlines, not the full package.[35]

- Our Father who is in heaven, hallowed be your name = Father's character

- Your kingdom come, your will be done on earth as it is in heaven = Father's kingdom

- Give us this day our daily bread = Father's provision

- Forgive us our sins as we forgive those who sin against us = Father's forgiveness

- Lead us not into temptation = Father's guidance

- Deliver us from the evil one = Father's protection

There are many teachings on using the Lord's Prayer as a framework for learning how to pray. Each section is taken as a springboard for praying through certain issues. It's a useful structure for those who are just learning to pray. I still find it a helpful fallback when my own more spontaneous style of praying seems to get stuck or loses its way.

For example, when praying for my family, the Father's character lens helped me to pray for one of them to know his love, be secure in his plan for their lives, and to experience His family to the full. The lens of the Father's kingdom reminds me to pray for those things that are blocking the Father's kingdom purpose in their lives to be aligned with the will of God. One of them was having a tough time in his job, and the kingdom lens allowed me to pray with authority over that situation. The Father's provision strengthened my prayers for one of them when they were looking to buy a house, and couldn't seem to get enough borrowing power to make it possible, etc. Each lens helps me to articulate prayers that are in line with the will of God, and in the way Jesus taught us to pray.

## WORSHIP

Developing a healthy heart of thanksgiving and worship are also priorities for the development of intimacy with the Father. They keep the new disciple in a good place to be hearing God and having faith for the challenges of the day. There is so much great music on CD and online that there really is no need to have any lack of resource in sung worship. Obviously there are many other ways to express our worship beside singing, but it is one of the key ways referenced in Scripture, as in the second half of Colossians 3:16 that I quoted earlier.

*"Let the message of Christ dwell among you richly as you teach and admonish one another with all wisdom through psalms, hymns, and songs from the Spirit, singing to God with gratitude in your hearts."*

It has always struck me that singing is such an amazing gift from God (whether you can sing in tune or not) because it uses another one of God's great gifts to us: music. I think that music is one of God's three unnecessary extravagancies in his creation, along with colour and taste. We could have lived without any of them, but God has blessed us with all of them. Amazing! The human voice is probably the greatest musical instrument of all time.

So it should not surprise us that singing is so prevalent in heaven. Chapter after chapter in the book of Revelation sees the angels, the elders, the living creatures, the nations, and in fact every created thing singing praise to God. Check out Revelation chapters 4, 5, 6, 7, 11, 15, and 19. We'd better get used to it!

I come across Christians who have almost begun to belittle sung worship. In their ignorance they believe they have found more superior ways of expressing worship. It's almost as though they think of singing as childish, and other more reflective, perhaps intellectual or creative ways of expressing worship as more adult. What a shame!

We want our young disciples to be in love with Jesus, to be filled with the Father's love on a daily basis, as they experience being continuously filled with God's Spirit:

"And hope does not put us to shame, because God's love has been poured out into our hearts through the Holy Spirit, who has been given to us." ~Romans 5:5

## OUR MOTIVES

The great commandment defines the why of our service:

> *"Jesus replied: 'Love the Lord your God with all your heart and with all your soul and with all your mind. This is the first and greatest commandment. And the second is like it: Love your neighbour as yourself.'" ~Matthew 22:37-39*

Love is the motivator and the method of our service, the why and the how. That's why it's so important that the new disciple immediately connects with their new God-given identity; and as His children, connects with the Father's unconditional love, acceptance and forgiveness in the up dimension.

## LEARNING

Growing in intimacy with God the Father needs to be matched by growing as a learner, a disciple. As we've already noted, the Greek word for disciple, *mathetes*, means a learner. This heart of a learner is first towards God as heavenly Father, but secondly to others who are becoming "spiritual parents" to the new disciple. We need to help them see that as with a newborn baby, they need others to help them grow. Others who will provide good spiritual nourishment for them, point them in the right direction, protect them with their prayers and advice, and who will help them engage with the Learning Circle process.

Spiritual parents will also help them engage in good predictable patterns, spiritual rhythms and with missionary purpose.

## IN

Learning to build community and grow in their identity as family will at first seem strange for those who have led a deeply individualistic life. But they will instinctively realize when they taste it that this is how we were designed to live. For the rest of the world, and through most of history, extended family has been the norm, not just for survival and efficient economics, but because it reflects the nature and heart of God in whose image we have been created. There is a great liberty and security in being deeply known by others. There is great joy in never feeling alone or isolated in life's challenges. There is great provision in the life of the family who *"has all things in common"* (Acts 2:44). This is not to say of course that community life is without its challenges. Jenny and I have lived with dozens and dozens of people over the years and have had many challenging moments when, for example, the lack of sensitivity on the part of someone in our house, the loss of privacy for our family, or just the inconvenience of meeting others needs, eats into our genuine love of this way of life. Even if others in our spiritual family don't live with us, just having an open home, a heart of hospitality and a generous attitude to including others can take its toll, and we need to make sure we also have good personal and family boundaries for our marriage's and children's sake.

Friendship and trust are at the heart of family. We need to nurture both. Those not used to being vulnerable will need to grow in confidence to be so. Equally the spiritual family will need to learn confidentiality, respect for, and responsibility towards each other. *"Am I my brother's keeper?"* (Genesis 4:9). I say a resounding, yes! We are called to care for and look out for one another. I believe there are 59 "one-anothers" in the New Testament.[36] That's a lot of interpersonal responsibility. But that's how a great family lives.

## WHAT WOULD A FAMILY DO?

The answer to most questions about the "In" dimension is quickly worked out by asking another question: "What would a family do?" It helps us figure out the answer to other questions about relationships, involvement in each other's lives, and decisions and dilemmas in community life. Clearly some of those who have grown up in a highly dysfunctional family will struggle to imagine what a great family would do. As they grow in understanding of God's family in Scripture, and in their own experience, that question will become easier to answer.

One example of using this question came up recently when we were wondering what to do about a couple who had been part of the community but had gone through a separation. One partner had to set up home separately from the original family home. What should we do – wag the finger and tell them this was no way to live, that God was not pleased with them, and that He hates divorce? As tempting as it was to read the riot act to them, when we asked what a family would do, the answer became obvious. We should love them unconditionally, support them individually and help the one to furnish their new house. If the opportunity came to help them reconcile we'd obviously take it, but for that moment we were to just love them where they were.

## REGULAR RHYTHMS

Rhythms of community life, if lived like a family, will involve more than weekly connection. Daily is ideal, but at least several times a week is needed if we are to truly build the kind of Acts 2 New Testament community life that led to the church being filled with missionary disciples and their places being filled with the gospel. The new member is introduced to this naturally by being drawn into the existing rhythms of the community. Geographical proximity makes this a whole lot easier.[37]

## GEOGRAPHICAL PROXIMITY

One family who lived a few miles away from us lived in a very comfortable neighborhood in a lovely house they had spent a lot of time and money on making just how they wanted. When God began to speak to them about moving into our immediate neighborhood (one street away), it was quite daunting, not only because the neighborhood was much more socially mixed but also because the Lord seemed to be directing them towards an old eight-bedroom convent that needed completing renovating. How they got the house was quite miraculous and a real confirmation that God was in the move. (It's good to have a clear word from God when making such big decisions). The result of their move has been that it's now so easy to pop in spontaneously and not to have to make an appointment to visit. We are able to have much more of a shared life and live more like extended family.

## HANDLING CRISES

Handling interpersonal crises are a normal part of family life. These come in all sorts of shapes and sizes. There is no silver bullet for dealing with them, but I have found a very useful framework for helping people process what is going on, one that doesn't leave them feeling powerless, a victim, or stuck in the situation. I call this framework "The Three Lenses",

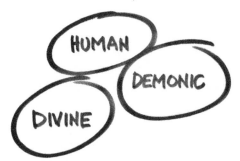

The *human* lens is the one most people focus on. He said... She did... etc. Human pride, insecurity, insensitivity, jealousy, miscommunication, weakness and failing is at the root of most interpersonal problems. And there is a need to deal with the situation through this lens.

Sometimes it feels like the church is one of the most dysfunctional families on earth! We hurt one another, we let others down, and we sin against each other. Often we cause offense without even realising it. The human dimension is real, powerful, and needs to be dealt with appropriately. There may be a need for a third party to get involved, as in Matthew 18:15-17. We have to learn to "speak the truth in love", but not use the truth as a weapon to inflict further hurt on each other. There will always be a need for repentance, as well as giving and receiving forgiveness. Forgiveness can be instant, but trust will take time to be rebuilt. Whatever we do, we mustn't just bury this stuff under the carpet.

But this isn't the only lens. The *demonic* lens helps us ask the question, what is the enemy trying to do here? It may of course be nothing, but in my experience there is usually a demonic element because the devil is an opportunist. He knows that if he can break relationships in the family he can rule in the situation (the "divide and conquer" principle). So we must take a step back from the human pain and confusion and start to see what is happening in the unseen realm. The enemy is usually at work when there is misunderstanding and miscommunication. It may be fanciful theology, but when I think of the devil being the prince of the power of the air (Ephesians 2:2), I imagine him messing with the airwaves of communication between brothers and sisters.

When we try to help someone unravel their traumatic, often complex and multifaceted situation, it's important we help them see where the devil is at work. Is he trying to break their relationship? Certainly, yes. Does he want to spread the seeds of offense and create a root of bitterness by which many others will be polluted (Hebrews 12:15)? Certainly, yes. Does he want to bring people into a destructive mindset of anger and unforgiveness that will lead to great unhappiness and isolation? Certainly, yes.

How we deal with the enemy is very different from how we deal with each other. The basis of our warfare will certainly start with whatever forgiveness is needed; otherwise the devil will retain legal rights in our situation (Ephesians 4:26-27). But then we need to stand alongside our brother or sister and face the enemy who intends to steal, kill and destroy. We need to rebuke him and his schemes. The apostle Paul said to the Corinthians, *"We are not unaware of his [the enemy's] schemes"* (2 Corinthians 2:11). We too must be equally aware of what the devil is up to. If we aren't, we will continue to fight the battle in the human dimension, causing greater damage. We need to bind (forbid / muzzle / choke off), break, and banish the work of the enemy in the name of Jesus. We need to stand against him commanding him to flee (James 4:7). And according to God's promise, he will. Having done so, we can be more alert to his schemes in the future, able to guard ourselves from the same pitfalls.

The final lens is the redemptive lens: the *divine* lens through which we begin to see what God is doing in the situation. The Father is always at work. We know that because of His infinite creative and generative power He is able to work *all things together for good* (Romans 8:28).

In my experience, few people look through the demonic lens, and even fewer through the divine lens. However, herein lies real victory. Satan always overplays his hand. But God always has the upper hand, and is ultimately bringing blessing in the situation. That may come by way of humbling us, disciplining us, and exposing stuff in our life that He wants to deal with. It may be that He is actually realigning some of our relationships for greater fruitfulness. He may be giving us deeper understanding of and love for one another. Let's embrace what the Father is doing, and in His love, be glad for it.

Not every situation has a happy ending. Sometimes one party will walk away before fully processing what has happened. Sometimes there is a failure of forgiveness, but God is always ready and willing to bring blessing out of our pain if we will work with Him. Use the lenses and don't give the devil a foothold. Let's be the best family we can be.

## THE HONESTY AND HONOR MATRIX

Another simple idea can help us calibrate our family relationships. I call it the honesty and honor matrix.

The idea is fairly self-explanatory. We need a healthy balance of honesty and honor in all our relationships. Too much honesty at the expense of honoring each other leads to aggressive communication, which leads to conflict or withdrawal. Too much honoring without any honesty leads to a kind of passivity in our communication and fails to develop a healthy and mutual understanding of where both parties are coming from. Discussions are somewhat fake and certainly ineffective. An absence of both honesty and honor leads to hidden agendas dominating without ever becoming visible. No one knows what is really going on, and it leads to the parties defending their own turf from the unknown threat in a passive aggressive manner.

Needless to say, when both honesty and honor are at work in a constructive way, it leads to healthy conflict, honest discussion, mutual understanding, and shared, agreed outcomes with high commitment from both parties, who are fully engaged in the process.

I hope both these simple tools will help you navigate well the terrain of family relationships in the In dimension.

## TRY THIS

Think of a time when you were involved in a conflict situation, either when trying to help two other parties, or when you were personally involved. How could either of these two tools ("The Three Lenses" and "The Honesty and Honor Matrix") have helped you get a better outcome?

## OUT

The new disciple will sooner or later want to be working out how they make a contribution. No one wants to feel they are constantly on the receiving end. As well as playing their part in community, they will also have the joy of discovering they are part of the mission of the group. As they connect in the out dimension with their wider circle of family and friends they realize they have a story to tell. Their own journey to Christ is a powerful tool in drawing others towards God. The new believer usually has a large contingent of non-Christian friends. These friends will be aware that something has happened to them, and will often be keen to hear their story.

Ben tells the Up, In and Out story of a young adult community in Deal:

*"We moved to Deal in 2011 with a remit to plant a young adult missional community. There was no university or college in the town but the church we were working with had noticed a few more young adults staying at home and getting jobs after school or commuting to Canterbury for college. The church had good youth work up to 18, so already had some good relationships with older teenagers. We started with a BBQ in our garden. It was October, and we had forgotten that it would get dark really early so we all ate burgers, got to know each other and stumbled around in the dark. It was lots of fun. From then, we began a weekly cell-type meeting where we would meet, worship and share what was going on in our lives with six or seven 18– 30 year olds.*

Our start was very much Up and In focussed, but fairly soon we moved to Out. We tried a few things to connect with people who weren't Christians. First of all we met in pubs locally but quickly realized that we didn't have enough friends between us to invite along. We needed to find a different way to connect. A number in our group were quite musical, so our prayers and ideas ended with a plan for an acoustic night at a local coffee bar every couple of months. We ran a few "Imagine" sessions – they were great fun and built our confidence. They also helped us connect with new people, some of who came to our church's Alpha course. We left Deal in 2013 and handed on the community to other leaders, who continued to meet weekly and look for ways to build a wider connection. They continued with the Imagine sessions for a while, and also tried other ideas, like a weekly football team. The community continued to grow, and they experimented with breaking up into smaller groupings (missional households). Every now and again I look on the community Facebook group page (no one has kicked me out yet) and get excited to see all the new people that have been added and have passed through that group."

## THE4POINTS

The out dimension is often the hardest to develop in the growing disciple and we need to help the new believer tell their story naturally, briefly and in a compelling manner. We also need to help them connect it to God's story. The4Points[38] is a simple tool to help them do both things.

This tool is a way of reminding people of their own story as well as helping people tell God's bigger story. The most basic explanation of The4Points is this:

- God loves me

- I have sinned

- Jesus died for me

- I need to decide to live for God

Whilst this is the essence of these symbols, we can't afford to reduce God's story to four simple statements when we are trying to communicate God's heart and His bigger story. The four symbols need to be the framework around which we tell God's amazing four-part story of:

1.  *Creation*: How God in His love created us for friendship, has a great plan for our lives, and wants to be with us at all times. We can all identify with the deeper ontological questions of "Why am I here? What does it all mean?" In His love He made us, and in His love he wants to know us and for us to be part of His family. We find out that He originally created everything perfect and that included a fitting purpose for our lives.

2.  *Fall:* How life in our world isn't working. We know that the world doesn't have the ability to sort out its own problems. If it did, it would have done so by now. We also know that because of our own selfishness we are part of the problem (the Bible calls it sin), and in many ways we feel powerless to change our basic self-orientated nature. We sense that we were created for something more, and wonder why we seem to be constantly missing the mark. The world is broken and needs someone to fix it.

3.  *Redemption:* Christ, as God in human form, entered sinful broken humanity. He saw our dilemma and need of being rescued. He lived a perfect life that demonstrated what God the Father was like. He ultimately gave His life on a cross in our place, taking the punishment we deserved. He rose from the dead proving that He has the power of life over death. He is able to offer each one of us forgiveness from the penalty of sin, freedom from the power of sin, and ultimately a place in His eternal heaven where we will also be free from the presence of sin. Because of this He offers us a new start, a new heart, a new family, a renewed purpose and plan for our lives.

4.  The cross also points us to a Christ who is Lord, one who has conquered sin and death. We cannot come to Him for forgiveness, freedom and fulfillment without surrendering our lives to His Lordship. That's just how it works. While we continue to try and stay in charge of our lives, we will continue to experience guilt, fear, insecurity and uncertainty. When we surrender, we discover He has the best possible plan for us. It's our joy and privilege to submit to that.

5.  *Restoration:* The final purpose of God is to restore humankind and the earth to its original joy-filled, pain-free, and beauty-infused creation. He wants to restore us to the purpose for which He created us. The question is will we

receive all that He offers, or will we continue in our own sweet (or not so sweet) way, thinking we will figure it out for ourselves and reach our full potential without Him? He stands waiting patiently for our response. The earth stands waiting for such a people to demonstrate what that amazing beautiful future reality could look like. When we receive Christ and follow Him as Lord, we bring that future kingdom to our present world.

Around these four points, we can also weave our own personal story, as we have experienced each of these parts of God's great story. The4Points is a simple and useful tool that each new believer can wear as a wristband, carry as a tract, put on their car with stickers, wear as a tee shirt, and share with others as opportunities arise. I regularly have people stop me in the street asking what the four symbols on my car mean. It's a joy to stop for a moment to share God's great story with them. When they ask, I usually start with, *"Well, let me tell you a story … or, well, let me tell you my story."*

Every new member can be encouraged to be a storyteller, inviting their family, friends and work colleagues to join the journey, the great adventure in following Christ.

As for vehicles, we can use the small groups, accountability groups, and missional community life to share and encourage the use of these tools. We will talk more about "family on mission" and missional communities in chapter seven.

## THE STORY OF GOD

Another opportunity to tell God's story is in the context of a wider group, perhaps the missional community that is growing out of your extended family on mission. This will include people of peace, new believers and established Christians.

*The Story of God,* or what is also known as *The Story-Formed Way*[39] is a great tool for equipping the new disciple. It takes them as part of a group through the bigger story of the Bible in a number of sessions (usually about ten sessions in ten to twelve weeks). It covers many of the major stories of the Bible and how they move through the four stages of Creation, Fall, Redemption and Restoration: the redemptive arc of Scripture.

It provides a great opportunity to discover who God is and how He works in history. It gives insights into human being's identity as created in His image; into the catastrophic consequences of the fall, into the development of God's covenant people through the history of the Old Testament, and the anticipation of the coming Messiah. Finally, Jesus is revealed against this backdrop, the church is born, and our appetite is whetted for the culmination of history in his return. It points us towards the future hope of the church in the world and God's ultimate purpose in creating humans.

Tools such as the Learning Circle and the Triangle, along with The4Points and The Story of God are great to introduce the new disciple to the life of faith, what it means to walk with Christ and to be part of His family.

## TRY THIS

Using the Triangle of Up, In and Out, do an audit on your own life. How balanced are your own relational priorities, and which dimension needs to be strengthened? If you are leading a small group, missional community or church, look at how the balance of the group as a whole works. Does it reflect your own bias and how could you correct that?

## SIMPLE. STICKY. REPRODUCIBLE.

- The Up, In and Out Triangle of relational priorities

- The Great Commission, and the Great Commandments, revealing the what, why and how of our calling

- The 3 lenses—human, demonic, and divine

- What would a family do?

- The4Points

# 6

# THE DISCIPLE-MAKERS JOURNEY

**Questions:** How do we stop the new disciple becoming content to spend the rest of their days fellowshipping with the saints? How can we equip the disciple to be confident to find their people of peace, and not get "stuck" in their existing, limited relationships?

Jesus sent His disciples out to preach the gospel, heal the sick, and find the people of peace in Luke 10:1-9. This was Jesus' strategy:

- Don't go alone; go in pairs for strength and protection (v1).

- Go in faith that there is a harvest to be had. Pray for the workers to get the job done, then be a worker (v2).

- Go to the places where the people are; don't expect them to come to you (v3).

- Don't rely on human wisdom or man-made stuff; trust in the power of the gospel and the Holy Spirit (v4).

- Find ways of connecting with large numbers of people (in this case by going from house to house) (v5).

- Identify the people of peace and stay with them, invest in them, accept their hospitality and let them serve you (v6-8).

- Proclaim the kingdom and heal the sick (v9).

This is in stark contrast to our usual approach of expecting people to come to our events, on our terms and on our turf. That invitation may be helpful at a certain stage, but not if we are going to reach everyone in our neighborhood, town or city with the gospel (see Section 3).

So, with our new disciple who is beginning to stabilize, be strengthened and is starting to grow as a disciple with some healthy, regular, and sustainable discipleship practices, we will want them to grow further in the Out dimension, into a missionary disciple. This is not necessarily a linear progression, and there will be much to be gained from equipping the new believer to enter the missionary lifestyle from the word go. But if the first challenge for the church leader is to help the member to enter into a lifestyle of discipleship, the next challenge is to equip that disciple to discover their missionary call, so that they become a missionary disciple. This means mobilizing the member into the mission field they are called to. I often talk about needing to know whom you are called to, but also knowing whom you are called with. It was never meant to be a solo sport.

Most churches are filled with cosy, comfortable, often complaining consumers but rarely with dedicated disciples. There are even fewer missionary disciples, those who have become part of the mission force of the local church, mobilized into the mission fields around them. Mobilization of all believers is a vital step, enabling a church to fulfill its calling to its neighborhoods and local places of work.

Establishing good discipleship practices so that every member is growing in God is hard enough. Getting each of them to become spiritually reproductive is a whole other challenge. As they are maturing they are growing in confidence in their new faith, growing in confidence in the gospel, growing in desire to affect others around them. We need to seize this opportunity early on to introduce them to the lifestyle of the missionary disciple, and the practices that go with it. If they fail to move quickly into this phase, a couple of things are likely to happen. They will become comfortable in being a consumer Christian who only thinks about ensuring their own needs are met, and more tragic still, they may lose all their non-Christian friends!

What do I mean by missionary? As you have probably guessed I'm not talking primarily about those who head off to other nations to serve God. Whilst we need to encourage and support those who have such a call, I am talking about those who have embraced the missionary lifestyle wherever they are, at home or overseas. I would say, however, that if someone hasn't learned to be a missionary in their own culture, what hope do they have of being a missionary in another culture where the challenges are so much greater? The missionary is one who is sent. It is the Latin equivalent of the Greek word apostle. Both mean the same thing: a sent one. Jesus was a sent one:

"For this is how God loved the world: He gave his one and only Son, so that everyone who believes in him will not perish but have eternal life. 17 God sent [apostello] his Son into the world not to judge the world, but to save the world through him" ~John 3:16-17 NLT

As followers of Jesus we are all sent. Jesus said to His disciples, "As the Father has sent me, I am sending you" (John 20:21). We are all called to be His witnesses, some to the equivalent of Jerusalem, others Judea, others Samaria, and some to the ends of the earth (Acts 1:8).

But again, it's important that we don't default to the individualistic mindset. Sadly, this is how we usually perceive the call to be a missionary, a kind of "one man against the odds", and part-human, part super hero!

Let's remind ourselves that we exist first as family. The call to be missionaries is a call we receive as family, as community. So as we unpack the equipping of the missionary, we will be looking at this not just as the individual, but also as missional household, or family on mission (see chapter seven).

The first tool I want to explore is one that we can use individually but works equally well as we work together as a missional household or community. We have covered some of the basic equipping for the missionary in the Out dimension of the Triangle using The4Points. So let's take it a step further.

## THE DISCIPLE-MAKER'S JOURNEY

One of the things I have observed over decades of watching people seek to live out the missionary call (the call to be his witnesses, the call to be good news people, to gospel our people and places) is that it's very easy to get stuck. People go so far in reaching out to non-Christians but are easily discouraged and at times feel they have no more contacts to invite to anything, or that the few friendships with not-yet-Christians that they have invested in for years are showing no signs of spiritual interest.

The disciple-maker's journey is designed to help us keep going when it seems difficult, and to avoid some of the easily identifiable roadblocks that can stop us in our tracks.

This journey is broken down into four parts as you can see. Each section describes a different part of the journey. It also helps us identify the roadblocks and how to navigate them and not get stuck. It also offers a very simple way of keeping going. It's not intended to be a method. It's not designed to describe the many ways you will navigate the different relationships God gives you. It's not intended to be a logical progression that you try and follow slavishly. It is intended to be a simple set of landmarks that help you navigate your way on this exciting journey and adventure. I hope it is a blessing to you.

## STAGE 1: CONNECTING

Every journey of the disciple-maker starts by connecting with people. As I like to say about most things in life, and especially in the kingdom, *"everything is relational"*. There are very few people who come to Christ by reading a tract, by watching a religious program on the TV, or by randomly wandering into a church and hearing the gospel being preached. Undoubtedly all these things do happen, but by far the majority of people come to faith through a relationship with someone who is already a Christ-follower. At the very least, this plays a very big part in the process.

This is not surprising considering the plural, relational, family nature of God's identity. God operates by means of relationships; and as those created in His image, we will too.

So the journey begins with making connections.

Connections happen in all sorts of predictable as well as unexpected ways. We meet people in the shops, at the bus stop, over the water cooler at work, in our street, at the school gates, in the park, at the gym, at the doctors, and at parties. The question is, will we make the most of every opportunity? Paul puts it this way in Colossians 4:5-6:

> *"Be wise in the way you act toward outsiders; make the most of every opportunity. Let your conversation be always full of grace, seasoned with salt, so that you may know how to answer everyone."*

We need to ask, *"Will we be intentional to create multiple opportunities for connections with people?"*

What I observe is that when people have been Christians for a few years, they often have very few non-Christian friends or contacts. The few they do have, at best, have failed to respond to multiple opportunities for spiritual conversations or invitations to events, or at worst, have never had an opportunity for spiritual engagement.

I remember a time in Frontline when we had been running with a very evangelistic and intentional cell group vision and structure. Over several years people had invited all their not-yet Christian friends to multiple events that we had put on over that time. The Christians felt they had exhausted all of these contacts, those naturally close to them in family, friendship or work. They had evangelism fatigue! And they had lost hope that their family or friends would ever show spiritual interest.

Reaching out to others requires that we break out of our comfortable and convenient circle of friends. This may be uncomfortable, but it's not difficult or complicated. We just need to be intentional about making new connections. So in reference to the disciple-maker's journey diagram, we see there is a mindset shift needed from few to *many*. We need to realize we can't just focus on a few, and that we need to make connections with many. If we don't make many connections, over time we are very unlikely to find people of peace (Luke 10:6), i.e. those who are spiritually open and *leaning into relationship with us.*

It's worth mentioning at this point that finding people of peace is a massively important part of our journey. We are not responsible to successfully persuade every one of the truth of the gospel, neither are we expected to invest the same amount of time in all our relationships. Jesus calls us to be available to all, to be a witness to all, but specifically to look for and invest more deeply in the people of peace as described in Luke 10. So focusing on finding those people of peace is both liberating and strategic.

Connecting with the many, not just the few (sounds a bit like a political slogan doesn't it) is a massive mindset shift from the early days of 1980s friendship evangelism, which encouraged us to just keep on blessing and loving the few people we already had connection with. Unfortunately, notwithstanding the rightness of continuing to be faithful with those friends, we need to understand that they may not be interested in God. We have to explore other ways of making many connections. By many I mean dozens, if not hundreds.

How do we do this? There are many simple ways. We can start to hang out where people in our neighborhoods or networks gather, like pubs, parks, cafes, coffee shops, book clubs, or football matches. We can be intentional to start speaking to those we don't know when we are at the school gates or shops. We can start to throw or attend more parties.

Our neighbors regularly put on Christmas parties so I make sure I prioritize them and deliberately speak to people I don't know. That's led to starting several relationships with people in our neighborhood I hadn't spoken to before. I discovered that I had a common interest with one who was in the Reserve Army for many years. We shared a common admiration for one of the greatest WWII heroes, Noel Chavasse, the only soldier to be awarded two Victoria Crosses (incidentally a great Christian man who spent time in Liverpool, training in what is now our church building, before enlisting). This led to us attending his memorial service in town together when the 100th anniversary of his death coincided with my birthday, and it led to some significant spiritual conversations.

Another young woman I met at the Christmas party the year after, who worked as a school teacher, allowed us to start to help her practically by providing food for kids in her class who came to school without breakfast. A simple connection at a party can lead to an enjoyable and fruitful relationship.

We can put on events in our street and invite everybody to them. I recently put out a drink and snack stall in our front driveway on a Sunday afternoon where I sat reading my book until someone passed by, and I was able to invite them to stop and have a drink with me. I wanted to make more connections in our street.

There are so many ways of going from few to many. Of course, we will then inevitably need to go from many to few as we start to discern whom the Father is working in and who are leaning into relationship with us. These are the ones with whom we will invest more time and energy. Others remain friends but don't get the same level of investment. In my opinion, we will need to have made contact with hundreds of people to find a handful of people of peace. It takes patience and persistence to do so.

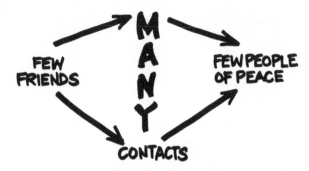

Some people may find this approach somewhat distasteful, even inauthentic, because if feels like we are using people. I don't believe this is true. When we look at the life of Jesus, we are persuaded that this is how He lived. He gave time to the crowds, but intentionally invested time in the seventy-two, a lot more time in the twelve and even more time in the three (Peter, James and John). If it is the way of Jesus, perhaps we should learn from that. "It is enough for the disciple to be like his master" (Matthew 10:25 ESV).

It's all about being intentional.

## STAGE 2: CHATTING

Having made connections with people we will inevitably start chatting with them. It really doesn't matter what we talk about. We are just trying to get to know them and to find out if they are interested in us at all. We can talk about whatever might be of common interest depending on context. If we're in the pub and there's a football match on, then we can talk about the game. If we are at the bus stop and it's raining, being British, we can of course talk about the weather!

It really doesn't matter where the conversation starts; it's where it leads that's more interesting. Sometimes we'll be snubbed and the person may refuse to talk to us. Fair enough. If they don't want to talk, we don't need to try and force something. I remember chatting to a couple at Runcorn train station late one night as we waited for a connection to Liverpool. At first the wife was just civil, but the husband wouldn't even look at me when I spoke – he deliberately looked in the opposite direction. That's just how it is sometimes. However, they turned out to be a captive audience, and with persistent friendliness they eventually thawed out, revealing that they had recently retired from being barristers and were now Welsh hill farmers! By the time we got back on the train, we were best buddies and had discovered we had a friend in the legal profession in common. It's fun making friends and finding points of common interest!

So if there is a response to our opening banter, we can start to find out a bit about them, where they work, what family they have. Most people like to talk about themselves. And most people are nosey enough to want to know something about you. You will usually get a chance to say something about yourself at some point.

The challenge here on the disciple-maker's journey is to see if the conversation can easily, in an unforced way, turn from *natural to spiritual* topics. Sometimes this happens easily. For example, when someone asks what you are doing over the weekend, it may give you an opportunity to talk about the church meeting you will attend and something of the life of your church community. If the conversation touches on your family, it may be easy to say something of your gratitude to God for the way He has helped you build a family or get through adversity together. I often say when talking about my marriage of forty-three years, that it if hadn't been for God's help, my marriage wouldn't have lasted one decade let alone four.

In all these opportunities we can look for an opening to tell our faith story. It has placed me in good stead to rehearse what I want to say in case the chance arises to tell my story. I can tell the brief version in about two minutes, and it's becomes easier and easier to weave it into many conversations. If anything of my faith comes into a conversation, it's easy to chip with, *"But I wasn't always a believer you know..."* and I'm off telling my story. Or if they simply ask me something about my life that is connected to my faith journey, I can simply say, *"Tell you what, can I just tell you my story."* There are plenty of natural segues in to spiritual conversation. Just be prepared! This happened to me last week when the magistrates I was sitting with in court asked me why I'd given up a career in general practice to go into church leadership. It was the easiest thing in the world for me to say, *"Tell you what, can I just tell you my story?"* and off I went. When we were interrupted by the case proceedings, they were quick to ask me to continue my story when we were in a position to do so later on.

## OUR TESTIMONY

Our faith story can either be crafted round the four stages of God's big story – Creation, Fall, Redemption, and Restoration; or it can be based around The4Points, or it can be simply crafted round these three sections – what my life was like beforehand, how I came to Christ, and what has changed since following Him.

Some who feel that they "have always been a Christian" aren't sure what to say about their life beforehand. It's important not to try and fabricate something to make it sound more dramatic. I became a Christian when I was twelve and didn't have any hell-raising tales of life beforehand. However, I was aware of a sense of alone-ness before I knew Christ; and this was followed by a deep sense of *belonging* afterwards. This has become an important part of my story. It's simple but real.

One way of helping to tell your story while keeping it simple is to do what I've just described above. To think of one word that typified life before and one that describes it afterwards. It may take time to figure that out, but once you have settled on a word for each part, then you can describe a few ways you experienced that to flesh it out.

Another way of telling your story is to try to tell it in six words. These then become the skeleton for telling the fuller story. So, for example, mine would be:

## BURIED ALIVE - ANSWERED PRAYER - ON FIRE

**Buried Alive:** This is the story of how I was buried under sand on a beach near Poole in Dorset, and nearly died at the age of fifteen. It was then I realized I was no longer afraid of dying. I experienced supernatural peace before I went unconscious.

**Answered prayer:** At the age of eight, I prayed a selfish prayer to come top of the class at school. It was the only time at that school that I ever came top. God certainly got my attention. So when I was twelve and heard about Jesus' death on a cross, His coming alive from the dead, and His offer of forgiveness, freedom and fulfillment, I jumped at it.

**On Fire:** At the age of nineteen, I realized I could never doubt again. God had answered so many prayers, had proved Himself to me over and over again. I realized I didn't want to live for anything but Him. I was on fire! And have been for the last forty-four years.

I have found over the years of telling my story through this framework that this order of events works good for me. People seem to understand and be curious to learn more. You may find that telling your six-word story in a more chronological order works better. It's up to you.

## TRY THIS

Try creating your own story based around six words and see if you can include the gospel as it was explained to you, or how you came to understand it.

When it comes to saying how you became a Christian, this is a good opportunity to talk about Jesus and what you did to become a Christ follower. It may have been gradual or sudden, it may have been structured or spontaneous, it doesn't matter. Talk about Jesus and what He's done for you. Describe it in your own words. I like to describe the impact of the gospel on me being as

- Forgiveness I could never deserve

- Freedom I could never attain

- Fulfilment I could never imagine

During this conversation about your faith story, or at a later date, you may get the opportunity to talk more about what Jesus has done on the cross. I recommend using a visual way of sharing the heart of the gospel. I like The4points as a way of doing that. It's very simple, works for any language and is a series of pictures on which you can both hang God's bigger gospel story, or weave your own story, or both.

I have the symbols on the side of my car as well as on a wristband. I love it when someone stops me (usually by in a supermarket parking lot - which happened twice in the last two days), and they say something like, *"Excuse me, but do you mind if I ask you what those signs on your car mean?"* No! Absolutely I don't mind. It is a great opportunity to share God's story with them, and I usually give them a small tract with the explanation so they can go away and think about it afterwards.

I love being a magistrate as I am always meeting new people, and often as we are chatting, waiting to go into court, I get the opportunity to tell my story One district judge ended up asking me to marry him and his girlfriend, and they went on to do an Alpha course in our home. Another magistrate took and read a copy of John's gospel from me. Many more have opened up spiritually as I've shared my story; one has allowed me to pray for him.

What we are looking for in all these is the opportunity to discern if God has led us to a person of peace. The person of peace is described in Luke 10 as the person who receives your peace, your shalom, your greeting and blessing. This is the person who is likely to welcome you into their heart and home, and probably wants to serve you in some way.

When the district judge I mentioned got married, instead of asking for presents for himself, he asked if all the guests would make a donation to our church's project in the Democratic Republic of Congo. Amazing! He continues to be a person of peace.

Relationships aren't built quickly. Trust takes time to establish. Wanting to know what you think about the deeper things of life isn't likely to be the first topic of conversation, but equally it's important not to wait for years before mentioning something to do with your faith or your story. It only needs to be a passing comment in an otherwise ordinary kind of conversation, but if you don't, it can seem strange to start inviting someone to something spiritual if you've never broached the subject in conversation.

However, when we have been able to chat at a spiritual level and have figured out who may be the people of peace, then we are ready to invite.

## STAGE 3: INVITING

It is remarkably simple to invite people to something, but most of us don't. We don't because we are afraid of the person saying no; or we don't have anything to invite people to, or anything we'd be confident to invite them to; or we don't want the responsibility of following them up if they say yes!

Many years ago, I remember going to get the sign for my medical practice made by an industrial engraver in Bristol. The boss, Nick, was intrigued by the fact that I wanted red Perspex one, rather than a brass plate. Those conversations led to me inviting him for a coffee. Intrigued, Nick agreed to come. Jenny and I struck up a friendship with him and his wife, Nikki (far too many Nicks in one room). The invitation to social contact led naturally to invitations to things that had spiritual content. Initially this was a Bible study exploring the claims of Christ. This was followed by an invitation to an evangelistic musical event called "Toymaker and Son", after which they both gave their lives to Christ. They have gone on to become disciple-makers in their own right. The challenge at the inviting stage of the disciple-maker's journey is to move from social invitation (e.g. come for a pint), to an invitation to a spiritual journey (e.g. come to Alpha, or our Christmas service).

Moving from *social contact to spiritual journey* is about helping to create an on-ramp to discipleship. The spiritual journey starts way before they come to Christ. It starts when they begin to engage with you at a spiritual level. It may be just watching how you live your life. It may be starting to ask spiritual questions. It may be experimenting with prayer. Whatever those first steps are, we want to create an intentional series of stepping-stones to faith and followership. If not, we may fail them in their yet-to-be-articulated desire to know God.

Invitations always start with friendship. We need to build friendship, to get to know the person, to find ways to bless them and if possible allow ourselves to be blessed by them. My friend with the interest in Noel Chavasse was keen to try and help me find a print of one of the portraits of the brave soldier. He turned up at my house bearing all sorts of offerings. I was blessed, and I think our relationship deepened, as he felt able to do something to bless me. It's a fallacy to believe we have to always be the giving one in the relationship. Often our friendships will grow faster and deeper when we allow others to meet our needs. This may seem counter-intuitive perhaps, but powerful nevertheless. When the 72 were sent out, they were dependent on people's hospitality. They had nothing of their own. It was part of Jesus strategy in sending them. Wanting to serve us is one of the signs of a possible person of peace. Mick and his wife subsequently came to an Alpha evening, and the journey continues.

The power of an invitation is simple, and quickly shows us, if we are not sure what the level of spiritual interest is, whether someone is a person of peace or not. It helps us calibrate how open they are to further spiritual conversations and an evolving spiritual journey.

Invitations are many and varied. We mustn't forget to offer to pick up the person if we are going to a venue other than our home. Do remember that if we are inviting them to a Christian event in our church, that it can be a very intimidating experience to go to a church building when they don't know anyone and have never been before. If we aren't taking them, we can at least meet them outside and go in with them.

Alpha, Christianity Explored, The Story of God, Journey's videos, and Seven Signs in John's Gospel are all spiritual journey tools that I have used.[40] If you are inviting people to something like this, tell them what to expect: leave as few surprises as possible.

Invitations should be completely un-pressured. We don't want people to feel press-ganged. We want them to feel that we want them to be there, but that we will love them just the same if they say no. If they say no and we leave the door open, they may well come to something on another occasion. If they have felt pressured, they are unlikely to stay in contact.

A friend of mine in our missional community decided to make a competition out of it when we first created an invitation opportunity for people in the community to invite their friends to. This was not one in which the person who got the most people there was the winner, completely the opposite. The winner was the person who got the most "no" responses to their initiations. This liberated everyone to have a go. The pressure was off. It became fun. The truth is, of course, that we can only ever make an invitation; God alone can move in their heart to create a spiritual hunger that would lead them to say "yes". Once we adopt this understanding of success it takes all the angst out of the situation. We can invite with impunity and just leave the rest to God.

Once someone has said "yes" to the spiritual journey, we should start to think of him or her as a disciple. Perhaps one that hasn't yet declared that Jesus is Lord, but nevertheless a learner, which is what *mathetes*, the Greek word for disciple means. If we think about it, the call to discipleship is the call to die! It is the call to follow Jesus wherever he leads us. It is the call to abandon all ideas of making it on our own and to trust in Him for every area of our life. How many of us came to Christ like that? I suspect none of us. When does a person become a follower of Christ? Is it when they say a prayer inviting Christ into their lives (of which there is actually no precedent in Scripture), or is it when they are showing the fruit of repentance in their lives? Food for thought.

So the journey of discipleship has begun. Game on!

How do we then help them towards a full understanding, acceptance, and experience of what it means to be a follower of Christ? How do we help them not just grow as a disciple, but also become a disciple-maker themselves, starting the cycle all over again with someone else. The answer to the first question has hopefully, to some extent, been answered in chapters four and five, but the latter question is answered in the final section of the disciple-makers journey.

## STAGE 4: MULTIPLYING

Whilst chapter nine deals more fully with Multipliers, this section starts to look at how a missionary disciple begins to multiply, by taking someone else on the disciple-makers journey. This final section of the journey is from *disciple to disciple-maker*. We help the person we have led to Christ, grow as a disciple and become a disciple-maker.

If a *member* is one who is learning the ropes of what it means to build their own practice of hearing and obeying (remember the wise and foolish man in Matthew 7), of intimacy with the Father, of becoming a learner from life, and of living out of the three relational priorities of up, in and out, then the *missionary* is first of all one who is looking outwards to make the gospel visible, audible, comprehendible and desirable. They do this as part of a missional household, a family on mission. But they embrace certain personal lifestyle habits on the way.

Taking someone from disciple to disciple-maker involves helping them discover the joy and privilege of pointing others to Christ. It has sometimes been described as one beggar telling another beggar where to find bread. I like the simplicity and compelling mind-picture that paints. It's also a process that describes the transition that they are making from missionary to *multiplier*...but more on that later.

As our young disciple, full of newfound enthusiasm shares their own experience with family and friends, they are having an impact whether they know it or not. In their zeal, some may be irritating, others may be engaging, but all who are truly discovering the reality of Christ's love and power cannot help but affect others. At this stage, they are at their most infectious. They will almost certainly have the greatest number of not-yet-Christian friends of anyone in their group. We need to do two things at the same time. Protect them and let them loose!

They need protecting, as they will almost certainly come under attack – in their job, their marriage, their finances, their health, or any other way the enemy can knock them off course. Once they are visible as followers of Christ (often after their public baptism), he will come after them and try to head off their newfound faith at the pass. He will seek to discourage them, bring them into conflict in their new relationships, or distract them with other "worthy" or "worldly" things.

We need to be protective by praying earnestly for them. Paul was at pains to describe some of the prayer protection effort made on behalf of the new believers in Colossae:

*"Epaphras [...] is always wrestling in prayer for you / praying earnestly for you / striving for you in his prayers / laboring earnestly for you in his prayers, that you may stand firm in all the will of God, mature and fully assured." ~Colossians 4:12 Composite translations*

As well as praying, we need to keep them close, in regular contact, daily if possible. A newborn baby shouldn't be left for long. Neither should a newborn Christian.

We also need to let them loose. We must help them infect as many people as possible with the gospel virus. They are at their most infectious, and it's not the time to quarantine them! Help them to have positive contact with their family and friends. Help them to be gracious and authentic in the way they tell their story. Above all, help them to connect their friends with the wider church family. Remember, "It's a family affair".

As they have influence in their circle of connections, they may not realize it, but they are starting to take others on the disciple-makers journey, and so the whole godly, gracious circle continues. (A gracious circle is the opposite of a vicious circle.) We can equip them to be intentional rather than random about the connections they are making. We end up making not just disciples but disciple-makers, which is exactly what Jesus had in mind when He told his disciples to *"teach them [their disciples] all I have commanded you"* (Matthew 28:20). Jesus intended the cycle of influence should grow and grow.

One young woman in our community who came to faith immediately invited her mom and grandmother to the community and the next Alpha course. She understood intuitively that it was something she didn't have to do, but got to do. The overflow of her life-change had a profound impact on her family.

## THE GLUE AND THE MAP

At the center of the circle diagram of the disciple-maker's journey are the three simple but life-changing words, "What's next, Lord?"[41]

The thing that gives the journey cohesion, momentum, and freedom are these three words. It gives cohesion because it is the one simple practice that is needed at every stage of the journey; it gives momentum because it stops us ever getting stuck; and it gives freedom because it stops us ever feeling we have to have it all figured out and create a game plan that takes each new contact from the A to Z of faith. We just need to know what to do next. Simple? I think so.

As we ask, "What's next, Lord?" it may be helpful to consider using the following map to figure out, to the best of our ability, where different people are on the journey.

## TRY THIS

Using the map below and the description above, plot which stage each of your discipling relationships are at.

WHO ARE THEY, WHERE
ARE THEY AND WHAT'S NEXT LORD?

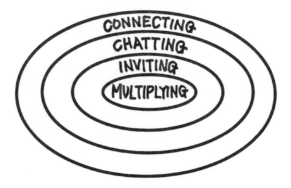

We will probably see dozens of people in the outer circle over a period of a year, and are likely to have just a couple of people who are in the inner circle of disciple-maker. This is how it works.

As we understand where each of our embryonic friendships is at, we simply ask the question, *"What's next, Lord?"* In other words, "What is the next thing you want me to do in this relationship, Lord?" It's not a hard prayer to pray, and perhaps surprisingly not difficult to hear God's reply. I think this is partly because He is so keen to help us in our joy-filled and challenge-infused adventure of making disciples, that He will help us willingly at every stage, gladly giving us the next idea.

Often the answers to our prayers come as a simple thought that pops into our mind as soon as we pray the prayer. I have found again and again that doing the next thing is a way of making the journey great fun and enjoying discovering what God does in response to my obedience.

It could be a thought as simple as...send them an encouraging text; "stop by and take them a cake; invite them to the pub; pray that you bump into them on the street; invite them to a BBQ or meal; invite them to the park with you and your kids; chat at the school gate; offer them help at work, or any one of a thousand different, but simple ideas.

A couple of weeks ago, I asked if anyone on our Home Watch group wanted to visit Williamsons Tunnels in Liverpool. One responded, and the "What's next, Lord?" I heard from God was to ask if I could get a lift with them. This gave opportunity to chat and get to know them more.

Our "What's next, Lord?" responses will usually be a mixture of invitation and challenge. We will gradually see if the person responds to spiritual conversation or hospitality. As we get to know them more, we can introduce more of the challenge, but initially it will all be simple invitation to relationship.

For those who are right in the bull's-eye of the map, they are up for lots of challenge, including starting them on the disciple-maker's journey. We can expect them to want to be challenged, as they will be keen to grow in their character and disciple-making skills.

The map will need to be updated every couple of months as it is always changing, both in terms of who is on it and where they are up to. This is the nature of life. Some will seem to have been inactive as contacts for some time. You may want to take them off the map for a while until God brings them back into your orbit again. You want to be giving your best time and energy to those who are "leaning in".

It's good to develop a weekly, or at the very least monthly practice of reviewing your "What's next, Lord?" actions. Sometimes you will find that you've completed the last thing God gave you to do, and other things you planned to do but haven't got round to yet, no longer seem relevant. It's all too easy for us to get sidetracked and lose momentum; so finding the right vehicle for accountability with the disciple-makers journey is really important. Missional accountability in a DNA triplet, or a small group is a game changer. It keeps the adventure factor high!

## TRY THIS

Make a list of everyone on your map, and each week pick a couple of them and ask God, "What's next, Lord?" It's likely that the first idea that comes to your mind is the right thing to do. Try it and see what happens. If it proves to be seriously unhelpful, then ask God so speak to you from that experience. In other words, go round the Learning Circle and ask a friend to help you process it.

## COMMUNITIES OF MISSIONARY DISCIPLES

The community aspect of the disciple-maker's journey is key to our fruitfulness and survival.

## FRUITFULNESS

Not one of us on our own has all the skills to raise a fully-fledged, fully mature disciple. We all bring different skills to the table, and we can draw on each other to help raise our missionary disciples. One may have great gathering abilities, others kindness and compassion, another a gift of hospitality, and yet another an ability to open and explain Scripture in an accessible and simple way. All will contribute to a person of peace coming on the journey of discovery to find faith, and everyone in the missional community helps that new believer grow as a disciple. The old African proverb saying that it takes a whole village to raise a child is very true. Similarly it takes a whole missional community to raise a missionary disciple. We have seen this again and again as we have watched different ones come on that journey of faith.

## SURVIVAL

The needs of newborn Christians are often overwhelming. In the early days of our community, we saw a young Somali asylum seeker come to faith. He was sitting round our table as we had been studying Scripture together. Half way through the evening he interrupted us to ask a question. Bear in mind that up until that time he had barely opened his mouth, and had only communicated with a few broken English words. His usual contribution to an evening was, *"My name is Kassim and I am a Muslim."*

What he said stunned us all. He said simply in broken English, *"I can see you are all happy. I think it is because you have Jesus. Can I have Jesus too?"*

The room went very quiet as we all realized the enormity of what he had said. Needless to say the Bible study got put on hold as we led him to put his trust in Christ. But it was only as the weeks unfolded that we discovered just how complex his situation was. We needed to give him help in so many areas. There were language lessons for a start, accommodation and food, help navigating the legal asylum system, transport, money, health issues and hospital appointments, ongoing education courses, not to mention helping him get his head round the decision he had made to follow Christ.

If any one of us had tried to do all this by ourselves, we would have been sunk. But as a community, as an extended family, we were able to cover all the bases and help him get established over the next nine months.

Eventually the government in its infinite wisdom (I don't think so) moved him to the other side of the country, away from all his support structures. He did, however, manage to get linked into a good church that continued to love and serve him.

*"We are ambassadors"* (2 Corinthians 5:20) is plural. *"You will be my witnesses"* (Acts 1:8) is plural. Church is plural. It's not a solo sport. It's a team game.

We are a family on mission. The members of a body (body parts) are no use on their own; they cannot function without the other members. Yes, we are individuals, but not at the expense of family. In God's creation, family comes first. Consider the Godhead, Adam and Eve, Noah and his whole family, Jacob and his twelve sons, the nation of Israel, and finally the church. As we think about being missionary disciples, we need to keep this family perspective and practice uppermost in all we do.

What would it look like if we always thought "family first"? Not just nuclear family, but God's extended family, our local expression of "family on mission". How would that change day-to-day decisions, use of finance, planning of time, and exercise of gifts? I suspect it would change just about everything.

We've talked about us all being witnesses, all being ambassadors, but what about the evangelists? Aren't they the ones who are meant to bring the new Christians in?

Certainly, they are key in our expressions of family on mission. They are catalysts to mission, they are trainers of troops, they equip the saints to be and do good news. They are the evangelistic conscience of the group. They will keep us focused when we want to veer off course. They will call us to sacrifice when we want comfort. They will advocate for the group to remain outward looking, and keep the missional purpose and purity of the group

We need the pastors, the teachers, and the prophets, but in my experience we need the apostles and evangelists in a more urgent way. Because of the intentionality required to maintain missional focus in any missional community, we need to especially look for and value the evangelists. Left to their own devices, most missional communities will, like any group, veer to the most comfortable option. *The missional energy in a group is like water; it always seeks the lowest level.* It's just human nature, fallen human nature, I'm afraid. That's why we so need the evangelists. They help us to aspire higher, even when it is costly.

It's not my purpose here to unpack all of the fivefold ministries of Ephesians 4:11-13, except to say that each of us is marked by one or more of these traits. Ephesians 4:7 says explicitly that *"He has given each one of us a special gift through the generosity of Christ'"(NLT).* Discovering the ministry traits of each individual is really helpful in building a mature community, as well as helping each person find their best contribution. It's also a way of discovering who the evangelists are.

I recommend the most recent fivefold survey from Alan Hirsch on his 5Q website – it's the best I have found so far. It is easy to do and relatively inexpensive: (https://5qcentral.com/product/apest-vocational-assessment/).

At the beginning of the house church movement, in the early '70s, we were strong on community but had little idea how to build either a missional or a discipling culture. We had the mistaken idea that if we just loved one another well enough the world would come running to our door. We were basing this belief on the prayer of Jesus *"that all of them may be one [...] that the world may believe that you have sent me" (John 17:21).* Sadly, it didn't work; we just produced a nice little Christian ghetto. I do think that our unity is very important in revealing Christ to the world, but not in the way we thought back then. (More of that in the final section of the book.)

Bill Hybels makes the astute observation that it takes far more energy and intentionality to build and maintain missional momentum and commitment in any congregation or staff body, compared with pastoral care or biblical knowledge for example. For every person we employ to help develop what we already have as a church, we need to invest more in those staff who are growing the church from new birth, not just recycling old saints. New birth growth is hard-won. We have to invest well our resource of time, money, staff, energy, platform opportunities, and social media content if we are to win the battle for mission and discipleship in our churches.

## SIMPLE. STICKY. REPRODUCIBLE.

- Everything is relational.

- The disciple-maker's journey of connecting, chatting, inviting, and multiplying, and the map.

- What's next, Lord?

- Your six-word testimony.

# 7

# LIVING OUT THIS LIFE TOGETHER

**Questions:** If the primary metaphor for church is "family", how much could that shape how we lead and build our churches and home-based groups? What are the tools and vehicles that will help us to grow extended families/communities of missionary disciples?

## FAMILY ON MISSION

Family on mission, or extended family on mission, is a term that Mike Breen has used extensively.[42] It is helpful in that it is easy to understand. But it describes more than defines, and it helps create culture more than structure. I want to use "family on mission" here to describe the best kind of culture or values of any community of believers that is serious about mission and discipleship.

Family on mission is another way of describing the ideal heart or values of any missional unit in a church that is serious about discipleship culture. This understanding of how both *family* and *mission* interact and combine at the heart of church life has evolved over the last couple of centuries.

Back in the day of the early pioneering missionaries, both local and international, the dominant mindset of the day was family or mission. Mission was the high calling of the few, and the pioneers were required to make huge sacrifices of family life in order to be true to this calling. Many amazing men and women left family behind to pioneer in some of the most hostile mission fields in the world. In contrast, those who put family first had no expectation of being missionaries in any context.

The next development was family *and* mission. This was an approach that required great discipline in time management, frequent burnout due to overload, and most often a failure in both family life and mission. Some of us have grown up in this culture and have the scars to show for it. We tried to have our cake and eat it. We hoped to successfully juggle the competing and demanding pressures of both family and mission. Very few have been able to make this work successfully.

Family *on* mission is different again.[43] It tries to express what an integrated life might look like. Family life fully connected to the family's mission. They aren't separate departments competing with each other but the two faces of family life. With this understanding, missional activities are not fitted around family life; they are the natural activities of a family's life bent towards its purpose and mission. So taking the children to the park becomes an opportunity to invite the neighbours and their kids. Friday night family tea becomes an opportunity to include some community members or unchurched friends. A trip to the cinema becomes a time for introverts to invite their work colleagues to a non-socially demanding time of fun and relaxation. All of these normal family times are being bent towards the family's mission. *It's one life. It's an integrated life. It's a joy-filled life.* If we can't say that it's a life that others would want, then we probably need to change something!

The word *family* is a great description of the culture of church. God is our Father; Jesus is our older brother, the Spirit is the Spirit of adoption (Rom 8:15); we have been adopted into this family and others are our spiritual brothers and sisters. One of the great New Testament ways of describing the church is the word family.

"For this reason I kneel before the Father, from whom the whole family in heaven and on earth derives its name." ~Ephesians 3:14-15

As I mentioned before, whenever we have a question about what is the right thing to do in the life of our household or missional community, then the best question to ask is, "What would a family do?" I have found that it is a remarkably releasing and useful question. For those of us who have grown up in broken or dysfunctional families, we may need to imagine what a good and healthy family would do.

Imagine a mother and father who are always there for their kids, always providing, protecting, nurturing, and releasing them as they get older to fully develop in their own personality and gifts. Imagine a sibling group who laugh together all the time, who support one another when there are tough times, when others pick on them at school, or when they have doubts about their value. Imagine this family gathered daily round the table to eat together, sharing news and praying together, making room for friends from outside. Imagine this family with a clear family identity and a sense of purpose, preferring one another, finding a place where they served others together, and brought the good news of Jesus to them when the opportunity arose. You might be getting close to the kind of family we need to be thinking of.

If this is so far from your own experience of family, take a look round at some of the most 'together' families in your church, they may not be perfect but you can probably identify things you can learn from them about what a healthy family looks like.

The Family on Mission Triangle looks like this:[44]

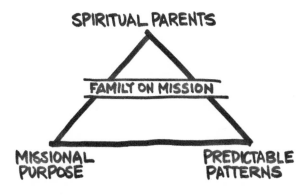

This depiction of family on mission identifies three areas that reflect the Up, In and Out Triangle. If we are to develop this culture in our different small group structures then we need to consider these three aspects.

## SPIRITUAL PARENTS

This is a way of understanding that someone has to take initiative, and someone has to take responsibility. My definition of leadership is this: *"leaders are those who take initiative and responsibility"*. Someone has to make the invitation for others to be part of the family; someone has to be the example, the model for others to imitate.

Each community of believers needs to be able to identify who the spiritual parents are. Generally they are the most mature, the furthest ahead on the journey of the disciple-maker, the most willing to gather and host, those who are committed to helping each one find their best contribution, those who will, in turn, raise up other leaders and spiritual parents. They are not, however, superstar saints or perfect. And if being a spiritual parent is not compatible with a busy job and family life with young children, then we are probably doing something wrong. It's about discovering that "one integrated life" way of living as a family on mission.

I've seen many groups where no one really wanted to take responsibility. The alternative is a kind of fuzzy shared cooperative leadership, which usually means no leadership. It rarely leads to anything healthy or vibrant and is hardly ever missional. It has a limited lifespan and often disintegrates with loss of good will and much disappointment. That which promised much delivered little.

To be spiritual parents is not limited to married couples. Single people are just as able to provide the leadership required. It's important to remember that the central character of the New Testament, Jesus, the perfect example of what God was like, was single. While single people can and do lead missional communities really well, it does usually help for it not to just be one person. So, for example, two single people who share a house or are in close proximity can provide great modelling of the life of a family on mission.

Those who lead missional communities benefit greatly from being in a coaching group (huddle) for both support and accountability (the low control sort of accountability that we talked about in chapter four). Because each missional community is given great freedom to express its own missional calling, have its own rhythms, style and flavour, it's vital that the leaders don't get cut off from the rest of the body or leadership of the church and that they remain accountable and teachable. This is where the huddle comes into its own.

## PREDICTABLE PATTERNS

This is another way of saying Spiritual Rhythms. The thing about predictable patterns is that they create a security that others can easily buy into. Every morning we do this; every Tuesday night we do that; every Sunday lunch we do the other. These kinds of predictable patterns not only create security because everyone knows what to expect, they also build good habits. It's very difficult to get into a habit of doing something that doesn't happen at the same time of day or week. Good habits are key stepping-stones to building the lifestyle of a missionary disciple, a primary goal of family on mission.

## TRY THIS

Predictable patterns can be developed round the Up, In and Out Triangle to help them reflect the three relational priorities of life. It's important to understand how our patterns reflect each of these priorities. Make an inventory of all the things your missional community or small group does. Mark each one with an Up, In or Out, depending on which dimension they most support. See if any of the Up, In or Out dimensions is poorly represented. Go back to God and ask Him what needs to stop and what needs to start. Take time to make these kinds of decisions. Involve all the people they will affect, as they will buy in much better to patterns they have helped to develop.

Sometimes creating predictable patterns can seem overly prescriptive, lacking room for the spontaneous. This can happen if we try to over-organize things. It's important that the patterns of life we are developing are sustainable and still give plenty of time and opportunity for the impromptu or unexpected. We talk about this as a *balance* between the *organized and the organic, the structured and the spontaneous.* Both are important.

It's also very important not to try and put everything of Up, In and Out into every regular missional community gathering (as some of us did in the days of cell groups, with the 4Ws of welcome, worship, word and witness). If we do this it creates an overload situation where nothing is done well, and subconsciously it says to members that the weekly gathering is where it all happens. We definitely don't want that to be the unspoken message. The balance of Up, In and Out needs to take place across a spectrum of organized and organic activity through the week and month. This naturally reinforces the message that *it is a lifestyle we are aiming for, not a meeting.* It's amazing how hard it is to pry Christians away from the midweek-meeting mindset (almost as difficult as the Sunday-service mindset).

## MISSIONAL PURPOSE

This is important for family on mission culture because it keeps the family both looking out and looking forward. Missional purpose is also a great means of pulling us together (In) and pushing us back into dependence on God (Up). A family that is working towards common ends will grow together in a much stronger way than one in which everyone is "doing their own thing". You can see the difference between two families in a restaurant. One family is at their table enjoying conversation, laughing and dreaming of "what could be" together. The other family is sitting in relative silence because each member is on their smart phone connecting to their friends on social media or checking their emails and texts.

Purpose is very energizing. It is motivating. People who have no purpose quickly lose any personal disciplines, for example around diet or exercise. They are often depressed and unmotivated. They may isolate themselves and become withdrawn. By contrast those who have purpose tend to be motivated and connected to others who share that purpose. We use the Philippians 2:2 verse from the NASB as a tag line for Together for the Harvest, the unity network of leaders in the Liverpool city region. Paul exhorts the Philippian believers to be "united in spirit, intent on one purpose". It is very motivating for us as church leaders to feel we share a common purpose for our city region. To be "intent on one purpose" means being *intentional*. To be intentional is in contrast to being unfocussed and random or reactive in the way we do life. It's also in contrast to being additional. By this I mean just adding more and more activity to an already busy life. To be intentional means using the things that are already part of our normal life and harnessing them for missional purpose. So a trip to the shops could be a time to buy something to bless a friend you are getting to know. It could be an opportunity to take one of the new disciples from your community to get quality time with them. Or it could be a chance to go with people of peace, if it coincides with them wanting to go to the shops too.

## OIKOS

*Oikos* is sometimes used to describe a specific household unit of church life that is embedding discipleship and missional practices, a missional household; and it can equally be used to describe a missional community. I will unpack both of these later in this chapter. However, I want to use it here to re-emphasise that it's culture, values and lifestyle more than structures that support mission and discipleship.

Oikos is a word that is used 120 times in the New Testament and is primarily translated as house, home, or household. It is the word used in Acts 2:46 when the newly birthed church was breaking bread and sharing meals from house to house (oikos to oikos). It is the word in the epistles when Paul describes the church in the house (oikos) of Philemon (Philemon v. 2), Priscilla and Aquila (Romans 16:5), and Nympha (Colossians 4:15). It describes the jailor and his household (oikos) when they are saved and baptised in Philippi (Acts 16:31). Likewise, in the same chapter, Paul encounters Lydia and her household (oikos). Her home then becomes the base for the church plant in Philippi (vv. 15, 40). In Acts 20:20 where Paul is summarising his ministry among the Ephesians he says:

> *"You know that I have not hesitated to preach anything that would be helpful to you but have taught you publicly and from house to house [Oikos to oikos]."*

The hugely important thing about the oikos is this. It was the primary unit of both mission and discipleship for the first 250 years of church history. Before public buildings could be legally owned by Christians, and under periods of severe persecution, the church continued to grow exponentially. It was something to do with the dynamics of the oikos.

Typically the New Testament home (oikos), in Greco-Roman style, would have consisted of a number of rooms round a central courtyard where extended family members lived. Such a set-up was almost certainly true of the household where Mary, John Mark's mother, lived. When Peter is broken out of prison by the Lord, he goes to Mary's house. Acts 12:13 states, *"He knocked at the door in the gate" (NLT)*. I imagine this as a large gate to an open courtyard. The smaller door within the gate would have been used to let individuals in and out without opening the larger gate, thus protecting the collection of rooms round the courtyard.

The household would usually have been the center of commerce or trade of the primary family. It would have been the gathering place not only for the extended family but also work colleagues, slaves, neighbours, friends and more distant family. The church commandeered this unit as the most natural vehicle for the gathering, equipping and sending of disciples into the world of the day. It proved to be mightily effective. By the time Emperor Constantine himself became a Christian, it is said that half of the entire empire had to some degree owned the name of Christ. In 313 AD, Constantine issued the Edict of Milan, decriminalizing Christian worship.

Coming back to Acts 2:42-47, the prototype church, we see a number of key activities which demonstrate the underlying set of values that the early church, under the influence of the Holy Spirit adopted. We can distill those activities and values down to five simple elements. These were the values and building blocks of the newly Christian household or oikos, and they can help us understand more of the practical outworking of family on mission values. Here's a simple picture of the elements of an *Oikos*

OIKOS HOUSE

Each of these elements is pretty self-explanatory. When the five elements are functioning effectively among a group of Christians, these believers are likely to be tapping in to something of the dynamic of the early church's community life. They also all fit around one another in aspect of the Up, In and Out Triangle.

The three keys that help to propel the development of oikos culture are added to the diagram below:

OIKOS HOUSE

I describe these as keys because they are simple ideas and practices that open up the broad spectrum of oikos life.

Jenny and I have for all of our marriage lived some variation of the oikos values. We have for forty-two of those forty-three years had extra people living with us. The numbers of those who have lived with us for extended periods is probably in excess of three figures. We didn't always know what we were doing, but we have certainly had a sense of living as an extended family with purpose, as well as a lot of fun! That purpose may not have always been purely missional, but it has been a deliberate attempt to live out some of the dynamics of the early church's lifestyle.

Our earliest attempts at this way of living involved a shared mortgage and a shared property with two other couples and a single guy (who actually provided the deposit). I was still a medical student at the time and it was quite a miracle that we were able to buy the property. When we bought our first house by ourselves it was a little two-up two-down with a small attic extension. At one point, we managed to accommodate Jenny and me, our first two children, three single girls who shared a room, and a young woman who I had invited to live with us having met her in the psychiatric unit I had been working in. Later on we gave a temporary home to an ex-convict (from the local prison) who slept on our lounge floor for a few weeks. I say this to make the point that "where there is a will, there is a way", and it doesn't depend on having a big income or a large house.

Sometimes people lived with us to help us at very busy stages of life. One New Zealand couple, Malcolm and Janice, were literally a lifesaver for us when our fourth child was born. For a season, we had four children under six years old. This wonderful couple moved in for three months and made life work for us.

Other people moved in simply because they needed accommodation. But by far the majority moved in because they needed the environment we provided, to find healing and stability in their lives, or because they wanted to be discipled by us. One day, one young woman was found standing on a windowsill ready to jump from one of our upstairs windows. Some of us were trying to coax her down from above, while others stood below in case she jumped. I'm not sure what we would have done if she had jumped – I don't think we'd have tried to catch her!

The man who had recently been saved in our prison outreach came out of the prison with nowhere to live. He had been the getaway driver in a less than successful bank robbery gang. Naïvely we offered him a place in our house. The gentleman wasn't very acquainted with the idea of personal hygiene, so Jenny would regularly put cotton wool balls soaked in perfume behind the storage heaters to try and mask the smell.

He took off a couple of times stealing Jenny's hand bag and then my camera, before he eventually returned and found a time of stability in a house of singles from the church, who lived down the road. Sometime later he moved away and we lost touch. God in his grace allowed us to see the long-term fruit in his life. On the very day we were moving to Liverpool, with the removal van in front of the house, he turned up on our doorstep and told us his story. God had kept him strong in his faith despite having experienced some sadness in his life. How good of God to let us see that. This is the power of living in community.

We learned a lot of lessons in those early days of how not to do community, but we also saw some great moments of breakthrough for many individuals. In recent years, we have been fine-tuning our practices of community-based mission and discipleship, as we have more clearly understood the worth and values of the New Testament oikos.

Let me state clearly that you don't have to have people live with you to practice oikos and family on mission. It is a very powerful way to live in community but not one that is either right or practical for everyone. But our homes and families are some of the most amazing resources God has given us to offer to a broken world looking for a place to belong and for spiritual reality. Our homes are also a great place of imitation for those who have never experienced a "normal" family. Many years ago, we had one particular young man live with us for a year. We had little idea that he was learning anything from us. Let's just say that he didn't wear his "teachability" on his sleeve! He recently admitted that everything he had learned about family life, he learned from living with us (much to our surprise). He now has a fabulous family of five in our neighborhood. They also interestingly have others living with them. It's the power of imitation – Jesus' greatest method for training his disciples.

Back to the three keys in the picture above which have been so helpful.

Having good *spiritual rhythms* in the life of our household has helped us to stay connected both to God and each other. This has included breakfast with the

Bible. We invite whoever is living or staying with us to share ten to fifteen minutes of reflection and prayer from the daily Moravian set Bible text.[45] We have also sought to eat together as often as possible in the evenings, inviting others from outside the home to eat with us frequently. In the evenings, we will try to break bread and pray after those meals whenever possible.

These rhythms, though far from perfect, are helping to build the oikos spiritual value of "Christ at the center". It's important to be intentional and have a go, and not to worry about having the perfect lifestyle! People sometimes like to tell me what they can't do because of their busy or complicated lifestyle. My response is usually to say, *"Don't focus on what you can't do, focus on what you can to."*

Other rhythms include eating and storytelling with the wider community twice a month. We do something one Sunday per month that connects us with our wider community and network of friends e.g. a brunch, a BBQ, a shared litter pick and picnic in the local park with the volunteer park organization, or lunch together in one of the eating establishments on High street. Some in the community will try to have a weekly "shared table" evening when others from the missional community or wider community can be invited.

The *people of peace* key has been massively important to us as we have tried to build the shared mission/shared resource piece of our missional community life. As I said before, it takes a whole community to raise a disciple. We have found this to be true in terms of time, giftings, finances, and material stuff. Sharing what we have for the sake of the mission has prevented any one person or household taking the brunt of the load. However, when it comes to seeing people come to faith (and the early church was seeing people added to their number daily –Acts 2:47), understanding the people of peace principle is very releasing. Whatever the context we are always looking for Luke 10 people of peace. It's part of the adventure, starting each day by asking God to bring me into contact with people of peace

Having a clearly defined missional purpose is not always easy to achieve for a group who don't necessarily live in the same street. I've found it helpful to think in terms of *common mission focus* and *shared mission focus*. The former is a place or group of people that we all agree are a common focus for everyone in the group. For example, Jenny and I live in Victoria Park in Liverpool. For everyone in our missional community, this is a primary focus for our MC whether they live in our area or not. Everyone agrees to invest in our activities in our neighborhood. That's why it's a common focus.

Another example of a common mission focus is the comedy club that a missional community of creative types decided they wanted to invest in. As they all attended the small club, they built relationship with the owners and others who went. After a while, the owner offered the main couple the opportunity to have a go at stand-up. The wife proved to be very good at it! They were also offered the opportunity to run some of the evenings. What a great chance to change the culture of the club. But this only worked because they all went; they all owned this *common mission focus.*

However, all of us have a circle of contacts at work or in the places we go. The various people of peace (or potential people of peace) that individuals are in contact with can be shared among all of us. This is what I mean by a *shared mission focus.* This happens as we introduce each other to our friends, and deliberately invest in forming friendships with those who others bring to our events. By doing this, our people of peace will see multiple examples of Jesus in different ones of us, and this will have a compounding impact on them.

Jesus was pretty at home at parties. Parties are a great way of meeting each other's friends and beginning to invest in each other's people of peace. This is a simple way of developing a *shared missional focus.*

The third key to developing Oikos culture is *shared life.* This is only really possible when there is reasonable proximity. As we like to say, "Proximity is powerful" when it comes to developing a shared life. If we want to have regular food and fun together, we will find it difficult if we always have to get in a car or on public transport to get to be with our extended family. The psychological barriers are too great for most of us to overcome, and the risk is that missional community life is reduced to some regular planned activities or meetings. We need the organized stuff, but we also need the organic, the spontaneous, where we can drop in unannounced for a cup of tea, to borrow some milk, stay for a bite to eat, or to ask for some prayer. This is a shared life.

To develop a shared life means that some people will move house, like the couple I mentioned who left their very comfortable house in a leafy suburb of Liverpool and moved into an old rundown convent round the corner from us because they knew they needed proximity to fully develop that shared life. We used to say in the early days of the house church movement, that carpet slipper distance was the gold standard for proximity!

Others won't move, but will stay where they are and try to build oikos lifestyle where they are with a view to eventually becoming the center of a new emerging missional community. This is one of the powerful ways of multiplying missional expressions of church (more of that later).

Another expression of the desire for shared life is the practice of knocking down internal dividing walls or building extensions on kitchen and eating areas. This enables the gathering spaces in our homes to specifically cater for the needs of and desires for extended family. I call this process "oikosification"! It's the nearest most of us are likely to get to the courtyard culture of the early church, based in households. A number of people in Frontline church have done just that.

So family on mission and oikos are tools for understanding the biblical culture of communities of missionary disciples, and the values that need to underpin all our small or mid-sized groups – the essential nature of the scattered life of the church.

## MISSIONAL COMMUNITY (MC)

Many leaders and church members have a tendency to gravitate towards MC as a useful structure for helping develop the life of the church, and as an alternative to other midweek groups. This focus on structure can often be a big mistake.

A Missional Community is usually a mid-sized group of between twelve and thirty people who can still squeeze into the biggest home at their disposal, or occasionally in a neutral public space like a coffee shop. They develop patterns of connecting around Up, In and Out. They facilitate discipleship, mission and community life. At their best, they are a healthy mixture of organized and organic activity. The organized makes sure there are regular touch points for specific kinds of activity. The organic ensures they develop the lifestyle of a "family on mission".

However, the organized frequently trumps the organic, due to the un-reformed "home group mentality". The members see the MC as a meeting, rather than an extended family. This also means that the structure of the organized activity is put before the culture of the extended family.

Rather than take the time and effort to understand and develop the culture, they default straight to structure. Because MC can all too easily be looked at through a structural lens – with components such as worship, prayer, Bible study, discipleship, fellowship, and missional projects – it is easy to see it as the silver bullet that will turn a dying home group program into a vibrant rejuvenated mission and discipleship structure. It just doesn't work this way. The testimony of every church that has tried this transitional approach is that it has failed to get the results they hoped for. Sadly, for some, this has tainted the wonderful potential of this biblical way of being and doing church.

## DON'T PUT STRUCTURE BEFORE CULTURE!

At Frontline, we made that mistake in our transition, and tried to backfill structure with culture for years. In fact, when John, the new senior pastor, took over in 2015 he wisely put all the MCs on hold for three or four months. He wanted to allow those that needed to close to do so, and those that were healthy to reopen and become the template for others that would grow out of them. It's so much easier to start with the right culture in a few pilot groups that can grow and multiply, than to create a master plan in which everyone is assigned to one of the new groups, and then expect them to "get" the new culture, the DNA. DNA is always best multiplied from an original. And if a group doesn't have the right DNA it won't multiply.

The secret is always to put culture before structure. And it's helpful to think how this happens at household level first. Let's call such a household that has this culture, built around shared rhythms of Up, In, and Out, a Missional Household

(MH). MHs have a much greater likelihood of getting the culture and lifestyle right because the life of a household is essentially organic rather than organized. The organized can be very helpful at MC level, but it easily becomes a replacement for the organic rhythms of mission and discipleship culture that are needed to underpin it.

Missional Households have fully embraced the lifestyle of the missionary disciple. The members of a MH will have gone on the disciple-maker's journey; they will have built their own spiritual rhythms or predictable patterns. They will have taken on board the values of oikos and family on mission. They can then become the healthy nucleus for the development of a MC.

So, who or what is a Missional Household? It is very simply those who live under the same roof and possibly the two, three, or four others who engage with them in a more than weekly rhythm of shared life i.e. those who are in and out of that home throughout the week. These may be natural family, neighbours or close friends. They may be people of peace or existing Christians. They may be new believers or seasoned disciples. The one thing they all have in common is the household they are connected to and the missional purpose of that household.

Despite our best efforts at oikosification we will never have the expansive courtyard based homes of the New Testament (not to mention the Mediterranean climate) capable of accommodating gatherings of up to fifty people. We don't usually have the shared commerce of the New Testament oikos, though this could change with more home-based working. So, necessarily, we will have smaller and more diverse units. But this can still be a powerfully effective unit of as few as three or four, or as large as seven or eight. It can still be a great incarnation of family on mission culture.

This missional unit or vehicle is well equipped to take on a much more organic, lifestyle-based way of being church. It will be a great culture engine, and template for a wider Missional Community as it evolves. When we think Missionary Household, think organic, lifestyle and rhythms, rather than structure, program or meetings.

Which comes first? A Missional Community can grow out of a Missional Household, or a MC can be formed from a larger gathered group of believers around a missional purpose who then build up the individual household's rhythms. Either way, the end is the same: multiple MHs that connect together in a larger MC, for the sake of mission, discipleship, and community.

As we build the culture of oikos/family on mission in our MH, this culture will affect and infect the whole of our emerging MC.

As a MH grows into a MC, it needs to provide a more structured way of including everyone, both those people of peace who are leaning in, and the other Christians who are starting to be drawn to the bright light of healthy oikos/family on mission culture. This is helpful in that it gives a greater pool of people for more ambitious missional activities. The MC also creates more opportunities for those connecting in order to grow in their discipleship as well as their gifts and contribution.

It's worth noting at this point that people will be drawn to our MC for all sorts of reasons, some good and some not so good. Some may just be looking for a place of connection without any thought of missional purpose. Others may be looking to find their sense of significance in their contribution. Neither of these types of people, or others who come with mixed motives are disqualified, but they can create a dilution of, or even damage to the DNA of the group. Because of this I have found it very useful to ask two questions of anyone wanting to join a MC from within the body of the church i.e. existing Christians.

The two questions are

- Are you willing to share our missional focus?

- Are you teachable?

No matter how I ask these questions, that's what I need to find out. If the answer to either of these is no, then I think twice about inviting them to join us. If the answer is yes, then I'm confident we can work with those people and help them to engage with, and be formed by, our DNA.

Where new people are being added as people of peace or as newborn Christians, these criteria are not relevant. We treat them as "in" unless or until they chose "out".

The MC size (twelve to thirty) is probably best suited to wider missional activities as well as extended family gatherings. By the time it reaches twelve people, it is probably already developing smaller structured groups of three to eight for discipling activities, closer fellowship and prayer. The bigger it gets, the less frequent its whole gathered activity will be, and the more frequent the smaller groups. The ideal size for a smaller group will depend on its purpose. For example, if it's a Discovery Bible study, then five or six is a good size. If for an accountability group, then three or four is a better size. Single sex groups can sometimes be helpful for allowing deeper and more personal levels of sharing. The size and make-up needs to be governed by the purpose.

The MC and small group will, by necessity, be more organized and structured than a MH. However, it's important that the organized doesn't suck the life out of the organic, oikos/family on mission lifestyle of both small group and MC, nor become a substitute for it. This can happen all too easily and we need to resist the drift back to the classic midweek meeting at all costs.

## THE 6 RHYTHMS

Because the heart of the life of a Missional Household or Missional Community is in its rhythms or predictable patterns, it is helpful to take a look at Caesar Kalinowski's teachings on *The 6 Rhythms* that he says are common to every culture. These are not so much around Up, In and Out, but are created by looking at what we naturally do all the time. It simply takes our normal rhythms and infuses them with intentionality.

This may not ultimately be the best set of rhythms for a particular community to adopt. A group may discover its own set of rhythms more suited to their context. However, there is much to learn from these. And if a MC doesn't know where to start in developing its own rhythms, these could be adopted until home grown ones are created.

Below are some extracts from Caesar's book Small Is Big, *Slow Is Fast*,[46] which summarise these six rhythms. Under each rhythm, I've shown how our missional community (Eat, Love, Pray = ELP) has processed and practiced the principles.

**Get a Rhythm.**

*I have learned that the secret to increasingly living our lives together on God's mission is to move away from seeing discipleship as something that needs to be tacked onto an already busy schedule, toward seeing all the normal stuff of life as full of opportunity for discipleship and growth in the gospel. This is not a call to life plus mission; rather, it is a call to life on mission. We have discovered six common rhythms that are found in every context and culture that we can intentionally engage in for the sake of making disciples. I have found that these six rhythms have been like handles I can hold onto, rather than a missional to-do list. In many ways you may already be living in some of these rhythms and just not have noticed. As you read through them, think about what each one might look like for you as a part of your daily and weekly cadence of life.*

1.  **Know the Story.** Everyone has a story (or many stories) to tell; we are "story-formed" people. Make it a habit to get to know the stories of the people in your life and community. They are dying to tell you! Help others to see how their stories intersect with and mirror God's story. In order to grow in this ability to listen and connect the stories of people with the story of God you will need to get more familiar with the narrative of the Bible and God's story

**ELP response:** As a community, we would love to make space to hear everyone's story over the shared meal table, to both truly know them, and see how their story reflects God's story, and weaves together with it. We'd love to do that with our people of peace too, as a way of helping them see themselves in God's story for their life. It would be great if we could finish going through the Story-formed-way to ensure we all have a good grasp of God's big story.

2.  **Listen.** We are all listening to something or someone. Set aside regular times to just listen to God. Try having times of prayer where all you do is listen for the voice of God to speak, resisting the urge to give God your to-do

list. Regularly practice listening "backward" by spending time in God's Word. And actively listen "forward" to hear what God is saying to you today through his Spirit and through your community. God is waiting to talk with us.

**ELP response:** We want to live a life that is hallmarked by God's kairos interventions. We want to read Scripture expecting God to speak, either on our own or in DBS (Discovery Bible Study) in our gatherings; and we want to listen to each other as if God might speak through any of us. We really want to be asking the "What's next, Lord?" question regarding all of our people of peace and those we are discipling on a regular basis. We also want to share what we think God is saying with each other. We recognise that we will need to make space for God to speak to us individually, as well as together as a community.

3. **Eat.** Regularly eat meals with others as a reminder of our common need for God and his faithfulness to provide for us both physically and spiritually. You are probably already eating around twenty-one meals each week. Start by consistently having at least one meal each week with a not-yet believer. Frequently invite others to have a seat at your Father's table!

**ELP response:** Wouldn't it be brilliant if we not only eat together on a Monday night, but also committed to each sharing one other meal per week with someone else in our community, or someone who might be or become a person of peace. If we did this together it might even be more fun.

4. **Bless**. God desires that all nations, all people would be blessed through Jesus. Seek God's direction for who He would have you tangibly bless each week. Intentionally bless others through words, gifts, and actions. You will be amazed at how many opportunities there are and what a difference it makes when a community is consistently blessing those around them.

**ELP response:** Imagine always having a personal blessing fund at our disposal, so we were always in a position to bless people in need, or people we just wanted to bless! We could make this part of our listening rhythm, listening for who God wants us to bless each week. A blessing could be given in any of the five love languages.[47] This could grow to become such an important part of our culture that it also becomes a natural part of how we do life together. As a whole community, we could be regularly looking for whom we could bless. It could lead to acts of service in our local communities. We could regularly ask, "Is there someone or a group of people in our spheres of influence that we want to bless together?"

5. **Celebrate.** Everyone is celebrating something; join them! Make celebrations and parties that you already attend a way to share the generosity God has shown you. Gather consistently throughout the week with your community to share stories and celebrate all that God is doing in and among you. Invite others to these celebrations as a way of displaying God's extravagant blessings.

**ELP response:** Imagine if we made celebration a hallmark of each time we met together. For example, we could always ask the question when we met, "Who has something they'd like to celebrate this week?" – allowing us to share in that person's joy. We could mark birthdays more significantly, either by using our Monday nights to remember them, or by holding simple parties at any point in the week, as an opportunity to invite our people of peace as well our community friends.

6. **ReCreate.** Take time each week to rest, play, create, and restore beauty in ways that display the gospel, resting in Jesus' completed work on your behalf. Cultivate this gospel rhythm of rest and create = ReCreate in your life. This is truly what it means to keep the Sabbath.

**ELP response:** Wouldn't it be great not only to practice ReCreation individually (Sabbathing etc.), but to also have times together with no agenda, time to simply recharge together where we can be creative and inclusive e.g. games nights, making stuff, or walks in the countryside.

Caesar says in conclusion:

*Each of these rhythms can be practiced in your life individually as well as in community, and they will help establish new organized opportunities for mission as well as occasions to be more present and find opportunities to share and model the gospel in more organic ways.*

*You might find it helpful to post these "rhythms" somewhere to remind you of these easy, daily opportunities you have to live out your gospel identity. What I am suggesting here is "recycling" your time: looking at the activities and normal stuff of life you are already involved in and seeking to bring a greater gospel and missional focus to them rather than adding more events and extra commitments to the calendar.*

*If life on mission, a life of discipleship, is too hard, or seems impossible with your schedule . . . Choose a different rhythm.*[48]

The beauty of these rhythms is that they force us to look at this life as "one life", not a series of disconnected activities. They also push us to think lifestyle not meetings.

## SIMPLE. STICKY. REPRODUCIBLE.

- Family on Mission and Oikos values

- Organized and organic patterns of activity

- Culture before structure

- Six rhythms of Story, Listen, Eat, Bless, Celebrate, and Recreate

# 8

# OTHER KEYS TO BUILDING EFFECTIVE COMMUNITIES ON MISSION

## INTRODUCTION

This chapter introduces a collection of ideas, practices, and tools that help our MCs to be effective in growing, or at least remove some of the barriers to growth. Over time I have observed all of these have a significant impact on different MCs, especially those that seem to have "got stuck".

**Questions:** Why are my missional communities not bearing fruit? Why do so many of them seem to revert so quickly to the old mindset of home group?

## BREAKING THE IDOLS

Building family on mission culture in our Missional Households and Missional Communities is no easy task. It's not a simple organizational task for church leadership, or in a bigger church perhaps for the pastor of small groups. Why is it such a challenge to us? I believe it is because it hits at the heart of our *independence* and *individualism*, two of the great idols of our time.

In most cultures, in most of history, extended family was the norm. Members of the extended family tended to live under the same roof, or certainly just down the road. It's only with the advent of new levels of wealth in Western culture over the last one hundred years that we have been given other options. Now we don't have to depend on each other for survival. We have moved up Maslow's hierarchy of needs.[49] Instead of our focus being on meeting our physical needs for food, clothing, shelter and safety, we have advanced to the so-called higher levels of meeting our needs for love, belonging, the respect of others and self, and beyond that to the highest levels of self-actualisation, significance and fulfilment.

You will notice that at the lower levels, we are much more dependent on each other, and this is where extended family thrives. At the higher levels, we are probably thinking much more individualistically, perhaps at times selfishly.

In our post-modern culture, we are inundated with self-help books designed to help *me* "be the best *me* I can be", to "help *me* find *my* true self and significance". As valuable as some of the insights of this narcissistic world may be, they tend to push us increasingly to the mindset of the unholy trinity of "me, myself and I", not us or we. They mitigate the possibility of living as God intended us to live, in community, and in extended family, as a first priority, and point of reference for anything we do as individuals.

Consequently, we have to go to developing countries and cultures, or first generation immigrant communities to rediscover what extended family looks like. This was the biblical culture of both Old and New Testaments. And it may just be that in embracing modern life, with all of the benefits it brings, we have overlooked something very precious.

We have become obsessed with *me*: my time, my space, my rights, my career, my fulfilment, my pleasure, my choices, my nuclear family which I must protect at all costs, my home, my castle. That's why it is so hard to rebuild according to biblical patterns and in the image of the triune community of the Godhead, who is family, who designed family and works primarily through extended families on mission.

Remember our foundations: "Be before do", and being made in the image of God. Who are we? How do our lives and relationships reflect the "family on mission" God? Our identity should be family before individual in all material ways. Yes, we are individuals, all with our unique relationship with God the Father, as his sons and daughters. We all have to come to God in our own right, receive our own forgiveness, and our own adoption as sons and daughters. But when it comes to figuring out how to live the life that God has given us, it should be done through the lens of family not of individual. Even salvation came to whole households in Philippi and other places (Acts 11:14; 16:31).

Does this start to explain our deep discomfort with the call to family on mission, to missional households? I think it does. It is why at almost every turn there is resistance to the call to this life on mission as communities of believers. It's why we can't possibly approach this as a structure to implement. Until we "get" the DNA and start to live it out, we will never persuade others around us that this is not just the next fad, but instead a recall to the Maker's original pattern and intention.

My VW Golf was recalled by the maker for a part of the emissions system to be reprogrammed. You may remember the outcry in the media when it was found that VW had conned the public and the authorities about the true nature of the VW emissions testing. They had deceived us by rigging the system so that it gave falsely low pollution readings. The reality was that the diesel emissions were far worse than reported, and they were getting away with murder. They were polluting our air and destroying our planet.

Similarly, I believe we have bought into the lie and idol of individualism; it's been polluting the church and destroying the family on mission that is God's answer to the world. It's time to get reprogrammed, to be recalled to the maker. We need to do this together and to become accountable to each other for the day-to-day decisions we make. We need to see the issues clearly and commit to changing our mindsets. It's a big job and one that will take time. Ironically, it's one that requires us all to work together, to pull down the idol and break down the mindset.

So we need all the help we can get!

As we start to implement this family on mission lifestyle, we need to think strategically as well as relationally. I say all the time that "everything in life is relational", and I deeply believe it. But if we don't also start to think strategically and intentionally, we will never see the needed change in church culture: the release of God's missionary heart through trained, mobilized family on mission units. It's not for the faint-hearted. To think strategically means to commit to working through some processes as Missional Households and Missional Communities. For example, it might involve looking at the six rhythms and coming up with a plan that we want to implement. Or we might choose to hold ourselves accountable to one another for reviewing how we are doing in building the family on mission culture with its predictable patterns around Up, In and Out. We just need to make a plan and stick to it!

*Materialism and Consumerism* are as lethal as independence and individualism when it comes to sabotaging family on mission culture. They are not only toxic in their own right, breeding an unhealthy addiction to stuff and comfort, but because they are some of the powerful drivers of our evermore busy lifestyles, working every hour God sent, they make it very difficult to build shared rhythms of life, to make time to be together, to do life together. We may just have to make some sacrifices in terms of our aspirations for material standards of living in order to gain something far more valuable - the culture of God's family on mission, the community values of the Godhead, the body of Christ functioning as it was intended, the lifestyle of the early church that changed the world. Radical? Maybe, but valuable beyond imagination.

Unless we grapple with these idols of independence and individualism, along with materialism and consumerism, we will find ourselves sailing happily out from the port of conventional church, only to discover a massive elasticized underwater rope pulling us back into the safety of the harbor. To travel to new lands, we must be prepared to cut that cord and sail into the unchartered territory of church as the New Testament modelled it. We must leave behind the safety of what we know. The dying cry of every institution is "but we've always done it this way". What will we do?

## TRY THIS

Look with others at the idols of independence and individualism, materialism and consumerism and imagine what church might look like if you were completely free from them. Make a plan of how together you would like to change the way you live so that you could develop the oikos/family on mission culture of the New Testament church. Remain accountable to each other for making those changes.

N.B. These changes will take months and years to fully develop. Don't give up at the first hurdle. Keep asking "What's next, Lord?" in the adventure and just doing the next thing God tells you to do.

## STEPPING STONES TO FAITH

Another way we think strategically is in using the disciple-maker's journey. As we consider how to make connections, start conversations and give invitations, we are inevitably thinking about a series of possible stepping-stones towards faith. It might look something like this:

- Say hi

- Start a conversation

- See if they pick up on any spiritual content that you drop in to that conversation

- Explore their faith background or lack of it

- Share your own faith story

- Connect them with God's story

- Make time to hang out

- Ask if they would like to chat more about spiritual things

- Make more explicit invitations to explore faith

- Guide them through a steps-to-faith process like Alpha or Story of God

- Ensure they understand the bigger gospel

- Deepen the discipling relationship and keep calibrating invitation and challenge

- Offer to pray with them and get them to try praying out loud

- Help them connect with God's saving grace

- Introduce them to the idea of being discipled in community

- Invite them to some of the organic and organized rhythms of the missional community life

- Get them started on the disciple-makers journey, making their own connections, conversations and invitations.

It's not rocket science, but we often drop the ball with those who are on their faith journey. Asking the "What's next, Lord?" question will definitely help. One thing that's clear from the above example of possible steps is that the "saving moment" of committing to Christ, asking Jesus into their heart, repenting of their sin etc, is just a small part of a much bigger saving journey to faith. We often put so much effort and energy into that moment, but easily forget the bigger process that it is part of.

Understanding that there are some obvious stepping-stones to faith will allow us to keep moving forward. Let me illustrate this with two current situations representing different journeys on these stepping-stones.

When I was prayer walking our local area in the summer I dropped into a new café/restaurant on High street. The couple that ran it were very friendly, offering me a free cup of tea or coffee. That immediately got my interest, wondering if they might be people of peace (remember they like to serve you). As I kept listening, the husband in particular wanted to engage with me in spiritual conversations. Jenny and I have taken different members of our missional community in to eat there. We wanted to bless them with our trade but also for them to meet others in our community.

Over the last few months, the husband has asked me to come in to see him to talk about a particular situation he is struggling with. As I've continued to ask "What's next, Lord?" I felt God said to "tell him your story", which I did; this led to explaining the gospel to him. He probably hasn't yet got a full on relationship with Jesus but he is drawing closer. Last week he let me pray with him for the first time. All I've done is pushed on an open door of relationship and asked "What's next, Lord?" The stepping-stones aren't set in stone (no pun intended), and every journey is different. But understanding the nature of the journey and looking for the next stepping-stone helps to keep us moving forward.

Interestingly, as I've got to know him and his wife I've been introduced to different members of his family, and it feels like I've become an honorary member!

Another man who has been helping with some building work is also taking steps of faith. It began with lots of "Hi, how are you?" type chats. Then a simple conversation about faith immediately drew his interest. He attended some of our last Alpha course in our home, and he is making clear noises about wanting to develop faith. I've taken that as an invitation to disciple him into the kingdom and we agreed that the first step would be teaching him how to pray, he's now asking me to teach him how to read the bible, and is saying he wants to start coming to a Sunday service once a month. He is much further on, and his stepping-stones have been different, but each one has helped him take another step closer to God

We need to think about how to deliberately raise the level of challenge when we get to the stage of inviting people to something, so that they keep moving towards the goal of knowing Christ and making him known.

This might start with an invitation to a coffee or beer. It may lead to an invitation to your home for a family meal (not a full on dinner party – we're not trying to impress but to connect). This may lead to an invitation to a community social (like a BBQ, walk, or party).

Eventually, you will be taking soundings to see if there is interest in being invited to something more spiritual and structured, like:

- Alpha https://alpha.org

- Christianity Explored http://christianityexplored.org

- Story of God http://www.caesarkalinowski.com/story-of-god-experience/

- Journeys video course http://willowcreek.org.uk/product/journeys/

- Seven sign in John's gospel https://www.cmaresources.org/files/SevenSigns-Church3.0.pdf

- A guest-friendly Sunday service

All of these are stepping-stones. Let's be ready to help people navigate the gulf between unbelief and faith using well-understood and accessible stepping-stones.

We understand that for people to come to faith there are stages they go through as they progress along what is known as the Engel scale[50] from "far from God", to "following God", to "bringing others to God". Stepping-stones help to define that process a little more clearly so that we don't get lost or stuck on the way. It also means we can have the resources available when needed.

There are things we can do to prepare for this life, the life of the missionary disciple. As someone has said, *"If we fail to prepare we are preparing to fail."* Why be caught out not knowing how to tell our story, when all it takes is a little practice? Why not be ready with a 4Points wristband or tract instead of kicking ourselves, wishing we had one with us? Why not be ready with an invitation because we have prepared for such opportunities, rather than having a great idea when it's too late?

## SEASONS OF COMMUNITY LIFE AND RHYTHMS OF CENTRALIZED INVITATION

It's not difficult to identify different seasons of missional community life. The seasons vary through the year; each one can have a definite emphasis. However there will always be overlap and it will never be neat and clear cut. We are always to some extent simultaneously sowing gospel seed, nurturing relationships with people of peace, and bringing people into a discipleship relationship. However, it helps to know the main emphasis of the current season.

For example, in our own community, ELP, using the three academic terms, we tend to find that the summer term is a good time for making new connections. The weather tends to help, and people are less busy. As I'm writing this, we are preparing for a BBQ and bouncy castle tomorrow in our back garden. It's not only for any of our MC who are around but also for neighbors and friends. As well as delivering personalised invitations round the neighborhood; I've also put the invite out on the local Homewatch WhatsApp group. I've then been able to invite various other potential people of peace from other walks of my life.

In the *autumn term,* we often invite people to some kind of a faith journey, usually an Alpha course in our home. In recent years, we have seen people come on this every year, and several have come to faith and connected to community life as result. We try to identify any people of peace in our lives. If we're not sure, we invite them anyway – it usually shows if they are people of peace or not.

The spring term tends to focus on building up the group, especially if we have new members joining. We don't try and do everything at once. We will prioritize those things that reflect the emphasis of that season. Then comes the summer when we look to expand our circle of connections again.

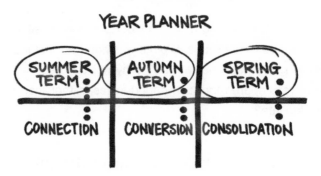

Alongside these seasons in the life of the MC, there can be rhythms of missional opportunities created by the central body of the church. Classically Easter and Christmas are the two used by most churches. But there are lots of other ways of creating missional invitational opportunities, for example around Remembrance Sunday, Lent, Harvest time, and summer fun days etc. In fact, anything that has national recognition can be turned into an opportunity to invite people to our centralized events.

These events can support the life of the MCs by creating invitational opportunities for those who we are getting to know on the disciple-maker's journey. It's good when centralized and decentralized, gathered and scattered can work together. Hope 2018 produced some excellent resources for local churches to embrace this idea.[51]

The other rhythm that we have found helpful here at Frontline is the rhythm of having the second Sunday of each month as a "Scattered Sunday". On those Sundays, every MC is encouraged not to come to the Sunday service but to organize their own activities over the weekend. These will often be missional in some way or perhaps a larger social gathering of the community to which friends can be invited. It would also give the opportunity for closely related MCs to do something together. One of our park clean up mornings was shared between three MCs on a scattered Sunday.

There is a lightweight, more acoustic service without children's work on those Sundays for those not in MC, and for visitors. This proves to be a good opportunity to welcome and recruit new folks to missional communities.

Having the scattered Sundays is a powerful message to the whole church, that MCs are important, and are the engine for mission and discipleship, as well as the place for belonging and care. It also frees space and time in the calendar for busy folk who want to explore new ways of being "extended families on mission".

## THE RHYTHMS OF REST AND WORK.

As a member starts to grow into a missionary and begins to build the lifestyle of a missionary disciple with rhythms of a missional household, it's tempting for them to keep adding new activities, commitments, gatherings, relationships, etc. It's here that it is so important to have understood that we are called to the one life of family on mission where everything is aligned, integrated and working together.

It's also vital that each person develops healthy rhythms of work and rest, embracing the Sabbath fully (Hebrews 4:1-11). They learn not only to take a day off, but also to build patterns of rest through their daily, weekly, monthly and yearly calendar. This rest may be physical, but also needs to be re-creational, restorative, and God-centered. It's crucial that the missionary disciple learns to work *from* rest and not *to* rest. In other words, they need to have a place of deep trust, dependence, and peace in God for the many areas of missional activity they are engaged in. If this is their starting point, they will not be striving to achieve, frustrated when they hit obstacles, or disappointed when things don't work out. They have already found rest and are working from it. They have learned to abide in Christ. Jesus in John's gospel said this:

*"Remain [or abide] in me, as I also remain in you. No branch can bear fruit by itself; it must remain in the vine. Neither can you bear fruit unless you remain in me." ~John 15:4*

In the same passage, Jesus says that after a time of bearing fruit, as a result of abiding in Him, the Father, as the gardener, will come and prune us.

*"He cuts off every branch in me that bears no fruit, while every branch that does bear fruit he prunes so that it will be even more fruitful." ~John 15:2*

We need to accept that there will be seasons of pruning. Jesus has said everything that is healthy and growing needs to be pruned so that it can bear more fruit. Ouch! No one likes the thought, or the reality of being pruned. It means to be cut back. It means we don't look so good. It means we have little to show for our work. It looks a lot like failure.

These seasons of pruning can be times of restriction and containment, when God keeps us hemmed in for a while. Often, He is dealing with heart issues. Sometimes He has us under His loving discipline (Hebrews 12:5-11). In these seasons of pruning we are often reduced to doing not very much. We learn to be still. We listen to His voice again. We cease from our "doings" and find a renewed rest in Him in our "being". The ground lies fallow for a season. Our missional community went through this.

The good news is that these seasons are for our blessing and ultimately for our greater fruitfulness. We can think of these rhythms of work and rest, fruitfulness and fallowness, growing and pruning, as alternating patterns of God at work in our lives. The Semicircle shape of the pendulum illustrates this rhythm (adapted from the 3DM Semicircle Lifeshape[52]). Work and rest, as well as growing and pruning need to find their natural rhythms over time.

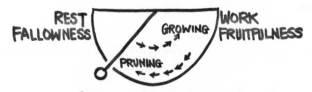

Some will try to fight this rhythm but will do so at their peril. The likelihood is that sooner or later they will burn up with exhaustion, give up with disappointment or puff up with pride. Either way, the enemy will use the situation to take them out of the game. Understanding the season and cooperating with God's Spirit in the process is the way to increasing levels of fruitfulness over time, and it ensures our survival as well. It is also key to bringing glory to the Father.

> *"This is to my Father's glory that you bear much fruit showing yourselves to be my disciples." ~John 15:8*

## FINDING/DEFINING/REFINING YOUR MISSIONAL PURPOSE

For every emerging MC, there is a need to find and define their missional purpose. For other more established MCs, there may be a need to refine it in some seasons. In either situation, it will be helpful to use these 7Ps to clarify the missional purpose.

The four Ps on the left identify which questions to ask, and the three Ps on the right help determine in what context that mission may be carried out.

The first question to ask of the spiritual parents, the missional household, or the emerging missional community is this, *"What are you passionate about, or what is your passion?"* If we use Jesus' manifesto in Luke 4:18-19 as a reference, we could say that one of his His passions was preaching. He said, "The Spirit of the Lord is upon me […] to preach" (v. 18 NASB).

What is your passion? What is it that gets you out of bed in the morning? Are you passionate about your neighborhood, about acting, about fixing cars, about working with young children, about your business or workplace, about the visual arts? This is the first and perhaps the most significant question to ask.

The next question is, *"What is the problem?"* In other words, what is it you want to fix, what injustice or discrimination makes you angry, where do you see a need you want to meet? For Jesus, it was the poor, the blind, the downtrodden, and the captives (Luke 4:18). He wanted to bias His preaching towards those disadvantaged groups. And He demonstrated this throughout His ministry.

What is it you want to help put right? What do you see around you that drives you want to do something about it? Is it the lack of any children's facilities in your neighborhood? Is it bullying at work? It is the homeless?

The next question is, *"What are your possessions?"* In other words, what resources has God given you? What material possessions, like your home and money; what other resources like influence, gifts and abilities do you have? It is no coincidence that you have the resources you have. If you remember in the oikos house picture, one of the rooms represented shared resources. God has entrusted these resources to you not just for you to enjoy, but also for you to share for the sake of His mission. As for Jesus, He clearly had an anointing from the Holy Spirit (Lk 4:18, Acts 10:38), and a huge reservoir of biblical (Old Testament) knowledge. He also had influence with His groups of twelve and seventy-two disciples who he was able to deploy in the mission. These were all resources.

You may have significant material/financial resources that can help make the mission fly. You may have a great home for hospitality. You may have significant influence and responsibility at work. How will you steward these resources for the sake of the mission?

The final question is, *"What evidence is there of God's providence in your life currently?"* In other words, which doors are God opening? Where are you already seeing fruit? How is God leading you? For Jesus, there was clearly no open door for Him in Nazareth (Luke 4:28-29), but by the time He got to Capernaum things were very different. He was casting out demons, healing the sick, and being welcomed. A door had opened wide and it seems that Peter's house in Capernaum became His base of operations for His Galilee ministry. This was the Father's providence.

How is God leading you and the groups you are working with? Is there evidence of God's providence in your life? Are there any open doors you have not yet seen? Are there ways that God's blessing has been visible in the past?

As you begin to process these questions, recognise that various bits of information will emerge. Not all of it will be relevant, but what you are looking for is any overlap between the answers, or any sense of convergence that might point you or your group in a particular direction.

When it comes to defining the missional purpose, it's helpful to think in terms of projects, people and places. You are likely to end up focusing on one or more of these. A project is often a good way to get started as a group because it gets everyone working together towards a particular outcome. It usually has a beginning and an end, which helps everyone muster the necessary energy and commitment. It is also a good way to get a group that has not functioned missionally before to start to think and act missionally. A project may only be for a limited period of time, or it may grow into something more permanent.

For example, in one missional community, they had been concerned that one of their neighbours had for years had a very overgrown, rubble and rubbish-strewn garden. The house looked very neglected. The community had a passion for their neighborhood, it was an obvious problem that needed fixing, they had members with gardening skills and tools as possessions, and they discovered that one of their members who was the captain of the local cricket club had already had contact with the homeowner as his house backed onto the cricket club. A sign of God's *providence*.

A *people* are a particular demographic, like single mums, schoolteachers, or the MC that I mentioned earlier who were focused on the attendees and staff of a comedy club. This kind of demographic missional focus is helpful in that it reflects a single-interest base for those involved. Its strength is in its clarity.

Those involved are usually passionate about this group of people. They often have some natural contact with them (*providence*) that has led them to want to reach out to them. It makes the mission very focussed. One example of this was a missional community that is reaching out to the homeless based in one particular hostel. They had a *passion*, in fact compassion, to reach the homeless. Their rejection by society and low self-esteem were *problems* they wanted to address. They had the resources / *possessions* of food and catering skills so they could provide meals for them,

It's worth mentioning that a demographic focussed MC may have a quick impact, but find it difficult to sustain long term because the members of the MC may have little else in common. They may not live near each other or spend much time together outside organized activities. Because of the difficulty of building strong authentic community between themselves, members are more likely to drift away, move on, or just drop out. The Out is strong, but the In and the Up may be weak. It doesn't detract from the value of this kind of MC, but it may be good to build in some timescales for review, either of the missional focus or of the MC itself, and be willing to refine the missional focus, or even allow the MC to disband and for members to re-gather round a number of other points of missional focus. Having said that, the example above of the MC focussed on the homeless hostel has been going strong for many years

A *place* is equally focused but in a different way. The geographic focus lends itself to many kinds of missional activity, from street cleaning, hosting parties, visiting the elderly, starting a neighborhood watch, or a kid's club. The two big advantages of a geographic focus are that the members, if they own their homes, are likely to be present over a long period of time. They are also likely to live near enough to be in and out of each other's houses in a more organic way, not just for organized activities. This leads to a stronger sense of family and community, which in turn leads to greater long-term commitment. Both of these factors lead to more stability and sustainability, and therefore longevity. We sometimes use the phrase when discussion missional focus that "proximity is king".

Our MC is focussed on a small geographic area of a few streets leading down to our local High Street. There are 4 families who live in the two main streets and others who live relatively nearby. Members have a passion for where they live; they see the problems first hand as they are in the area all the time. Doors have opened to shops on High Street and to a small primary school in our road. These are signs of God's *providence* in the situation.

## WHEN IT COMES TO BUILDING STRONG MISSIONAL COMMUNITIES WITH SUSTAINABLE MISSIONAL FOCUS...
# PROXIMITY IS KING

Putting all these 7Ps together will help any individual, household, or missional community figure out the answer to the question, *"To who am I called?"* And as they process the same questions with others, they will eventually be able to answer the second key question, *"With whom am I called?"* This happens as those with clarity about their missional focus start to let others know what they are thinking. They may invite specific friends to be involved with them. Others who hear about it and are drawn to the same people, place or project then start to gravitate to them. Gradually a team is formed to launch the MC.

As is implicit from the "refine" part of the title to this section, any MCs purpose may drift over time, projects may be completed, and/or members of the group may change. For whatever reason, it's good to review the missional purpose from time to time and check it's still the right one. Just go through the same questions as above, and see what God is saying.

## TRY THIS

Spend some time going through the 7Ps with your group and see what you come up with at the end of the process. Does it give you a clear missional purpose? Is this new, and if so does it change what you have been doing? If so, what's the new plan?

## MC VARIANTS

As well as the geographic and demographic variants of classic missional communities that are described earlier (see pictures below – Classic MC), there are also other variations of groups that may emerge, as a church is moving more towards a missional community culture and structure.

When a church is making the transition towards missional communities, it is hard sometimes to know what to do with some of the existing groups of volunteers who have a shared missional purpose. Should they be stopped, or can they be channelled into missional community life? A typical example most churches encounter is a ministry or social action outreach project team (see picture below – Ministry MC)) that has highly committed volunteers who are passionate about the people they are serving, and the needs they are meeting. In terms of *passion* and *problem*, it ticks both the boxes. But when we measure what they have against the three dimensions of the Triangle, Up, In and Out, they are very one-sided, one-dimensional. As a community, they may have a great team spirit but no actual genuine community (In dimension), other than around the task in hand. They are also unlikely to have much of an Up dimension, of prayer, worship, discipleship, or breaking bread.

The truth is that many communities that have a good Up and In dimension often lack a strong or effective Out dimension. So it cuts both ways!

For a team that is working together in a food bank, an outreach to sex workers, or in a parent and toddler group, they will need to be willing to develop the other two dimensions if they want to experience the benefits and blessings of missional community life. To do this may mean reducing the frequency of their involvement in the social action project to free up time for the other dimensions. Though it might feel costly to do less outreach, it's important to engage with all three aspects, it's following the pattern of Jesus, it's being before doing. It's not just because we need to tick the boxes of all three elements happening – there is vision, a reason behind the decision to start doing less outreach.

In order to build the Up and In dimensions, such a group will probably need to set up some kind of regular times together when they are developing prayer, discipleship, mutual support, family, eating and fun together.

If they are willing to do this, there is no reason why a ministry or social action project team can't make the transition. In fact, it is probably best for the project as well as the people involved. There will be many logistical obstacles to work through, but the biggest resistance is likely to come from the people involved. They didn't originally sign up for this and so are not likely to jump at the opportunity. It remains an ideal, however, and for the reasons given above is worth persisting with. Here at Frontline a "Healing Rooms" team has successfully transitioned to a MC.

Other variants are workplace based (see pictures below – Marketplace MC). Either people in the same kind of work but in different places e.g. schoolteachers in a variety of different schools. Or people all working in the same office block/ business/local government building. In the case of the former, the opportunities for outreach are harder because there is less support on site for any such activities, but in the latter, there is no reason why several members of staff can't just start something like a prayer meeting, Alpha or a Christianity Explored course in the workplace.

Those who make the workplace their missional focus also need to make space to develop the discipleship dimensions, such as accountability triplets. They will need to all gather regularly to maintain any sense of real community together. For those who are all from the same place of work, they can fulfill some of those functions on the site in their breaks, or before/after work. For those working in different places, it requires more intention to build the other dimensions.

As God raises up people of increasing influence and significant responsibility in the workplace, there will need to be support for them and others who are carrying similar kinds of responsibility. So, for example, leaders in education, healthcare, business, media, and local government etc. will need to take time out to be replenished and meet with others from the same sector.

There are many ways to skin a cat, and there are many ways to build three-dimensional missional community. Some are easier than others, and some have more permanence than others. Some of the variants are good ways to get moving, even if they aren't the final expression. We need to try out a few things and see what works. Innovation is the key to revolution. More of the same isn't going to get us to the glorious church that Jesus had in mind when He said, *"I will build my church and the gates of Hades will not overcome it" (Matthew 16:18).*

The following pictures may help imagine what some of these variants might look like.

# 1. CLASSIC (MC)

### (A) GEOGRAPHIC FOCUS   (B) DEMOGRAPHIC FOCUS

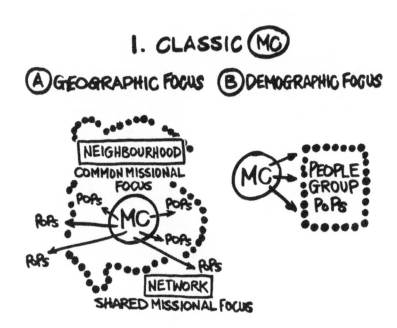

# 2. MINISTRY (MC)

## 3. MARKETPLACE (MC)

Ⓐ LOCALIZED/SINGLE PLACE OF WORK

Ⓑ DISPERSED EG... THOSE WORKING IN SCHOOLS

**TRY THIS**

Look at any projects or groupings in your church that have a clear missional focus, but don't meet the normal criteria for MCs. See if there is any way you could help them to become three-dimensional missional communities and explore it with the leaders of those groups.

**SIMPLE. STICKY. REPRODUCIBLE.**

- The idols of independence, individualism, materialism and consumerism

- MC Seasons of connection, conversion and consolidation

- The Semicircle rhythms of rest and work, pruning and growing, fallowness and fruitfulness

- The 7Ps of finding your missional purpose

# 9

# THE HOLY GRAIL OF MULTIPLICATION

**Questions:** How can we start to multiply disciples and missional communities? Why can't I raise world-class leaders by simply creating a world-class leadership course?

## INTRODUCTION

The challenge with the *member* is to help them engage with a lifestyle of discipleship, and the challenge with the *missionary* is to train and mobilize them into their missional calling. The challenge with the *multiplier* is to enable them to become an equipper and not just a doer. Most church attendees are loathe to either get their hands dirty in any kind of ministry, or if they do, they want to stay at the sharp productive end of "doing something useful", rather than seeing how they could multiply their impact by training and equipping others. For many leaders, the idea of multiplication is great but the practice of it seems very elusive.

The vehicles for this part of the journey are likely to be similar to those for members and missionaries i.e. accountability triplets, huddle, Missional Household and Missional Community, but will also include the learning community vehicle, and all will focus on leadership and multiplication.

First, before we get into the specific tools that we want to use to equip multipliers, let me talk a little bit about the biblical journey from addition to multiplication.

## FROM ADDITION TO MULTIPLICATION

As I read the book of Acts, I see a most remarkable development in both the exponential growth of the church and the language that is used to describe the process.

We start in Acts 2 following the day of Pentecost and Peter's first sermon where 3000 were added to the number of believers:

*"Those who accepted his message were baptized, and about three thousand were added to their number that day." ~Acts 2:41*

The word in the Greek for added is the word *prostithemi*. It carries the sense of laying one thing alongside another, and so adding to the original.

This same word is found several more times in the Acts story. It occurs again at the end of the same chapter, "the Lord added to their number daily those who were being saved" (v. 47). We see the same word prostithemi in Acts 5:14, "Nevertheless, more and more men and women believed in the Lord and were added to their number."

Addition was the norm for the first five chapters in Acts. But then, in the next chapter, we see an interesting development. As the church grows there are two key words that change as the story moves into chapter six. Firstly, "persons" in chapter two and "men and women" in chapter five, change to "disciples", (*mathetes* in the Greek) in chapter six. Secondly, instead of them growing by addition, *prostithemi*, they are now growing by multiplication, the Greek word *plethyno*.

A plethora of followers:

*Now in those days, when the number of the disciples (mathetes) was multiplying [plethyno] ... ~Acts 6:1a NKJV*

This is a completely different idea and dynamic. In many Bible versions, it is simply translated as "increase". But in the New King James version it is much more clearly translated as "multiplying". Clearly there is something about the (missionary) disciple that has the potential not just to add a few more men and women, but to multiply themselves. This is key to understanding the possibilities of discipleship and the potential of *"disciples who make disciples"*. The same word is used of the rapidly increasing number of disciples in Jerusalem in Acts 6:7.

The same work plethyno is used in the well-known passage in 2 Corinthians:

> *"Now He who supplies seed to the sower and bread for food will supply and multiply your seed for sowing and increase the harvest of your righteousness." ~2 Corinthians 9:10 (NASB)*

The idea of multiplication is built into the practice of seed sowing. You sow ten seeds and reap hundreds of seeds.

But the language of multiplication doesn't stop there – it continues over the coming chapters. We start with multiplying *disciples*, and then we move on to multiplying *churches*.

A church that multiplies:

> *"Then the **churches** throughout all Judea, Galilee, and Samaria had peace and were edified. And walking in the fear of the Lord and in the comfort of the Holy Spirit, they were **multiplied** [plethyno]." ~Acts 9:31 (NKJV)*

When disciples multiply, so do churches. It's been said that if we make disciples, Jesus will build His church. I believe that. I'd add that *if we multiply disciples, Jesus will multiply His church*. Where there are mature expressions of disciple-making movements in Africa and Asia, this phenomenon is very evident. For more information, take a look at Steve Addison's seminal work, *Movements That Change the World* [53] and *Miraculous Movements* by Jerry Trousdale.[54]

We have yet to see this scale of multiplication in Western culture. But the potential of the church is the same in every part of the world.

Remember that in the New Testament the basic unit of church life was the Greco-Roman household, the oikos. These extended family units were the natural expressions of church for the first 300 years of church history. So when we think of church, think home-based extended families on mission. Units of say fifteen to fifty people. If we think of multiplying churches, we tend to default to thinking buildings, Sunday services, professional leaders, and full-on programs. Not so in the book of Acts. These households were the primary place of discipleship, mission and multiplication. How could that change our view of church planting or church multiplication?

The best example in the book of Acts is in chapter 19, where Paul establishes the church at Ephesus. This beachhead of apostolic movement leads to the rapid training and deployment of disciples to plant churches all across Asia, modern-day Western Turkey. It is likely that this two-year period is when the church at Colossae and the seven churches of Revelation were all planted.

Once we have the multiplication of disciples and churches, then a new dynamic emerges in the book of Acts, and this is potentially the most exciting. In Acts 12, the apostle James is beheaded in prison, and it looks like Peter will be next. The church, we are told in v. 5, started to "pray for him fervently". One wonders if there was a lack of prayer beforehand. Maybe the praying hadn't been up to much until the church saw what happened to James. Whatever the reason, they started praying up a storm. They prayed fervently, earnestly, and zealously for Peter.

*"So Peter was kept in prison, but fervent and persistent prayer for him was being made to God by the church. ~Acts 12:5 (AMP)*

When we read on in Acts 12, we see that the result was a miraculous escape for Peter, facilitated by an angel. Peter walks out of prison and turns up at Mary's house, John Mark's mother. The servant, Rhoda, who answers the door is amazed that Peter could be standing outside and instead of opening the gate to the compound, runs back to tell the others, who can't believe it's Peter (so much for their faith in prayer!).

Anyway, after joyful reunions, Herod orders the execution of the prison guards. We subsequently read that Herod is consumed by worms and dies for allowing the people to worship him. The chapter concludes with these words, "But the word of the Lord continued to grow and to be *multiplied* [plethyno]" (Acts 12:24 NASB).

In my words, *the gospel went viral*. It was like the movement reached a tipping point. It became unstoppable. It was naturally and spontaneously multiplying and spreading across the known world.

It's this potential of multiplying disciples, churches and the gospel that gives me courage to dream of a reality that the vision statement of Kairos Connexion expresses: *seeing our nation transformed by the gospel through a movement of missionary disciples.*

In the next chapter, Paul and Barnabus start their first missionary journey from Antioch, and by the end of Paul's life, he is able to say to the believers in Rome,

> "So from Jerusalem all the way around to Illyricum [modern Albania], I have fully proclaimed the gospel of Christ." ~Romans 15:19b

True movement had begun. And it continued to expand exponentially for the next 250 years. **If** *we want movement we have to understand multiplication.*

We must go on the journey from *prostithemi* to *plethyno*: from *addition* to *multiplication*. If I'm honest, I know that I and many other church leaders would be happy just to have a bit of addition (avoiding the dreaded subtraction or worse still, division). While that may make us feel better in the short term, it will not get us to where we want to go. It will not release a movement of missionary disciples who can transform our nation with the gospel. We will talk about more of that later.

This kind of multiplication is happening in many parts of the world. In Western culture not so much, but there are early signs of hope where church leaders have taken the bull by the horns and refused to settle for safe, comfortable, consumer-based, centralized, attractional churches – where instead the leader is committed to helping members become missionaries, and missionaries to become multipliers.

So how do we help our members and missionaries become multipliers and ultimately movement builders?

## THE JOURNEY FROM DISCIPLE TO LEADER

We have looked at the journey from person of peace to disciple-maker in the disciple-makers journey. But we need to look more specifically at how this works in raising leaders who not only lead self, and lead others, but who move to the next level of leading leaders. In other words, they become multipliers.

The Square has become a staple in the diet of those who have done any sort of 3DM training or reading.[55] It is a brilliant tool to describe the simple process in which Jesus takes His disciples on their journey from lost to leader, from member to multiplier.

When Jesus first encounters those who became His followers, they were regular men and women in a variety of jobs and from many different backgrounds. There were obviously plenty of fishermen in His group of followers, but also tax collectors, prostitutes, a doctor, zealots, other tradesmen, and wealthy women. The thing they all had in common was that they were willing to leave their comfortable context and job security to follow Jesus. They embarked on a journey of becoming learners at His feet. They were willing to assume they didn't know it all, that they needed to be taught. They were willing to follow without knowing where they were going, or where it would all end.

We describe the phases of this journey using the four sides of the Square:

The initial leg of the journey, disciple stage one (D1), for the first disciples describes the first phase of meeting Jesus. They had a sense of excitement that they had met someone very special, maybe even the Messiah. They were quick to invite their family members to come and meet Him. In John 1:40-45, in their excitement in finding the Messiah, Andrew goes to find Simon Peter and Philip goes to find Nathaniel. Jesus was demonstrating the lifestyle He was about to lead them into, modelling something for them to imitate. He said, *"Follow me and I will make you fishers of men"*, Matthew 4:19.

For us this is often the honeymoon phase of our becoming disciples of Jesus, where everything is wonderful and new. We believe we can conquer the world. Certainly the first followers must have thought that. They watched Jesus do miracles, give the Pharisees a good telling off, and wow the crowds with His teaching. They would have felt invincible.

The truth is they didn't know what they didn't know; they were living in what we call "unconscious incompetence". They were like the kid with the new bike on Christmas day, marvelling at its beautiful red frame and shiny chrome wheels. The kid has never tried to ride a bike. He has no idea of the grazed knees and hurt pride that lies ahead! The disciples had no idea they were being trained, apprenticed to do the works that Jesus did. If they did they may have been less enthusiastic to sign up.

Sooner or later, Jesus began to deploy and train His followers to do kingdom stuff – casting out demons, healing the sick (Luke 9:1), multiplying loaves and fishes (Luke 9:10-17), and walking on water (Matthew 14:22-33). They quickly realized they had a lot to learn. They complained they didn't have enough to feed the crowd; the demon didn't come out when they tried to eject it from the boy (Matthew 17:14-18); Peter started to sink when Jesus invited him to come to Him on the water. They were entering disciple stage two (D2) the phase where we feel like giving up and going home.

They needed lots of extra support and encouragement from Jesus as well as a little rebuke for their lack of faith. Jesus, as spiritual parent, was there for them. He picked them up and set them on their feet again to have another go, this time a little wiser and humbler (Matthew 17:19-21). This is the "consciously incompetent" phase. The disciples now know what they don't know. They are painfully aware of their inadequacies. They have entered the true learning phase. Failure is a fast, if painful, teacher. The kid on the bike realizes that balance is not a God-given right, but must be mastered by practice. He learns that grazed knees and elbows are not fatal!

Disciple stage three (D3) represents the phase where the disciples start to master some of the basic skills and grow in godly character. It is the phase of "conscious competence". They know what they know, but are still having to concentrate hard to master the moves, just like the boy on the bike who is managing to stay upright but still with great effort and concentration. His grip on the handlebars is vice-like in his attempt to stay upright. There is quietly growing confidence in this phase.

The disciples return from their evangelistic campaign in the towns and villages with great joy reporting to Jesus that "even the demons submit to us" (Luke 10:17). Jesus smiles knowingly at their newfound confidence, and gently reminds them that it's actually more important to remember that their names are written in the book of life (Luke 10:20). Jesus as coach is less involved and is operating more from a distance, just keeping a watchful eye on them. He still gives them feedback and they still need Him, but no longer as intensely as in their great failures.

Finally the disciples reach Disciple stage four (D4) and are ready to do the job by themselves. Jesus is telling them He is going back to heaven. He promises them they will receive the Holy Spirit who will continue to lead and empower them (John 14:15-28). He gives them the great commission explaining to them that they will now be the ones to train others to be disciples and disciple-makers. *"Go and make disciples of all nations ... teaching them to obey all that I have commanded you" (Matthew 28:19-20).* And He leaves them to go back to the Father.

The disciples are now ready, trained, armed and dangerous! They are in the phase of "unconscious competence". What they know has become instinctive. They are no longer having to think about how do preach the gospel or heal the sick. They are trained. The boy on the bike no longer thinks about how to balance, he is operating instinctively. He rides with confidence, "look no hands!"

The journey round the Square is complete. This is the journey from disciple to leader. We take someone who knows nothing, but thinks they know everything. We help them through the early stages of disappointment and failure, through to the stage of growing in skill-based confidence and character maturity. We release them finally to do for others what we have done for them. They emerge from an intense discipleship experience to become disciple-makers, leaders.

The beauty of the Square is that it helps us calibrate where our disciples are at and what kind of support is needed. In fact it determines our leadership style at each stage. *Directing* at D1, *Mentoring* at D2, *Coaching* at D3, and *Consulting* at D4. The style of leadership at each stage becomes increasingly hands-off. For this reason, it is also sometimes called *The Leadership Square* as well as *The Discipleship Square.* This tool also helps the disciple to be realistic about the journey they are on, and see how to take others on the same journey. It is the journey towards leadership and multiplying leaders.

Caesar Kalinowski and others mirror these same four stages in the acronym MAWL.

**M**odel = show them how to do it. Be the example

**A**ssist = help them as they struggle in their first attempts to do the stuff

**W**atch = delegate and give them space to grow in confidence

**L**eave = hand on the responsibility and leave them to raise other disciples and leaders

Who are you MAWLing?

## TRY THIS

Think about the people you are discipling or giving input to. Where are they on the Square? Are you preparing them to do the same with others? How could you develop with them a new approach that embodies multiplication? Make a "note to self" to have those conversations with the few you are investing in.

## COACHING LEADERS

Coaching is a powerful tool in growing and multiplying leaders. It became obvious to me that coaching purely on a one-to-one basis was never going to allow me to multiply leaders. It was too time intensive. Whilst there will be a need to occasionally use a one to one approach for coaching, the general principle is that we need to develop group-based leadership coaching. We call this kind of group a huddle. Picture penguins huddling together on the ice floes, drawing strength from each other. Picture American footballers or British rugby players huddling together on the pitch, devising strategy and putting a game plan together. Both these images contribute to our understanding of what a huddle can be.

### Example of A Huddle In Action

George is a great MC leader who tends to over commit. In the context of a huddle, when the leader was talking about the inner drivers of ambition, appetite, and approval, based on the three temptations of Jesus (see chapter one), and the 4Gs (of God being Great, Glorious Good and Gracious), George began to think that God might be trying to get his attention (a kairos moment). George had been worrying about what other people had been thinking about him recently, and with the stress of some things happening in his family, had realized he'd been using inappropriate late night TV and food as a way of de-stressing.

As the leader shared about these three areas that tend to trip us up, George began to see that he had been covering up what had been happening in his wider family, carrying a sense of shame on their behalf. He had internalised his pain rather than sharing it with his bothers and sisters. As others in the huddle began to help him by asking questions to tease out his feelings, he realized that the fear of man and his need for approval had been controlling him. Someone suggested that he needed to reflect on God's glorious nature, so that others opinions had less influence over him. George also realized that his way of dealing with stress was to do what he often did when under pressure, to resort to feeding an appetite to feel better about life, he would binge eat. He realized it was only a short-term fix, and that only Jesus could fully satisfy his need for peace, fulfillment and satisfaction. The huddle leader asked what George thought God was saying, and what he (George) was going to do about it. He was pretty clear that need for approval and the seduction of appetite were both tempting him to ungodly responses. He needed to focus on God's grace and glory over coming weeks. Others in the huddle prayed for him, and the leader gave him the opportunity to feedback next time they met, to let them know how he was doing (accountability).

It's easy to see how the Learning Circle, and the two discipleship questions were at work here. This is typical of many huddles. In this situation the focus had been on a character issue.

A huddle is a well-established vehicle for growing and multiplying leaders. The huddle leader will regularly be helping the leaders apply their learning to their context. This person is committed to helping other leaders grow in both character (discipleship) and competency (leadership). Often this will be the rhythm of huddle sessions, one or two sessions on character issues, one or two on competence in leadership skills and one or two on context applications.

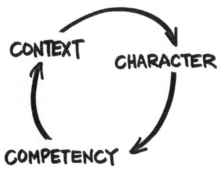

The huddle leader will need to be competent in all the tools and applications that have become the mainstay of training for members and missionaries. He or she will need to have been part of a huddle where they will have observed and understood the dynamics of huddle. It's easy to understand the simple idea behind a huddle but much harder to do it well.

I started the transition to the culture of mission and discipleship by huddling a number of my senior leaders, who in turn were to huddle the other MC leaders. I'd read the book. It seemed straightforward. But it was like the blind leading the blind. Not surprisingly many of those who were in the early days of my huddle found reasons not to remain in it. I can fully understand why!

It wasn't till I was invited to be part of a huddle led by Paul Maconochie that I finally began to understand the unique dynamic of huddle that I was being apprenticed in. After a year or so I finally "got it", and my own huddles started to be transformational. I reckon that in the first two years of being huddled by Paul I grew as a disciple and leader more than I had grown in the previous ten years. I will try and explain why and how that happens. But please don't make the same mistake I did and think you can do it just from reading about it. It's one of those situations where learning really has to take place by imitation, not just information (remember the Training Triangle).

The training process is a mixture of gaining sufficient *information* (too little is probably better than too much), observing by *imitation*. But it's not until we get to have a go ourselves, *innovation*, and learn by doing, failing, reflecting and readjusting that we truly grow. The whole process is best described as an apprenticeship. It was the way the Jewish Rabbi's trained their disciples. It was the way Jesus trained his disciples. It is the most effective way for us to train our missionary disciples today.

So recognising that huddle itself is learned by imitation, it's important to realize the huddle is also a place of imitation. This initially seems strange as it is not an obvious "on the job" situation. However, what we can do in a huddle is put our current and past experience of life and leadership "out there", on the line, with transparency and honesty, making ourselves vulnerable, the good the bad and the ugly, so others can learn from us by imitating our lives, or avoiding our mistakes! It is actually a surprisingly powerful imitation context.

No two huddles are the same but the typical pattern of a huddle is as follows: It usually lasts a strict hour. Participants normally appreciate the well-defined timeframe because multipliers (who are by definition leaders) are usually busy people and value making the most of their time. One hour is a good length of time to process what God is saying and help each person come to some clarity about the two discipleship questions (What is God saying? and What am I going to do about it?). The aim of every huddle is to get to this point. The process is based round the dynamics of the Learning Circle. We give some input on a particular topic whether it is a *character, competence* or *context* topic. We give time for the members of the huddle to discuss and process it. We encourage peer sharing and learning. We give comment and ongoing input as necessary, but where possible and appropriate we allow the learning to come from the group.

In the last 10-15 minutes, we ask the members to try and answer the two discipleship questions. In situations where the kairos' are negative revelations about themselves, issues they are struggling with, fears and frustrations, or challenges they are facing, we may choose to use the identity-based Learning Circle. In this context, we will ask questions like:

- What is it about God that you are not believing?

- What is the lie about God that you have believed?

- In the light of who God is, what is it that you need to know about Him?

- How has God demonstrated that aspect of His nature before – in Scripture, at the cross, and in your own experience?

- In the light of your kairos and who God is, what is now true of you (identity, authority, and privilege)?

- In the light of that, how do you now get to live?

These questions will dig to the heart of identity-type issues.

If the kairos relates to a revelation of some truth about life, or leadership, it may be more appropriate to go straight to the two discipleship questions.

In the light of what God has said to someone and what they have said they are going to do about it, one simple question that creates a great accountability opportunity is to ask, "What question do you want me to ask at the next huddle that shows you have taken action?"

*Accountability* is the hidden power of the huddle.

By starting each week with feedback on the previous huddle's accountability questions, it creates a great motivation for each person to see through what they have committed to. The aim is always to help them do what they have believed God wants them to do. Beyond this, the hope is that one-off choices become regular patterns of behavior, or habits. Eventually a lifestyle is formed. This is the gold standard of transformation. Thanks to Rich Robinson for this helpful understanding of how lifestyles are created.

## DISCIPLINE → HABIT → LIFESTYLE

### TRY THIS

Keep a note on your phone (or somewhere easily accessed) of all the kairos-based actions you are keeping track of and implementing. Review them regularly so that the most important ones don't get lost over time, but build towards good habits and permanent lifestyle changes.

Accountability is always by permission of the multiplier you are training. It is always about what they believe God is saying to them, not what you think they should be doing! That's why we talk about creating a culture of "low control but high accountability". Too often we come across church cultures that have high control but low or no accountability. Not healthy.

The huddle is a great way of forming multipliers of disciple-makers, leaders of leaders. It is one of the main tools and vehicles for the multiplier stage. Huddle is ideally done face-to-face, but if some have to travel a distance it may be more practical to do the huddle on a web-based platform, like Skype or Zoom. I believe that 80-90% of the value of a face-to-face huddle can be experienced on a Zoom call. However, there are times when being in the same literal room, not just a virtual room, creates opportunity for greater connection and bonding, and whenever possible this should complement an online huddle.

Huddle is not primarily a place of pastoral care, but we are human, and difficult stuff happens to us all, so it's good to make sure no one is really hurting when we connect. It's never time wasted to pray for one or two individuals. It's also an opportunity for other members of the huddle to contribute by praying for their colleagues or getting an encouraging word from God for them. I usually start a huddle with a time of catch-up in the first few minutes; this gives me the opportunity to see if anyone is struggling.

A huddle should run for at least a year to be of value and at a minimum frequency of every two weeks. A huddle will reap maximum benefit if it is weekly, though this is often impractical. I have also run monthly huddles. These are not ideal, as they tend to lose momentum and people forget their accountability points from the previous time. And if they miss one huddle, it's two months before they reconnect. However a monthly huddle is better than no huddle, and is still of significant value. Some huddles will last a lot longer than one year, but it's good to at least review each year and decide if it should continue for a further year. If some members need to leave and others join at that stage, it can be helpful to have created that opportunity for change.

It is a privilege to be in a huddle and they are by invitation only. This is important, as we need people in the huddle who are roughly at similar stages of maturity and responsibility, so they can relate to and support each other. We also need to know that the people we invite have a teachable heart, and don't just want somewhere to air their own very definite opinions! The huddle leader needs to decide whom God is calling him or her to invest in. Jesus picked his twelve, responding to what he saw the Father doing. To invest in a multiplier is a great joy but it is also costly. It is a significant investment in a relationship that may last many years, and involve a lot of our time and energy. We need to have faith that God is in the process, so that when it feels tough to invest in others, we can be sure that we are being obedient to what God has called us to do, rather than simply executing a good idea. We're much more likely to persevere through challenging situations when we're certain we're responding to where the Father is at work.

Choosing which topic to input into the huddle requires a number of sensitivities,

- To the needs and different stages of development of the multipliers

- To the common themes of challenge emerging in the whole group

- To what has come up in a previous huddle

- To the contexts of the people being huddled

- To the voice of the Holy Spirit speaking

Discerning this is, in my opinion, one of the most demanding parts of leading a huddle. Second to that is facilitating the discussion in such a way that each person, as far as possible, gets his or her own kairos.

There is a whole huddle curriculum in the 3DM huddle leaders guide, for those who want to unpack all the 3DM Lifeshapes.[56] This can take a year or two to go through.

A sustainable rhythm of huddle is the backbone of training the multiplier, enabling them to raise missionary disciples. Once this is in place, many other less structured inputs and opportunities to shape the multiplier will emerge in a more organic way. Doing stuff together is a great time for organic input. I recently took another church leader with me to a leaders day in another city. We talked for the hour all the way there. On the way home we were in such depth of conversation that I overshot our motorway turn off by three junctions! These were precious moments of input to his life. Any training needs to be organized and organic, formal and informal, to create the best opportunities for information and imitation, and for review of innovation to take place. So if they are someone who has, for example, just started leading a small group or MC, we get to ask how the new thing they are doing is going. It's a chance to hear any of their struggles, answer any questions they have, and to encourage them to keep going.

Opportunities to take part in shared mission experiences will be invaluable to bonding, training, and growing in faith and leadership. A huddle could organize its own mission experience. It could be as simple as joining a day's mission that another church is running, an outreach in a local city center, or being part of a national mission that an organization is running. Or it could be as adventurous as jumping on a plane to another city in another country for 3 days, just being led by God as to who to go to, where to stay and what to do. The more risky and unknown, the better the experience is likely to be. These kind of experiences tend to push everyone out of their comfort zone, and it's here that many kairos' will be experienced, many areas of character will be exposed, and many new skills be developed. Alan Hirsch describes this as one of the strands of missional DNA that help to build genuine movement. He calls it "liminality and communitas"[57]: the place where, in the marginal risky places of mission, true brotherhood and sisterhood is formed.

## THE LEADERSHIP JOURNEY

There are a few different ideas here about the journey of leadership development, in relation to multiplication.

I have found that the word *leader* is often laden with apprehension for those being trained. As I have mentioned previously, my definition of leadership is "the ability and motivation to take initiative and responsibility". Others would add, "for the sake of others". This seems like a much more attainable aspiration.

When it comes to releasing leadership in others, it's about giving them permission to have a go, to fail, to experiment, to innovate, and to learn from experience. It's also about giving support in the process. So leadership is about *giving permission and support,* so that others can *take initiative and responsibility.*

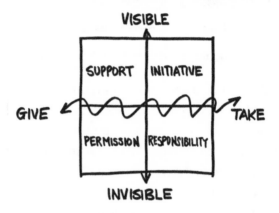

As I mentioned in chapter three, we can view the multiplier as the culmination of the leadership pathway – from leading self, through leading others, to leading leaders.

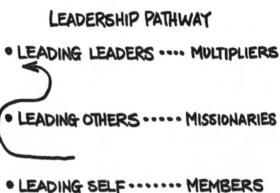

The leadership pathway highlights the focus for each stage of the journey from member through to multiplier:

For the new *member* (think body part not organizational subscriber), the focus is going to be on *leading themselves*. This is the starting point for discipleship. Toddlers have to learn to feed themselves, walk without falling over, share their toys, and effectively communicate their needs. Similarly, the newly born-again disciple (member) has to learn to lead themselves. In terms of initiative and responsibility, they start to take initiative in growing their own soul, growing in spiritual disciplines, finding their best contribution to the body of Christ and how they as a member fit into the bigger picture. They are also learning to walk in the Spirit and live their life from love, for the benefit of others. They are discovering they can take kingdom initiatives as the Spirit directs them. New disciples begin to take responsibility for keeping healthy relationships, for letting others know of their needs, for becoming net contributors rather than consumers, for finding the people they are called to serve alongside in community. They are taking responsibility for being an ambassador for Christ.

The *missionary disciple,* operating out of a missionary household, is learning to lead others. They understand that they are called, not only as individuals, to love and serve God, but to operate as part of a spiritual family on mission, as part of an oikos, a household of faith, a community of believers who share a focus of mission. They are called to lead others in this missionary household (as single or married people); they are called on the disciple-makers journey to make and multiply disciples.

The missionary disciple is always taking the initiative in asking "What's next, Lord?" with all those that God is drawing to them on the disciple-maker's journey. They are taking responsibility as spiritual parents for those God is drawing to be part of their spiritual family. They are taking responsibility for helping others in their household grow in their discipleship/followership.

The *multiplier* is taking that a step further in terms of looking to raise others into leadership. They lead leaders. They take initiative in finding those with leadership gifts around them and releasing them. They take responsibility for the process of multiplication. They know that the only way that the great commission is going to be completed is if we move beyond subtraction and division, even beyond addition, to multiplication. From *prostithemi* to *plethyno.*

They are functioning in all four quadrants of the 4 elements of leadership. As well as taking initiative and responsibility, they are also giving permission and support to others to grow into their leadership, so they too can become multipliers. Multipliers beget multipliers. They have discovered that leadership is both give and take. Giving permission and support. Taking initiative and responsibility.

## THE LEADERSHIP PIPELINE

The Leadership Pipeline helps us move people from members, to missionaries to multipliers. Operating in all growing organizations, the leadership pipeline is by no means a new concept. It generally works around a number of key functions: recruit, train, and deploy. For our purposes, we add a review element to ensure continued learning.

The three key tools of the Learning Circle, the Training Triangle of Information, Imitation and Innovation, and the Discipleship/Leadership Square, come together to form the training engine for the pipeline. As these three tools operate in sync, they act like a pump and generate momentum for the pipeline.

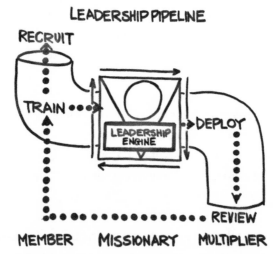

The pipeline is vital to any growing organization. I believe it was Peter Wagner who said that the rate-limiting factor of any church's growth would be the rate at which it can produce new leaders. In fact, it maybe that the rate of development of those leaders actually drives the growth of the church.

Each part of the pipeline is vital. The wide funnel of entry to it is where we can afford to be most generous. If anyone shows initiative or takes responsibility, or even if they simply express a desire for more opportunity, it's worth taking a risk on them and inviting them into the pipeline process, usually in a huddle within a MC.[58] It's important that we help them understand that there will be points of exit from the process if it's not working. Either side must be free to activate that exit. If the leader feels that the individual is not making the most of the investment, he can challenge their attitude, commitment or application of what they are learning. If the individual feels he or she is not ready, or that circumstances have changed making their involvement practically very difficult, they too must be free to leave the process without feeling awkward or like a failure. Sometimes it's just a matter of getting the timing right. We must help them see that it's not a failure to have tried even if it doesn't work out. Timing or other factors beyond their control may intervene. Sometimes the person shows that at a particular point in time they are not able to step up to the new opportunities that are coming their way. Every effort must be applauded.

We need to ensure there are plenty of deployment opportunities for those we are training to experience hands-on leadership in practical settings. Through this they will learn by doing, and grow from their failures. These opportunities can vary from a small single task responsibility, say leading in prayer in a small group, to much bigger long-term responsibilities for an individual or a group's welfare.

## REVIEWING PEOPLE AND PROCESS

The review part may actually be the least utilised but most important part of the pipeline. In fact, review needs to be all through the process, not just at the end.

One way to work on review is to focus not just on the leaders being produced from the pipeline, but on the pipeline itself. In other words, to look at reviewing people and process.

**People**: are we producing healthy, happy leaders?

**Process**: are the parts of the pipeline joined up and working effectively together?

Let's take a moment to think about how we can review the people, the leaders emerging from the training and deployment process. We can use the Up, In and Out Triangle to assess the effectiveness of what we are doing.

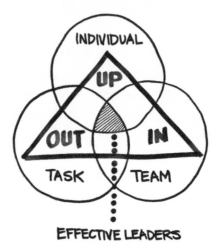

Back in the '70s, John Adair in his classic book, *Action-Centered Leadership,*[59] defined three key dimensions that every successful leader needs to take note of and develop well. These are task, team, and individual. The overlap of these three aspects is the sweet spot for any leader. They also map well on to our Triangle of Up, In and Out.

We can ask the following questions to assess a leader's engagement in each dimension:

- Is the leader as an *individual "growing"* in self-awareness, as evidenced by a teachable heart?

- Is the leader *"gathering"* with others with *team*-orientation, as evidenced by time invested those relationships?

- Is the leader's task flourishing in *"going"* with missional-purpose, as evidenced by the leader taking initiative?

There are plenty of ways of reviewing the pipeline process (as opposed to people), but the important thing is that it is reviewed. One of the simplest ways is to ask two questions:

- What are we doing well?

- What could we be doing better?

Getting feedback from a number of different people is invaluable – from the leader going through the process, those who are involved in training them, and those who are on the receiving end of their deployment.

As the leader in training enters the pipeline, they will need to commit to some kind of responsibility. Initially we can just ask them to take on a few specific tasks. For example, we may ask them to organize the hospitality for a missional community meeting, to choose a passage for and lead a Discovery Bible Study, or just to give some time to a new Christian.

As they prove responsible we will start to give them medium-term assignments such as planning and communicating the MC program for the next term, organizing a missional project for the community, or leading an Alpha course or *The Story of God.*

The further they go on the pipeline, the clearer we need to be about the process they have embarked on. It needs to be undertaken with increasing permission and agreement. They will almost certainly need to be huddled.

As they demonstrate their engagement with the Circle, Square, and Training Triangle, and as they show their willingness to lead or be part of a missionary household, we will be deploying them to more significant responsibility. Eventually they will reach D4 on the Square and the innovation part of the Training Triangle, and we will need to give them something of their own to lead.

As the pipeline moves from recruit towards deploy, the number of people in the pipeline will naturally decrease. This is normal.

Assuming the emerging leader is already leading a missionary household, the most obvious thing is to see if God is leading them to build a new MC around their MH, one that has a distinct missional purpose, specific to them as a spiritual parent. Eventually the time comes to release them from your reducing oversight to operate more autonomously. You hope they will want to stay connected and part of a wider family of MCs that you have given birth to.

## TRY THIS

Discuss with one of your co-leaders: Have you got a leadership pipeline? Is it working? What do you need to change?

## MULTIPLYING MCs

This leads to some thoughts about how a MC multiplies. As we will see in our final section on reaching a whole town or city, the multiplication of missional expressions of church is vital to the vision. In fact, it is vital that no MC is able to start without the vision for multiplication sown in at the outset. Many people will just be looking for a safe place to belong and be cared for. This is not wrong, but it's not complete. They will ultimately not be fulfilled if they are not part of something that is growing and multiplying. If the vision and hope for this is not declared openly from day one, the members of the group may feel they have been duped when you later start to talk about it. Thankfully the larger size of most MCs means that when multiplication takes place, everyone will have the opportunity of staying with those they are most closely bonded to, and with whom they share a missional focus, as they form the nucleus of the next MC. The DNA for multiplication is key to the health of every MC.

*There are four main ways a MC can multiply (using organic language):*

1.      **Mitosis:** When a MC approaches a certain size, usually about thirty people, it becomes impossible for it to remain home-based. This pushes the MC to multiply along relational, geographical, or preferably missional focus lines. The latter is the most useful, but when different parts of the MC have distinct and strong relational connections or different areas of geography in common, it's quite normal for either of these to become the basis of multiplication. The two groups may be similar in size or one may be a little bigger than the other, but both will be big enough to function immediately as a MC. The multiplication is driven here by size. It is similar to the process of cell division that happens in nature, a process called mitosis.

STAGES OF MITOSIS

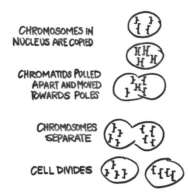

CHROMOSOMES IN NUCLEUS ARE COPIED

CHROMATIDS PULLED APART AND MOVED TOWARDS POLES

CHROMOSOMES SEPARATE

CELL DIVIDES

2.      **Budding:** Whatever the size of the MC, it may be that an emerging leader has a significantly different missional vision from the parent MC. This gives the new leader the opportunity to share what God is speaking to him or her about and to see if there are others who identify with them in that new missional focus. This needs to be done with the agreement of the spiritual parents of the main MC so that it doesn't cause confusion or competition, and so that they are able to affirm that the timing is right. The new group may only be a few people. It may or may not be a single missionary household, so it's probably best to think of it as a small group (4-8) rather than a MC (12-30). The small group can then "bud off" and set about growing to become a MC. The multiplication here is driven by new missional vision. Budding is similar to how an amoeba multiplies.

AMOEBA BUDDING

3.      **Reproducing:** The parent MC may have a number of missional households in it, and these households are like seeds in a fruit. The time may come for each or any of those households to become a MC in their own right. This will depend on the geography of the MH or the level of connectedness to the spiritual parents of the original MC. When the MH is geographically distant from the parent MC, it makes perfect sense for the MH to grow into its own MC.

In fact, this may have been the intention from the day they joined the original MC. We sometimes invite someone to join a MC with a view to developing as a MH and then into their own MC. Some MHs may want to stay long-term part of the parent MC, and this can be very helpful for the healthy sustainability of that MC. The "reproducing" multiplication here is driven by the strategic development of MHs.

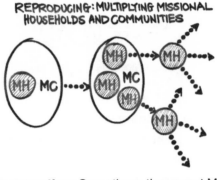

REPRODUCING: MULTIPLYING MISSIONAL HOUSEHOLDS AND COMMUNITIES

4.      **Death and Resurrection:** Sometimes the parent MC comes to a natural end. This can be because members move on to new things, or the spiritual parents move away. Sometimes a MC has a natural lifespan due to the life stage of most of its members. A demographically focused MC, i.e. one that is not geographical but is reaching out to a particular type of or group of people, is likely to have a shorter lifespan, as previously explained in chapter 8. Geography and proximity give much greater stability and longevity to a MC. Whatever the reason, the ending of one MC can lead to the birth of others. As the remaining members consider their options, there may be a number of groups that emerge with different missional visions. This "re-birthing" multiplication here is driven by the death of one community giving birth to others, ("Unless a kernel of wheat falls to the ground and dies, it remains only a single seed. But if it dies, it produces many seeds" John 12:24).

DEATH AND RESURRECTION

Several of these MCs may want to stay connected as part of a family of MCs that have a shared a common history. This may also be a natural stepping-stone to church planting.

The Greek word for synagogue is *sunagoge* and literally means "coming together". There seems to be no set size for a synagogue building, but one could not even be formed unless there was a cohort of at least ten men (with their families). It seems likely, looking at the archaeological footprint of synagogues from New Testament times, that many synagogues could accommodate up to 150 people - some even more. In any case, this size gathering of MCs may be a very useful adjunct to church life. It provides a helpful connection between the MCs and larger citywide gatherings, if such exist.

It is very hard to know everyone's name at a gathering once numbers go above 150. Thus, below that size still allows for a meaningful expression of family. As I have suggested, this emerging expression of church life is also a useful vehicle and strategy for church planting where smaller church planting is part of the parent church vision.

## INTERNAL LEARNING COMMUNITIES

In addition to huddle and other more informal "apprenticing" approaches, one other vehicle that is helpful in the development of multipliers is that of the internal learning community. 3DM has pioneered the use of the learning community model for helping leadership teams and churches that want to transition from a more traditional way of being and doing church to become churches that have put mission and discipleship front and center of their agenda – the engine under the hood.

The same principles that have been so effective over several days with churches in transition can be pared down to a more simple practice for emerging missional leaders within a church.

The heart of the process involves:

- Leaders prioritizing and setting aside time from their busy schedules to grow and learn from more mature leaders, and from each other. Four to six hours is usually a minimum of time needed every six months.

- Working through a three-stage process. The aim of this process is to be hearing from God throughout it.

  - It starts with *"What is?"* and is a time to reflect on how things are going with the MCs. This may be in general terms or in relation to a specific topic being covered that day. We are looking for insights from God and learning from what we have done. There will always be things we could have done differently or better, things we feel God had asked us to do that we didn't manage, or conversely things where we feel God really came through and helped us achieve something significant. Sometimes we use a SWOT analysis[60] to help mine the gold from this process.

  - The process moves on to *"What could be?"* which is time set aside to consider some fresh input to the group. This is a blue-sky thinking time when leaders are encouraged to dream about the future of their MCs. It is an opportunity to take note of the teaching input of the day, to discuss with each other how that could apply to their own missional context, and to listen to God though that process, aiming to answer the first discipleship question *"What is God saying to us?"*

  - It concludes with *"What will be?"* and this is time to make some specific plans for the next six months. This is where the MC team tries to answer the second discipleship question, *"What are we going to do about it?"*

- Building in accountability opportunities for plans made from previous learning community gatherings. This is usually part of the "What is?" assessment at the outset.

- Formal opportunities for leaders to present their learning or plans to each other.

- Informal opportunities for the leaders gathered to interact with each other, usually done over food!

The learning community is one of the most structured and organized parts of the multiplier's training. By contrast, the bulk of the learning is done "on the job" with regular opportunities for review, feedback, and discussion about what has worked and what could have been done differently or better.

The wise multiplier will provoke as many opportunities as possible for such times of review. As Ken Blanchard says, *"Feedback is the breakfast of champions!"* [61]

## FORM

One of the tools that has been pivotal in raising up young leaders within Kx churches is the national intern program called FORM.[62] These potential multipliers are those who have set aside a year or more of their lives for the sake of learning the art and skills of the missionary disciple. This program is running at an increasing number of centers across the UK. It allows younger people[63] who generally have more flexibility to work part-time and study/apprentice part-time, to prepare themselves for pioneering roles in their local churches or for church planting. I love the Scripture in Psalm 110:3 which speaks to me of this generation of younger people:

*"Your troops will be willing on your day of battle. Arrayed in holy splendour, your young men will come to you like dew from the morning's womb."*

There is no bar on age, gender, social background, or race when it comes to becoming a multiplier. The whole vision and structure of missional communities is designed to help every person who aspires to serve God's purpose fully to be trained to the full potential of their leadership. Each one can become a multiplier.

## TRY THIS

Who are your leaders? Make a list of those you want to invest in. Put a plan together to invest in them.

Having given some thought to the three stages of growth, from member to missionary to multiplier, I want to move on to consider where all this may lead to. It may even bring us to a fourth *M* – the movement builder.

## SIMPLE. STICKY. REPRODUCIBLE.

- Disciples who make disciples

- Transforming our nation with the gospel through a movement of missionary disciples

- Multiplication leads to movement

- The Discipleship/Leadership Square

- Huddle, a tool for discipling leaders

- Leadership is give and take. *Giving* permission and support for other leaders to grow, and *taking* initiative and responsibility.

# SECTION 3

## Future Vision:
## Reaching and Transforming our
## Towns, Cities and Nations

# 10

# GET A BIG VISION

## INTRODUCTION

If we are going to arrive at any destination, we need to know where we are going. What information will we program our spiritual navigator with? As we move into the final section of the book, I want to look beyond the local church to the church in a town, city or region. This was the perspective of the church planters in the book of Acts and of the New Testament epistle writers. If we want to be "the church that Jesus died for and is coming back for", I believe we need to make this shift of perspective. It's a move from dance floor to balcony. We need to start looking down on what is happening from the balcony, not just keep moving ever more frantically round the dance floor.

**Questions:** Where is this all going? Why do we need to look beyond our local church's ministry? How do we know when we've completed God's work? Is it possible to reach a whole city with the gospel?

A clear and compelling vision is essential if we want to see people mobilized into the great commission. The following I believe is clear and compelling as well as biblical.

Steven R. Covey, who wrote *The 7 Habits of Highly Effective People*,[64] begins with the principle of "starting with the end in mind". This is what one of my past mentors, Dwight Smith, calls "A to Z thinking". We need to understand where this is all going, where we are heading, what God is trying to achieve through us, His people, His church, prior to Christ's return. If not, we may well find ourselves running after goals or achievements that are, at best, valid but not crucial to His plans, or at worst, "vain pursuits", monuments to ourselves that have no eternal value.

So how do we ensure that our plans are in line with the Father's plans? How do we have confidence, like Jesus, that we are only doing what we see the Father doing? Maybe God's Word is a good place to start, and a good plumb line for our plans. Woody Allen said, *"If you want to make God laugh, tell Him about your plans."* Proverbs tells us, *"Many are the plans in a person's heart, but it is the Lord's purpose that prevails" (Proverbs 19:21).*

God is gracious and knows that we will only ever understand and see in part. We will never fully grasp all that is in the Father's heart and mind for His church and His creation. But He has chosen to reveal a remarkable part of His heart and plan to us through Scripture.

Jesus, as the full representation and manifestation of God in a human body (Hebrews 1:3) is always going to be our starting point for understanding God's heart. So it's important to examine why Christ came, and what He entrusted to His disciples when He went back to the Father.

Jesus makes a number of core purpose statements through the gospels. Here are a few.

> *"The Spirit of the Lord is on me, because he has anointed me **to proclaim good** news to the poor. He has sent me to proclaim freedom for the prisoners and recovery of sight for the blind, to set the oppressed free, to proclaim the year of the Lord's favor." ~Luke 4:18-19*

And when the disciples try to keep Him in Capernaum, He says,

*"I must preach the kingdom of God to the other cities also, for I was sent for this **purpose**." ~Luke 4:43 NASB*

After inviting the loathed tax collector Zacchaeus into a relationship with Himself, He explains to the disciples,

*"For the Son of Man came to **seek and to save the lost**."*
*~Luke 19:10*

When Paul comes to explain God's heart to Timothy, he says,

*"This is good, and pleases God our Saviour, who wants **all people to be saved** and to come to knowledge of the truth."*
*~1 Timothy 2:3-4*

And finally Peter, the disciple who knew as much as anyone about Jesus' heart for the lost, says,

*"The Lord is not slow in keeping his promise, as some understand slowness. Instead he is patient with you, **not wanting anyone to perish, but everyone to come to repentance**."*
*~2 Peter 3:9:*

It is no surprise then that in his gospel, the apostle John records these words just as Jesus is about to go to back to the Father:

*"Again Jesus said, 'Peace be with you! As the Father has sent me, I am sending you.'" ~John 20:21*

And Matthew in his gospel makes the commissioning of the disciples more explicit still.

*"Then Jesus came to them and said, 'All authority in heaven and on earth has been given to me. Therefore **go and make disciples** of all nations, baptizing them in the name of the Father and of the Son and of the Holy Spirit, and teaching them to obey everything I have commanded*

*you. And surely I am with you always, to the very end of the age.'"*
*~Matthew 28:18-20*

However you cut it, it seems that Jesus' main concern was for those who had yet to come into a saving relationship with the Father, and receive the abundant life He promises those who follow Him. This primary concern is passed on to the disciples, who in turn were instructed to pass it on to us.

Whilst we can say along with the shorter Westminster Catechism that "the chief end of man is to glorify God and enjoy him for ever", an astute person will ask "how are we intended to glorify God?" Again if we look to Jesus as our example, we see that He had one clear way of glorifying the Father. We find this statement in His prayer in Gethsemane as He reflects on His life's work:

*"I have brought you glory on earth by finishing the work you gave me to do." ~John 17:4*

Jesus understood that the way we can glorify the Father, is not so much by our worship services, as wonderful as they may be, but by simply finishing the work He has given us to do. And what is that work?

It is to complete the great commission, and in so doing prepare a beautiful bride for the Bridegroom at Jesus' return. So we come back to where we started our thinking in chapter one. I suggest that the church that has been able to complete the great commission will of necessity become everything else it needs to be in the process. It will be a church that has understood the why, the when, the what, who and how of the great commission. Expanding on my comments in chapter 5 about our motivation:

**Why?** Love for God and people is the "why?" of the great commission:

*"Jesus replied: 'Love the Lord your God with all your heart and with all your soul and with all your mind. This is the first and greatest commandment. And the second is like it: 'Love your neighbour as yourself.'" ~Matthew 22:37-39*

**When?** The great commission will be completed before Christ's return:

> *"'And this gospel of the kingdom will be preached in the whole world as a testimony to all nations, and then the end will come."* ~Matthew 24:14

**What, Who, How?** The great commission is to make disciples of the nations. We are called to go and complete it. We fulfill the great commission by making disciples who make disciples:

> *"Therefore go and make disciples of all nations, baptizing them in the name of the Father and of the Son and of the Holy Spirit, and teaching them to obey everything I have commanded you."* ~Matthew 28:19-20

I believe the missional (apostolic) vision of the church energizes the pastoral vision, defines the prophetic vision, gives content to the teaching vision, and harnesses the power of the evangelistic vision.

In other words, it is the missional / apostolic vision of church, entrusted to us by the Father, modelled for us by Jesus and for which we are specifically empowered by the Holy Spirit, that gives context for all of the other ministry callings of Ephesians 4 (The five-fold callings of apostle, prophet, evangelist, shepherd and teacher).

It is the *apostolic* working with the *prophetic* that provides the necessary foundation for the life of the church (Ephesians 2:20). The apostolic is vital to providing a framework of understanding within which the prophetic calls the church to obedience and spotlights the specific issues that need to be focussed on at any particular moment.

It is the *apostolic* that validates the vital importance of the evangelistic gifts and callings in the church for the purpose of growth and expansion. Without this the evangelists will quickly become marginalised or worse still made to feel unwelcome. They so often end up in para-church organizations because they don't know where they fit in the local church. I'm not in any way decrying the great job that para-church organizations do, just that many more evangelists could be wonderfully raised, released and used to resource a church that has a clear missional mandate at its heart.

The missional vision of church keeps us going when we are tempted to get bogged down with the entire *pastoral / shepherding* implications and responsibilities of building church. The pastoral dimension needs the energy and bigger picture vision of the *apostolic* to rise above the maintenance mindset and keep moving forward with the mission entrusted to us. It keeps the church looking outwards when we are tempted to just look in. It keeps the church pioneering, taking new ground, and growing when we want just to settle.

The *apostolic* draws on the *teaching* gifts in a local church to teach and train the saints for the specific work they will be involved in, skills they will need, and character God will form in them in the context of the mission. In the training triangle of information, imitation, and innovation, the teacher will provide much of the information needed. The apostolic vision will help inform the particular emphasis of teaching needed in any particular season. Without this the teaching and preaching pattern of a local church will likely be somewhat random, at the whim of the pastor's current fad, or just follow the lead of popular preachers' podcasts.

A church that has fulfilled the great commission will have had to put aside its petty differences. It will have had to strive for the unity of the Spirit mentioned in Ephesians 4:3. It will have had to train and mobilize all its members. It will have had to become powerful in its prayer life and gifts of the Spirit. It cannot complete the great commission without these vital elements and characteristics. But don't mistake any of these as an end in and of themselves. They are all a means to finishing the work that Jesus began 2000 years ago, and will be completed before He returns. This is an event that we expect to be soon. We carry the urgency that Paul spoke of in 2 Corinthians 5:11, 14-15, 19b-20:

*"Since, then, we know what it is to fear the Lord, we try to persuade others [...] "*

*"For Christ's love compels us, because we are convinced that one died for all, and therefore all died. And he died for all, that those who live should no longer live for themselves but for him who died for them and was raised again [...]"*

*"And he has committed to us the message of reconciliation. **We are therefore Christ's ambassadors**, as though God were making his appeal through us. We implore you on Christ's behalf: Be reconciled to God."*

I remember well the sense that I had after that first YWAM mission in 1973, from many missions since then, and also from the daily attempts to be, do, and say good news wherever I am – that sense of "this is what we were made for"; that sense of knowing I'm delighting the heart of God; that sense of connecting with divine purpose. I'm not a raving evangelist who loves nothing more than to blast people with the gospel. I'm usually timid about sharing my faith, as apprehensive as the next person, as fearful of rejection as anyone. But the idea that I am aligning with God's main purpose for the church on earth is reward in itself. And it's not just me. Whenever I talk to someone who puts himself or herself out there to be, do and say good news, they offer similar testimony, however timid they may be.

I hope you are persuaded that whatever your personal preferences, gifts, and callings are, and whatever your Ephesians 4 ministry bias is,[65] that the missional vision of the church, the call to complete the great commission requires all of us to work together to this one end, so that the Father may be glorified, Jesus will return, and we will get to "enjoy Him forever".

We have eternity to perfect our worship of God. We have eternity to understand all the revelations and mysteries of heaven. We have eternity to be Christ's ultimate co-regents in ruling His kingdom in a new heavens and a new earth. But we have one short life to fulfill the great commission.

## A WORD ABOUT THE KINGDOM

I consider that the church is the primary (though perhaps not exclusive) vehicle through which God's kingdom comes to earth, and through which our prayers for "his kingdom to come" are answered.

Much has been written about what it means to see God's kingdom come on earth as it is in heaven. I have much sympathy with Bill Johnson of Bethel Church, Redding, California. When asked how much of the kingdom we can expect to see this side of Christ's return, he answers in typical Bill fashion by asking, "Well how much do you want to see?" A frustrating, if not provoking answer.

The truth, I believe, is that we will see a whole lot more than we see now, but we will not see it all. As the theologian George Eldon Ladd says, we are living in the overlap between the "now" and the "not yet".[66] We are called to pray "your kingdom come on earth as it is in heaven". We are called to proclaim, "The kingdom of heaven is at hand, repent and believe the good news" (Mk 1:15). We are called to work for kingdom issues through social action and social justice. But we clearly will not see the full manifestation of the kingdom here and now.[67]

Jesus has been described as prophet, priest and king.[68]

I believe in this age that the church, as Jesus' body on earth, is called to be primarily prophetic and priestly in the way that it embodies the kingdom. As a prophetic people, others should be able to look at the church and say "Ah, that's what the King and His kingdom are like', full of love, faith, truth and justice." They are also called into relationship with the Father by a priestly people who take on the burden of prayer and the responsibility of being agents of reconciliation, of being His ambassadors.

After Christ returns, we will be primarily kingly, ruling in His kingdom, fulfilling the mandate to Adam and Eve at the beginning in Genesis 1:27 "to subdue the earth and rule over it". We do of course exercise that kingly rule now, in terms of casting out demons, taking authority over sickness, bringing His kingdom to individuals and families who are caught in the domain of darkness. We will also see His kingdom power have a transforming impact on our culture and society through its impact on businesses, schools, hospitals, media outlets, sporting bodies, local communities, city authorities, and even national governments. But I do not believe it will be our primary expression this side of Christ's return. If it were so then the Scriptures that talk about a great falling away, a great persecution prior to Christ's return (eg Matt 24:9-14, 2 Tim 3:1-13) would probably not be true. It is true that the light will shine brighter against increasing darkness, but that is unlikely to mean that the church is universally welcomed in its kingly influence in this age.

And the reason is this – our enemy, Satan, the accuser, liar, deceiver, tempter and destroyer is still at work, and his mission is to thwart all that God's people are doing. We know he is defeated, but not yet destroyed. He will continue to exert influence wherever we allow him to. Our expression of God's kingdom will only be in part, until that great day when Christ returns to gather His own to Himself in the sky as His precious bride; that day when Satan and his demons are finally thrown into the lake of fire; and when God's people, His church, are given the ultimate responsibility for the kingly manifestation of His kingdom in new heavens and a new earth.

Worth waiting for? Worth working for? Absolutely!

So, in answer to the question "Where is it all going?" we can say with some confidence that it is all heading to a completed great commission, the return of Christ, and the fulfillment of His kingdom on earth.

So with that in mind, let's consider the *implications* for our towns, cities and nations.

## BIG VISION - TIGHT FOCUS:

If we accept this premise, then we need to think through our *ecclesiology in the light of our eschatology.* How are we meant to live as the people of God prior to Christ's return?

Looking at the New Testament model of church is revealing. I am conscious that we are not them, and now is not then. Their time and context was unique, so I'm wary of making too many parallels with the way the New Testament apostles built church.

However, what stands out to me is that the church was originally one body in any town or city. There may have been many house churches, but they were all, as far as we can tell, linked together with singular purpose, and shared leadership. They clearly had their issues around unity and discord between individuals and probably house churches. Many of Paul's letters make reference to these. But the intention was clear, "Make every effort to keep the unity of the Spirit through the bond of peace" (Ephesians 4:3).

If that same unity of Spirit is as accessible today as it was then, imagine what we could achieve together. I'm not suggesting we should close down all our existing local churches, or abolish denominations (though the thought does occur to me sometimes). It is still possible for all of us to put a kingdom agenda, and a town or citywide vision before our own, more limited, vision for our local church, or the particular distinctives of our denomination or stream. I love the Moravian church's tag line of "in essentials unity, in non-essentials liberty, in all things love." Now that would be a good mantra for churches working together.

Is that same unity of the Spirit available today? Of course it is. We just need to get over ourselves, our own agendas, our personal fiefdoms, and our need for significance, security or self-worth in our local work, and start to ask the right questions.

I once had the temerity to ask a local church leader in Bristol if his reaction to a particular situation revealed a certain insecurity in his attitude to his own church. His response was illuminating. He literally shouted at me, in my face, "I am not insecure!" Insecurity is unfortunately like a plague on church leaders.

I find that most of the best decisions in life are made not by having the right answers, but by asking the right questions. What might those be for our town, city or regional context? I think about these things for our Liverpool city region. 1.5 million people across the six boroughs of Sefton, Knowsley, St Helens, Halton, Liverpool and Wirral, the vast majority of whom live in spiritual darkness, are heading to a lost eternity, and often living miserable broken lives as part of highly dysfunctional families.

Does this region need to see, hear, and taste the good news of Jesus? Most certainly. Who is responsible? Who is called to complete this assignment? To whom has God entrusted this great privilege? Surely it is to us, His people, the church in the city region.

Is it worth us thinking how we could achieve this by working more closely together? To me it's a "no-brainer". Of course it is. Why wouldn't we? Well for some, it's the things I've listed above like personal agendas or insecurities. For others it's just genuine busyness. Which pastor, minister, or vicar has the luxury of free time to readily consider working with other leaders and churches? Very few of us. It will only happen if we consider it a key part of our job in leading our own local church, to work with other local churches for the sake of the kingdom and the town, city, or region.

It will only happen if we see the priority of, and purpose in, being part of something bigger (this is always a mark of a healthy person, church or organization). It will only happen if we get the agreement of our elder boards and leadership teams to give some of our time, resources, administrative support, church agenda, and calendar to that end. Could it be the enemy's strategy to keep us so busy with good works, pastoral problems, or internal divisions, that we feel it's impossible to look above the parapet and see the wider landscape, to make time for God's bigger purpose in our town, city or region?

I know that during our first few years in Liverpool, we had to just keep our heads down to get Frontline church established – to get a clear vision and a good leadership team in place; to get the church members engaging with the missional purpose of the church. But after about four years, I felt God say, *"Now is the time to look beyond the local work, and see what I'm doing across the city."* And that became the start of wanting to work more collaboratively with other churches. *Together for the Harvest* (TFH) came into being soon after that, and has been one of the main vehicles for shared church mission across the city and region for over twenty years. Since then I have always made time to be part of that mission and vision.

Because of the tendency for denominations to only work with their own kind, the ability to work across these boundaries has been limited. In some parts of the UK, *Churches Together* has been a useful instrument, but in others it has been little more than a talking shop.

In the Liverpool City Region, TFH has been a significant vehicle for inter-church cooperation, for the encouragement of leaders, and for shared mission projects. Over the years there have been a number of major mission initiatives. There was J. John's *"Just 10"* series in Liverpool Cathedral. This was followed by Merseyfest across the Mersey region with a hundred or more churches putting on a week of social action projects, followed by a huge celebration in one of Liverpool's biggest parks, where over 80,000 attended across the weekend. Hope '08 took place in Hope Street in the city center, and many other smaller projects have happened over the last twenty years.

There has also been a proliferation of local church social action projects stimulated in part by TFH's promotion, training, and brokering of the opportunities that have existed, to partner with national organizations. The most recent audit done in partnership with TFH and the Cinnamon Network has demonstrated an amazing impact by the church across the city of Liverpool: 600 such projects from just under 100 churches, adding £10 million to the local economy each year. There are more details of the national statistics of the Cinnamon Network Faith Action Audit on their website.[69]

TFH has also been a champion of prayer for the last twenty years, with big prayer gatherings in the early days. In recent years, churches have participated in a prayer relay, with each church taking responsibility for praying for the city or region for a week of each year, and then handing on the prayer journal / baton to the next church.

Leaders' lunches for encouragement, shared learning, prayer and worship have also played their part in fostering meaningful relationship between leaders.

With all this activity, you'd expect some evidence of Liverpool's transformation. The truth is that the city has seen remarkable change in the last twenty years, not only in gaining the status of Capital of Culture in 2008, but also a general stimulation of the local economy, more jobs coming to the city with reducing unemployment, reduction in crime, and a complete renewal of the city center following nearly £1 billion of investment by the Duke of Westminster.

While difficult to prove, we believe prayer and local churches' "on the ground" actions have played a significant part in this.

However, as TFH reconsidered its vision in 2015/16, we came to some sobering conclusions. While all this activity and physical evidence of transformation had been encouraging, we had not seen any apparent net growth in church attendance, or the forming of more disciples, as evidence of increasing penetration of the gospel in our culture.

This brings us back to our core conviction about the missional purpose of the church – to be, do and say good news, such that we are making disciples who make disciples. Some may argue that it's about quality not quantity. Well I would say, let's look at the early church and Scripture again for our inspiration. Paul and the other Bible writers clearly contended for the quality of discipleship and unity of church life. But they equally expected the church to be constantly mobilized into its mission.

The result of this was massive quantitative growth for the first 300 years of the church's history. The growth during this period against a backdrop of persecution was almost certainly exponential. We can't use the "quality not quantity" argument as justification for lack of growth in the number of disciples in our city region.

So coming back to the Scriptures quoted earlier in this chapter, who are we responsible for reaching with the gospel? Is it just a few, or is it every man, woman and child? From 1 Timothy 2:4 and 2 Peter 3:9, it is clear that God want all to be saved and for *none* to perish. The gospel is for *everyone*. That's why Jesus commanded the disciples to "Go and preach the gospel to every creature" (NKJV), or "Go and preach the good news to everyone in the world." (CEV), Mark 16:15.

We, the church in the Liverpool city region, are responsible for reaching every man, woman and child with a living demonstration and winsome declaration of the gospel. Period! (As the Americans would say.) And I would suggest that you are too, for your neighborhood, village, town, city or region.

## KEEP THE END IN MIND

Coming back to our eschatology, we must remind ourselves that this is our great task, our great privilege, and our great commission: to fully preach the gospel so that Jesus can return to a bride that is full of true disciples, full of purity and passion, and is filling the earth with His glory. This is how Jesus put,

> *"And this gospel of the Kingdom will be preached in the whole world as a testimony to all nations, and then the end will come." ~Matthew 24:14*

"And *then* the end will come". Not before and not after. When we the church have done what we have been commanded and commissioned to do.

How do we know when that task is complete? Well there are many gospel indicators. Let me suggest a few:

- When the Jewish nation has been grafted back in to the vine, i.e. we have seen a great returning of Jewish people to Jesus (Romans 11:25-29).

- When the gospel has been preached to every people group in their heart language (Matthew 24:14). The word nations in v.14 is the Greek ethnos which means distinct tribe or ethnic people group, not the modern geo-political nation.

- When there is an established witness in every people group, i.e. a church, a true gospel community. I believe this means a permanent incarnation of the gospel embodied in a community of believers in every people group. Bear in mind that this understanding of church has little to do with our current obsession with buildings and programs, or even dare I say Sunday services, but is much more about communities of believers living out their faith in the context of the world they live in, as living demonstrations (testimonies) of the gospel 24/7.

- Some would build on the latter point to say that another indicator is when there is a viable church planting movement in every nation capable of achieving gospel saturation. I'm inclined to agree.

- When everyone in a nation has seen, heard, and had the opportunity to respond to the gospel through such incarnational communities of believers, in line with I Timothy 2:3-4 and 2 Peter 3:9.

- When, in any one generation, the church has flooded every neighborhood, town or city with gospel witness, i.e. when everyone in a neighborhood knows someone who knows, loves and follows Jesus. When everyone in that neighborhood knows they are invited to be part of that gospel community through following Jesus.

Jesus said, "*This* generation will certainly not pass away until all these things have happened", i.e. the things that lead to Christ's return (Matthew 24:34).

It seemed that the early church believed it likely that Jesus would come back in their lifetime. They certainly lived for that great hope, the hope of Christ's return and the hope of resurrection. They also lived out the command to go and make disciples of all nations in the understanding that this was part of the deal.

So we see a number of statements in Acts and Romans that suggests that it was part of the disciples' strategy to reach the whole of the known world with the gospel. In fact, it mirrors Jesus' promise in Acts 1:8 that the disciples would be His witnesses in Jerusalem, Judea, Samaria and to the ends of the earth.

In Acts 5:28, the Jewish leaders complained that the disciples had "*filled* Jerusalem with [their] teaching".

In Acts 19:10, in a chapter that describes Paul's training of disciples and church planters in the hall of Tyrannus in Ephesus, and their being sent out church planting all over Asia (modern Western Turkey), Luke, the author, states that, "*all* [...] who lived in the province of Asia heard the word of the Lord".

In Romans 15:19, where Paul is describing his life's mission, he says, "From Jerusalem all the way round to Illyricum [modern Albania] I have *fully proclaimed the gospel of Christ.*"

I believe to the best of their ability they sought to fulfill the great commission in their generation in the hope of seeing Christ's return. For whatever reason, they clearly didn't complete it, and Christ is still waiting to return 2000 years later. Will we be the generation to complete the task? Will we see Christ return in "this generation"? Why not? So much biblical prophecy has been fulfilled. So much of the world has already been reached.

For those interested in how far we have got, there are different ways of measuring our global progress. If we measure simply in terms of the gospel communicated in the heart language of the people group, then we are doing well, and the pioneer missionary Bible translators are doing an amazing job. If we measure by how many people groups have any Christians in them, the job is nearly complete. However, if we measure by the establishment of a permanent community of believers, meaning others in that people group are in reach of the gospel, the answer is more challenging. The Joshua project has sought to measure our progress more along these lines.

> "The definition used by mission strategists for people group is 'a significantly large grouping of individuals who perceive themselves to have a common affinity for one another because of their shared language, religion, ethnicity, residence, occupation, class or caste, situation, etc., or combinations of these.' For evangelistic purposes it is 'the largest group within which the gospel can spread as a church planting movement

*without encountering barriers of understanding or acceptance" (Ralph Winter).*[70]

The Joshua Project goes on to define an unreached people group as "a people group within which there is no indigenous community of believing Christians able to evangelize this people group."

The article continues by analysing the number of people groups who have less than 2% Christ followers, this being the percentage that would be required to evangelize that people group. It says that of the 16,600 people groups 6,700 would be considered "unreached" on this basis. And 42% of the world's population live in those 6,700 people groups.

And so the article goes on to give more details of the challenge ahead in completing the great commission in the light of these definitions.

So, next, let's consider some of the strategic implications of this for our towns, cities, and regions.

## SIMPLE. STICKY. REPRODUCIBLE.

- Start with the end in mind.

- God wants all to be saved, and none to perish.

- United in spirit, intent on one purpose.

- In essentials unity, in non-essentials liberty, in all things love.

# 11

# WHAT SHOULD WE DO THEN?

**Questions:** What is a unity movement meant to be and do? Is there a way of mobilizing the whole church in to its mission to reach a whole city?

I am a keen observer of what other cities and towns are doing by way of unity movements, particularly as documented by Roger Sutton and the Gather network in the UK. At the time of writing he has connected with and documented more than 120 of such "unity for mission" networks in the UK. I have great admiration for this work and want to be a part of it.[71]

If anything surprises me it is the lack of clear evangelistic / missional strategy to emerge from the majority of these unity movements. I expect to be proved wrong in the coming days, and indeed hope to be. Up to now my observation is that most unity movements revolve around one of several things:

- Inter-denominational leaders' gatherings for mutual support

- Prayer or worship gatherings

- Joint social action projects

- Occasional evangelistic events

None of these are bad or to be discouraged. However, if my missional understanding from the previous chapter has validity, none of these are enough. There is a lost world waiting to hear a message of hope. The gospel has yet to reach every man, woman and child in such a way that everyone has the opportunity to become a disciple of Jesus and part of a community of believers.

Building strong relationships is foundational (remember "everything is relational"), as is prayer ("praying before doing"), but neither is enough. We need to get our missional hands dirty. We need to be good news people who both demonstrate and declare a message of great hope of abundant and eternal life.

That demonstration is manifest through many of our social action projects, but it needs to also be visible in the way we all live our everyday lives. Lives of great generosity, inclusion, kindness, compassion, and selflessness. We're not just to be visible at the organized project level, but also at the organic lifestyle level.

Jesus said, *"By this everyone will know that you are my disciples, if you love one another."* (John 13:35). Jesus also prayed that, *"They [all believers] may be brought to complete unity. Then the world will know that you sent me."* (John 17:23).

As I mentioned in chapter six, in the early days of the house church movement (early 1970s) we believed that this unity and love for each other was not only a valid, but also a sufficient expression of the gospel to bring people to faith in Christ. We discovered to our disappointment that it wasn't. In my opinion, it was one of the death knells of the house church movement. Ultimately we failed to any great extent to see new birth (there were some notable exceptions).

Our love for one another and our unity may well point people towards a God of love and unity, but it does little to call people to a life of discipleship. There *must* be a gospel declared as well as demonstrated.

What does that look like at a town or citywide level?

I've developed a simple picture of what a strategic framework for inter-church, inter-denominational, inter-leader cooperation to reach a whole town or city could look like.

CITY-REGION REACHING STRATEGIC FRAMEWORK

'BE STRONG, AND LET US SHOW OURSELVES COURAGEOUS, FOR THE SAKE OF OUR PEOPLE AND THE CITIES OF GOD.' 2 SAM 10:12

## THE ARROWHEAD OVERVIEW

The arrowhead represents the full gospel mobilization of the body of Christ in any town, city or region. I am convinced it takes the whole church to reach the whole city.

I recognise that the evangelistic component of this framework will usually be the toughest to see established. The gospel declared will be the thing that gets us rejected by others (friends, neighbours, family, and work colleagues). It will often be the thing that gets us in trouble. It may even be the thing that ultimately gets us put in prison.

The gospel declared will be the hardest for most of us. Unless we are a rabid evangelist who has thick skin and a delight in being rejected, most of us will avoid confrontation or rejection and so will skirt round the opportunities that exist for us to be good news "say-ers" as well as good news "do-ers". The irony is that the gospel declared is not only vital; it is also very powerful. I think it's what the apostle Paul had in mind when he wrote to the church in Rome:

> "For I am not ashamed of the gospel, because it is the power of God that brings salvation to everyone who believes: first to the Jew, then to the Gentile." ~Romans 1:16

It's why Timothy, who was almost certainly not a natural evangelist (though was called to do the work of an evangelist, 2 Timothy 4:5), was exhorted by Paul to be full of courage in his declaration of the gospel.

> *"For the Spirit God gave us does not make us timid, but gives us power, love and self-discipline. So do not be ashamed of the testimony about our Lord or of me his prisoner. Rather, join with me in suffering for the gospel, by the power of God." ~2 Timothy 1:7-8*

I never think of myself as a natural evangelist, and have to take courage every time I deliberately open my mouth to share some aspect of the good news. I have to accept that my words may be misunderstood, I may experience rejection, even anger, but the love of Christ compels me (2 Corinthians 5:14).

Because of its vital and powerful nature, I have put the gospel declared, or what I have *called confident personal witness* (confidence to share our story and speak of the good news) at the front end of the arrowhead. I have also put *missional expressions of church* alongside it. Because we were never meant to function on our own but always as part of a family, a community of believers, this missional expression of church is vital for nurturing missionally confident Christians, and their working together to be, do, and say good news using their complementary gifts. I will talk about more of this later.

As you can see, the arrowhead is also made up of two other components: *community social action projects and marketplace kingdom endeavors.*

In the 1990s, I think the argument for the church's need to become missional was to a large extent won, at least in theory. In the 2000s we became good at developing social action projects, both as a way for a somewhat discredited institution to regain some relevance and credibility, but also as a way to express our mission, the good news, our gospel. In fact, we have become so good at these projects that both national and local governments rely on churches to be one of the biggest providers of social action, social support and social glue. In Liverpool, for example, the Lord Mayors fund has been used generously to support a number of church-run Food banks, as have funds from Housing Associations. The Cinnamon Network has become excellent at documenting this social impact in towns and cities across the UK as previously mentioned.

*Marketplace kingdom* endeavors seeks to recognise a different gospel dynamic. For some people their primary calling in expressing the gospel and the kingdom is in the market place. It is especially true for those who are called to lead in the spheres of society and culture. So this would be true for Christians in positions of leadership in business, healthcare, education, local or national government, the arts and entertainment, media, sport, etc. Such leaders are bringing a vital kingdom influence to our culture. They are not exempt from bringing a declared gospel to those they work with, but they have a wider calling and responsibility. With the understanding we have from the previous discussion on how far we can expect kingdom influence and extension to go prior to Jesus' return, I believe we should give such individuals all the support we can.

In some cities, such groups have been formed linking those who lead in specific spheres. One of the problems is that those who are in these positions of influence have often kept their light somewhat hidden for fear of being "outed" as Christian, and therefore discredited. It's time for us to say that "our faith informs every aspect of our lives", including our work, our areas of influence, and therefore not to be ashamed of it. We should be able to point to a track record of integrity, hard work, good team building, creativity, optimism and vision for our spheres, as evidence that our faith is a positive influence.

But we need to help those in these spheres connect with each other for encouragement, and where appropriate, for cooperation and leveraging impact. I believe that church leaders should be fostering such connections, though it is vital that they don't try to lead the groupings that emerge. It is not their calling, and they should leave it to those who are leading in the spheres to lead the groupings that emerge. Church leaders need to be there to support and encourage those with such callings in their churches, not try to control them. We need to release them from some of the expectations we place on others in our churches, without allowing them to become disconnected to the vital supplies that body connections bring:

*"[Christ,] from whom the whole body, being fitted and held together by*

*what every joint supplies, according to the proper working of each individual part, causes the growth of the body for the building up of itself in love." ~Ephesians 4:16 (NASB)*

## THE SHAFT OF THE ARROW

The shaft is vital to any arrow, giving it weight, straight flight, and distance. The arrowhead will go nowhere without the shaft. The same is true of evangelistic efforts that are not underpinned by relationship and prayer.

Relationships between church leaders of trust, gospel partnership, mutual respect, and deference to each other's gifting are needed if we are to see the gospel reach every man, woman and child in our cities. Typically, insecurity, mistrust, competition and comparison wreck any chance of working together for the sake of the gospel. There is a spiritual battle to deal with suspicions, past hurts, and the fear of others prospering at our expense.

## DEALING WITH TRANSFERS

Having been in the city of Liverpool for twenty-seven years, I am very aware of how miscommunication and suspicion can so quickly control our leadership relationships. Most leaders at some point have had members of our church leave us to join other churches. In different seasons, one particular church has become the "flavor of the month" and many from other churches mysteriously seem to be 'called' to be part of that church. But what comes around goes around. Usually that church sees members move on when they realize the grass isn't perhaps as green as they thought.

At Frontline church I've been on both ends of the exchange, and I've certainly not always handled it well. It's painful when people you have invested in move on for what seems like no good reason. Often they leave with little explanation or thanks. It is always painful when someone you have nurtured and for whom you've poured out your life decides to move on. We don't help each other when we glibly accept those from other churches without going back to their previous pastor and checking that they have left on good terms. If they have left with issues, they will certainly bring those issues with them. It is much better to encourage them to go back and sort out whatever they have taken offense at. Whatever the "given" reason for their leaving, there is often offense at the root of it.

We need to be transparent with each other in leadership and honoring of each other in the way we deal with transfers. It's not always wrong to move church, but it is always wrong to do it badly. Many times a member who has decided to move on has presented me with a fait accompli. If I'd been given the opportunity to be involved in discussing their thoughts and feelings before they made a decision, there could have been a much more constructive outcome.

However, we don't live in a perfect world, and people will come and go for all sorts of dubious reasons. We need to be big enough and secure enough to trust that "Jesus is building His church" despite our human weaknesses.

We need to learn to forgive where we have felt other church leaders have not dealt with us very honorably. Treat others as you would want to be treated. Look to see the bigger picture, particularly the tens of thousands who don't know Jesus. Let's not fight over the few that are already in the sheepfold; let's put our energy into looking for those who are still out wandering, lost and looking for hope, meaning, and security.

## BE A TEAM

As church leaders, we need to also value each other's gifts and abilities. I know there are some areas that I don't thrive in. I'm not a great events person. I often feel inadequate when it comes to organizing a great event. Others around me are much better at it. But when it comes to understanding the strategic process needed to get from A to B, then count me in. That's where I give of my best. When it comes to networking, to sharing vision, to gathering leaders to a common cause, and to training leaders, then I'm in my element.

As we have worked together for many years as a group of leaders in Liverpool in TFH, we have grown in this kind of understanding and deference. It's a big relief not to have to be great at everything but to be able to defer to each other's area of strength. It helps to build a great team. We need each other. We need strong trusting relationships around a shared vision.

For many of the last twenty years, we have had monthly leaders' lunches. They have taken on different formats and have had varying measures of success. We have run retreats and socials. We have done whatever we felt would help us build strong, healthy, robust relationships. No leader is an island. We need each other.

One thing I've noticed is that denominational structures designed to give support to their clergy often fail to do so because they are administratively organized, not relationally prioritized. It's one way that TFH has added value to many who are also part of such institutions, offering a place of genuine friendship and mutual support.

I remember when Jenny and I unintentionally got into a large amount of debt (as mentioned in chapter 4). The TFH prayer group that I had been meeting with most months for the best part of ten years was an incredible support to me as I let out all my fears and frustrations. They stood with me, spoke God's word to me and let me borrow some of their courage for a season, until I was able to find my own in God again. I value relationship.

## THE IMPORTANCE OF PRAYER

We've spoken about prayer in section one on foundations. Over the years, we have engaged with many prayer practices to express our belief in the importance of prayer in TFH. There have been leaders meeting in different parts of the city region to support each other in prayer. There have been large prayer gatherings bringing churches together. There has been coordinated prayer, with different churches taking their turn, covering the region in prayer fifty-two weeks a year. There is a regular core leaders' prayer gathering. And we will need to continue innovating and developing a prayer strategy to match any emerging evangelistic strategy.

One of the needs that have become evident in most cities where there are growing "unity for mission" movements, is the need for some joined-up thinking and practice between church leaders and prayer leaders. For whatever reason, the two groups have historically found it difficult to forge a good cooperative working relationship. This must be a great strategy of the enemy. If prayer is foundational to everything, what a great plan of Satan to separate and isolate the air force (intercessors) from the ground troops (church leaders and members who are witnesses). In modern warfare strategy, the coordination and cooperation between air and ground forces is critical to success.

How do we achieve the desired partnership? I use the word partnership as I think one of the problems in the past has been the expectation that prayer leaders would simply do whatever the church leaders asked of them. There is some legitimacy in this; however, it doesn't really give the appropriate respect and deference that prayer leaders deserve. Partnership in some measure restores this balance.

Prayer leaders are usually quite prophetic in their gifting and outlook. Local church leaders are more often pastors, teachers, evangelists or apostles. So it's perhaps not surprising that there is often misunderstanding and breakdown of relationship with prophetically orientated prayer leaders. We need to listen to, and hear each other, deeply. We need to ask forgiveness where we have jumped to conclusions about the other. We need to start again and rebuild partnerships that are fit for the battles that lie ahead.

Both evangelists and prophetically gifted and motivated leaders have a tendency to build their own organizations, usually because they have not felt there was room for them to flourish in a local church context. And this may be a reality they have had to deal with. However, the need to develop separate legal, organizational, and financial entities, the need to have autonomous and independent leadership, I believe, are in some measure a failure of both church leaders and evangelists, and prayer leaders. We need to repent of our separateness, and where possible and where helpful, find new ways of working together, where these separate entities are not barriers but blessings to the overall work of the gospel in our towns and cities. We need to find what cooperation not competition looks like.

## A NETWORK OF NETWORKS

Within the Liverpool city region, there are many moving parts. They include the six boroughs, separate towns like St Helens and Runcorn, large geographical areas like the Wirral, and the city of Liverpool itself. Liverpool is a city of many villages, many areas like Anfield, Everton, Toxteth, Speke, Childwall, Walton and Woolton. To take account of the varied geography across the region, one of the things we are doing is establishing a network of networks. The city region is far too big to be reached by one single network of leaders working together, and needs networks of leaders who identify with a given geographical area, with each other, and with the vision to reach every man, woman and child.

Such networks need to operate somewhat independently so they can contextualise the vision and mission to their area; and so they can tailor the strategy to work with their group of leaders and churches. But there will need to be certain things that each network has in common if they are going to be part of the mission force across our shared mission field, the city region. It may be helpful for any group of leaders working together to bring gospel saturation to any town, city or region to consider this.

### Four Functions Of An Effective Missional Network Of Leaders

I believe these leaders will need to:

- Meet regularly to pray, encourage each other, and build friendship.

- Meet to plan missionally together and review progress.

- Meet to share innovations and figure out what is working.

- Connect to the bigger entity that is tracking and mapping progress across the region, taking advantage of training, and the ongoing development of strategy.

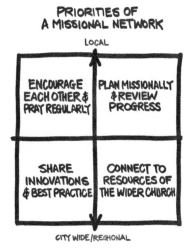

PRIORITIES OF
A MISSIONAL NETWORK

LOCAL

| ENCOURAGE EACH OTHER & PRAY REGULARLY | PLAN MISSIONALLY & REVIEW PROGRESS |
| SHARE INNOVATIONS & BEST PRACTICE | CONNECT TO RESOURCES OF THE WIDER CHURCH |

CITY WIDE/REGIONAL

Without these four elements, they will not achieve the goal of fully reaching their area with the gospel, or be part of the bigger picture. The network should be as inclusive as possible, not excluding anyone who shares the vision for reaching every man, woman and child. The vision itself will be self-selecting. It will not attract those who see the church as primarily institutional rather than missional. It is unlikely to draw those with a low view of Scripture, or Jesus call to unity. It should still draw churches with differing views on issues like gifts of the Spirit or women in leadership. As we have said before, we would do well to embrace the Moravian church movement's motto, "In essentials unity, in non-essentials liberty, in all things love".

It will be up to each network to interpret the strategic framework for its own local strategy but it will probably need to have something in place that takes note of every element of that framework if it is to be effective.

## LIVERPOOL CITY REGION TRAINING

As we have sought to interpret confident personal witness in our region, we have recognised that this will not be achieved without some quite specific training. Most churches are not full of people brimming over with confidence to talk about their faith at the water cooler at work, over the garden fence or at the Christmas party. We have developed some tailored training in this area, and at the time of writing have completed courses for a number churches in the Toxteth, Runcorn,

Wirral, Waterloo and Tuebrook areas of Liverpool, with a number more planned for the coming year across the region.

The training is over four evenings and covers three key confidences. We have tried to reduce this to its simplest form, so as not to overcomplicate the issues or intimidate people. We want everyone, whatever their background, whatever their gifting, whatever their stage of life to be able to think, "Yes, I could do that."

The three confidences (I call them *the three confidences of missionally effective Christians*) are as follows:

- Confidence to share your faith story
- Confidence to talk about Jesus and His good news
- Confidence to invite people to something

We summarise it as – my story, God's story, our story.

We call this training "Brighter ... good news habits to help you shine"

Doesn't sound like rocket science, does it? But we believe it could transform a church's ability to reach out with the gospel if a majority of its members went through the training and started to put it into practice.

Each member will be given training in each of these areas including some simple homework to be done by the next session. At the start of each session there will be an opportunity for feedback on what God has been doing. This element of accountability is vital to the effectiveness of the training. As the saying goes "people don't do what you expect, they do what you inspect". The homework involves a low bar task. For example, after week one the task may be to pray every day for someone to share your story with, and when the opportunity arises to have a go. No one will be made to feel inadequate or a failure. Everyone will be learning together. I believe there will be many stories to encourage everyone to keep going.

One participant said this,

> *"It has been encouraging to hear more testimonies in church as a result of the course. It made me re-evaluate the power and grace of God in my own testimony, and it has caused me to pray more for people I know who don't know Jesus."*

We are starting to measure, with a simple online tool, the increase in missional confidence during and beyond the training period. The aim of the training is to ultimately build a lifestyle of witness, not just to have a short burst of evangelistic activity, as is the norm for many evangelistic events. This will take time and ongoing encouragement to achieve, but is entirely possible, desirable, and I believe essential if we are to see our dream fulfilled. The church is the great sleeping giant. It's time for us to wake up to the wonder of the gospel and get ourselves equipped and confident to share it wherever we go.

## MULTIPLYING MISSIONAL EXPRESSIONS OF CHURCH

One of the hardest questions to answer is, "How will you know when you have reached every man, woman and child in the city region?" In fact it's almost impossible to answer this question to everyone's satisfaction. One of the difficulties is that the population is always changing. People move in and out of cities, people die and new children are born every day. In other words, the population is not static and we cannot be sure at any one moment that "everyone is reached". And even if we were by some statistical miracle able to achieve that, the population would have changed by the next day. This, in itself, suggests that a numerical measure of this nature is not only unachievable but also unhelpful.

What I would like to suggest is that we aim for a generational goal. We read earlier that "this generation will certainly not pass away until all these things have happened" (Matthew 24:34). What if we could say that, as far as our generation is concerned, we have saturated our city region with the gospel by so mobilizing and multiplying the church that every person was in easy reach of a vibrant incarnated gospel witness or testimony, as Matthew 24:14 puts it? Witness is the Greek word (*martyrion*) from which we get martyr (might suggest that some sacrifice will be needed!). That witness would need to look like a healthy community of believers visibly living out the gospel in their daily lives. And what if every person in their area had first-hand experience of those people, i.e. had had contact with them, and knew them to be people of good character, full of love, willing to serve, and carrying a message of hope for all people.

When Jenny and I moved to Liverpool in 1991, Lord David Alton (just David Alton then) was our local MP. At election times his billboard advertising slogan was: "Everyone knows someone who's been helped by David Alton". He was such a great local constituency MP that the slogan was absolutely true. I have often dreamed of a day when people in our city region are able to say, "Everyone knows someone whose life has been transformed by Jesus."

What if these communities of mission / missional expressions of church were so growing and multiplying that over a ten-year period, every neighborhood in the city region had such a group present in it. I believe it would be possible to say that we were, in that generation, reaching every man, woman and child with the gospel.

It of course raises 101 questions, but the basic idea is, I believe, both *biblical* and *achievable*.

I say biblical because I believe that is what happened in Jerusalem and all the major cities and towns that the gospel came to in the Acts of the Apostles. *"You have filled Jerusalem with your teaching"* (Acts 5:28); *"All who lived in Asia heard the word of the Lord"* (Acts 19:10).

I say *achievable* because in very approximate terms there are enough Christian households in the Liverpool city region for there to be one per street. If all of those households were part of a local expression of church in the neighborhood, then gospel penetration, and saturation would be possible.

I believe that these gospel communities will need to be home-based, simply because if it requires a building, a professional paid leader, and a Sunday service to achieve this goal, it will never happen. It's too expensive, too complicated, and too clergy dependent.

It's possible that some of these "missional expressions of church" could be a localised church plant, a new congregation, a fresh expression, a multisite campus, or simply a small local congregation that takes full gospel responsibility for its immediate neighborhood. But the vast majority of such multiplying missional expressions of church will need to be home-based, lay-led, and not Sunday-dependent. They will need to be informal but highly intentional, outwardly focussed and discipleship-orientated, geographically stable and yet rapidly multiplying.

## FIVE CHARACTERISTICS OF AN EFFECTIVE MISSIONAL EXPRES-SION OF CHURCH

I believe that each of these gospel communities will need to display the following characteristics if they are to be successful in reaching their entire neighborhood with the gospel:

1.  **Prayer:** Praying for every household in that neighborhood, where possible by name

2.  **Presence:** Being present and accessible. Serving the neighborhood in a variety of practical ways. As well as demonstrating the gospel, this is also a way of connecting with many people in the local area (remember the disciple-maker's journey)

3.  **People of peace:** Befriending many, and looking prayerfully for the people of peace, i.e. those who are "leaning in", spiritually open, and may be doorways to families or sections of the local community

4.  **Pathways to faith:** Creating pathways to faith for those who want to know more e.g. Alpha or similar

5.  **Producing disciple-makers:** Developing ways of growing new Christians to become disciple-makers themselves.

THE ⑤ P's OF MULTIPLYING MISSIONAL EXPRESSIONS OF CHURCH...

① PRAYER
② PRESENCE
⑤ PRODUCING DISCIPLE MAKERS
③ PEOPLE OF PEACE
④ PATHWAYS TO FAITH

While the approach I've described above is dependent on a geographical neighborhood approach, we know that many people don't connect much in their local community and instead make more of their friendships at work or in social settings. For this reason it is likely that we will also need to develop demographic equivalents to these missional expressions of church for the workplace and other social gathering places.

Having said that, it is instinctively understood that most people are looking for genuine community in their locality, but because of the fragmentation of family structure, and the individualisation of society, they find it increasingly difficult to find it there. Enter the church! We are probably the best-placed group of people to reintroduce community values to a neighborhood. We understand hospitality, we are already part of loving communities, we should be some of the most inclusive people around, and wouldn't it be great if we could say that we also know how to have fun!

Neighborhood watch, Homewatch and other similar groups have started out with security in mind, but have, in some places, actually been unexpectedly successful in re-creating a sense of community, simply because there is an appetite for it. The chance to rebuild a sense of community where we live is our big opportunity I believe.

As missional expressions of church grow and multiply, we are in reality describing a church planting strategy. We could think of these expressions of church as in some way equivalent to the New Testament "church in the house", as seen in Romans 16:5, Colossians 4:15, and Philemon 1:2.

Such missional communities, I believe, are the backbone of any strategy to effectively reach an entire town, city or region with the gospel. They will require support, training, encouragement, and leadership development. This is where the centralized resources of a local church are most needed. Instead of deploying the vast majority of its resources to Sunday services, pastoral care, and social programs, it could instead prioritize the growth and multiplication of such missional communities. Imagine a local church that dedicated 50% of its resources to this end. Imagine how much impact it could have in its decentralized, scattered context. Imagine how this might then feed into its gathered centralized activities. It could be a winning combination if the investment levels for both scattered and gathered were adjusted for this purpose.

As mentioned earlier in the disciple-maker's journey, one of the strategies that we are nurturing through TFH is the Hope 2018 initiative that, amongst other things, is encouraging and resourcing local churches to build a rhythm of invitational opportunities through the seasons of the year. The idea is that there is always something that members of a gospel community can invite people to, where they know they will be exposed to the gospel as well as the wider church family. Christmas and Easter are the low-hanging fruit of centralized gospel invitational opportunities, but what if every local church also developed such opportunities around Lent, summer fun days, harvest events, and Remembrance Sunday?

Having such a rhythm of invitational opportunities would also play well into the member training around the three confidences of sharing their faith story, talking about Jesus, and inviting to something.

## MOVEMENT BUILDERS

And this is where it's appropriate to consider the idea of becoming movement builders: from members to missionaries to multipliers and now to movement builders.

Everyone who is multiplying others to lead their own missional households is also preparing them to leading a growing "church in the house". As they do so, they are not just adding to the growth of the body, but they are multiplying its potential impact and reach.

Once these gospel communities start to multiply and the leadership pipeline is full of emerging missionary disciples, then we have the potential for unlimited growth and genuine movement. Movement happens when there is such momentum that the growth feels unstoppable, and there is very little "stirring" from the center needed to keep things moving forwards in the right direction. The more our activities need prodding and poking by church leaders and their core staff to keep moving, the further from real movement we actually are.

By working in this way to multiply these missional expressions of church, gospel communities, missional communities, church in the house, whatever you want to call them, we will eventually be able to saturate the region with a patchwork of such communities of believers so that every neighborhood is covered, and every person is being reached.

## 1 IN 1000

A simply way of expressing this desire is to think of this patchwork expressed as 1 missional community for every 1000 people. Clearly the exact number is not as important as the understanding that comes from it: we need to multiply our gospel communities such that we have something of this number in relation to the overall population. It gives us a realistic and measurable goal to aim for. Some gospel communities may only be reaching out to 300 people, others may be bigger or stronger and be able to reach 1000 or even 1500. Some people will like this idea and some will hate it. Let's use it to the degree that it serves us, not in such a way that we feel we are slavishly bound to the mathematical exactness of it!

Some households may adopt the street they live in as part of this strategy. There is a national Neighborhood Prayer Network that is fostering praying, caring and sharing in local communities.[72] This could be a powerful part of the overall strategy and would give the added bonus of seeing our local efforts as part of a national initiative. If it falls short in anyway, it does so in terms of the needs of discipleship, leadership development, inter-church cooperation, and the potential for multiplication and gospel saturation. However, I thoroughly commend it as a great step in the right direction.

As we begin to see these gospel communities multiply, we will be able to map them and chart the coverage of the region. This is when it will start to get exciting, and when we will probably need to be ready for some opposition.

It has been asked if people in one missional community can be members of different local churches (or no church), as long as they all live in the same neighborhood and want to work together to reach it with the gospel. In theory this shouldn't be a problem, but in practice it becomes difficult if the different local churches have different approaches to say, discipleship, leader training, pastoral care, or moral issues.

For example, if a member of a missional community is struggling with severe mental health issues, it is likely to be beyond the competence or capacity of the local missional community leader. Who do they contact for support?

What if there is a discipline issue over an immoral relationship and the church the MC leader belongs to has a stricter policy than the one that the individual attends on Sundays? What if there is a false accusation by a member towards an MC leader, and they both are members of different churches?

None of these things are irreconcilable, but it requires much closer cooperation between church leaders. Ultimately this is a good thing, but may not be simple to achieve.

However, this question does help us consider the degree of inter-church cooperation that is possible. Where leaders of local churches have bought into the idea of reaching every man, woman and child with the gospel, where they are all trying to work to a similar shared strategy, such levels of cooperation should be possible. It will be one of the marks of the church coming to maturity when we see this taking place. It comes back to some of the issues we touched on earlier such as leadership insecurities, personal agendas and empire-building mindsets.

It's good to be reminded of the intended result of the equipping impact of the Ephesians 4 ministries of apostle, prophet, evangelist, shepherd and teacher (APEST):

> "Instead, we will speak the truth in love, growing in every way more and more like Christ, who is the head of his body, the church. He makes the whole body fit together perfectly. As each part does its own special work, it helps the other parts grow, so that the whole body is healthy and growing and full of love." ~Ephesians 4:15-16 NLT

Wouldn't it be amazing if leaders of local churches were less focused on the understandable desire to grow their own church, and instead prioritized the growth of the whole church? It will take the whole church to reach the whole of a town or city. We need to keep working at our relationships, our understanding and respect for each other, our willingness to trust, and put the kingdom before our local responsibilities. Could it be that one of the schemes of the enemy (2 Corinthians 2:11) is to keep us separate in our own silos, rather than be a meaningful whole expression of the church in a town or city, as seems to have been the norm in the New Testament.

In Frontline church we had a period in our history when I would regularly ask the congregation in the middle of a sermon, "How many churches are there in Liverpool?" Eventually they learned that the right reply was, "There is one church in Liverpool" (and we are just part of it). I can't say I always lived fully to that ideal, or that I was always free from personal agendas, but as a church we were always supportive of the citywide inter-church activities. There is much more to do on this front for all of us, if we are truly to reach every man, woman and child with the gospel by 2026 (ten years from when we started).

## SIMPLE. STICKY. REPRODUCIBLE.

- The arrowhead strategic framework.

- Brighter, good news habits to help you shine.

- 5 characteristics of effective missional expressions of church.

- 1 in 1000

# 12

# GOD'S GLORY IN THE NATIONS

It has always been God's intention that the earth would once again reflect and be filled with God's glory, goodness and grace, as it was in the beginning. Currently corrupted by sin and death, we are told by Paul that, *"Creation itself will be liberated from its bondage to decay and brought into the freedom and glory of the children of God"* (Romans 8:21).

That's why Romans 8:19 says *"For the creation waits in eager expectation for the children of God to be revealed".* We, God's children, are the agents of change; we herald the setting free of creation itself. I don't know if that sends tingles down your spine but it does mine. There is a huge sense of privilege that we have as his children in being "the first fruits of all he created" (James 1:18). J. B. Philips translation of Romans 8:19 says that, *"The whole creation is on tiptoe to see the wonderful sight of the sons of God coming into their own."*

God is preparing the world to be restored to its original design, free from sin, free from corruption, and free from death. In that world we will no longer experience suffering, pain, or tears (Revelation 21:4). All of this comes to its fulfillment at Christ's return. The bride is caught up to meet Him in the air (1 Thessalonians 4:16-17). The living and the dead are judged (1 Peter 4:5), Satan and his demons are destroyed (Revelation 20:10), and God's new heavens and new earth will be ruled over by His saints (Revelation 5:9-10).

All of this is heady stuff, and some may be tempted just to see salvation as a ticket to a secured eternity, which of course it is. But any idea that we should hide away from an evil world and hang on "till Christ returns" is defeatist, escapist and contrary to Scripture.

What does it look like for "the sons of God to come into their own"? I believe we can understand this best in the context of God's glory filling the earth.

Some like to think of God's glory in transcendent terms, as in the dedication of Solomon's temple in 2 Chronicles 5:14:

> "And the priests could not perform their service because of the cloud, for the glory of the LORD filled the temple of God."

Or as in Acts 2:2-3 when the Spirit was poured out as wind and fire on the day of Pentecost.

Or as when Stephen was being interrogated in Acts 6:15 and the ruling Jewish council witnessed his face "like the face of an angel". And just before his stoning when Stephen looks up to heaven (Acts 7:55) and sees the glory of God.

We cannot control such transcendent experiences, but we can welcome them whenever God reveals himself in such a way.

However, as mentioned in the introduction, another description of God's glory is given in Exodus 33. Moses has asked to see God's glory. God says,

> "I Myself will make all My goodness pass before you, and will proclaim the name of the LORD before you; and I will be gracious to whom I will be gracious, and will show compassion on whom I will show compassion."
> ~Exodus 33:18-19 NASB

God's glory is revealed in His goodness, His compassion, and His grace and in the proclamation of His name. While God reveals all of these in His own sovereign way, His people, we who are the current bearers of such glory, primarily demonstrate them. The Apostle Paul says of the church,

> "To them (the saints) God has chosen to make known among the Gentiles the glorious riches of this mystery, which is Christ in you, the hope of glory." ~Colossians 1:27

I like to say that Christ is our hope of glory in heaven, and we are *His hope of glory on earth.*

We are living in the day when God is doing just this, revealing His glory on earth through His saints. We may not always have eyes to see it, but the evidence is compelling when we look at the global church, especially in parts of Asia, Africa, and South America. There are vast swathes of the world where God's glory is indeed filling nations. How is He doing this? Through multitudes of radical missionary disciples. Women and men of God who have abandoned all desire to live comfortable and convenient lives in this world. Those who have seen themselves as citizens of heaven, who think of their life in this world in the way Abraham's was described in Hebrews 11:9-10:

> "By faith he made his home in the promised land like a stranger in a foreign country; he lived in tents, as did Isaac and Jacob, who were heirs with him of the same promise. For he was looking forward to the city with foundations, whose architect and builder is God".

These missionary disciples, these ambassadors of another kingdom, are not content on "getting by for their comfort", but intent on "going big for the king". The Apostle Paul puts it this way:

> "So whether we are here in this body or away from this body, our goal is to please him. For we must all stand before Christ to be judged. We will each receive whatever we deserve for the good or evil we have done in this earthly body. Because we understand our fearful responsibility to the Lord, we work hard to persuade others[...] So we are Christ's ambassadors; God is making his appeal through us. We speak for Christ

*when we plead, 'Come back to God!"* ~2 Corinthians 5:9-11, 20 NLT

*As his ambassadors, we fill the earth with His glory* when we flood our places with the good news, both demonstrated and declared, that Jesus is here, and through us His family, that His goodness, compassion and grace reach out to every man, woman and child. As good news people, our eyes are filled with the love of God, our hands are filled with the practical goodness of God, and our mouths filled with the invitation of God, "be reconciled to Him". If God is light and God is love, let's expect both the transcendent and the incarnational to be revealed as we give ourselves to His purpose in our time.

Many of you will have had people say to you something like, "There's something in your eyes, something shining, like a light." Or perhaps, "You know when you helped me through that difficult time, I experienced God's love through you." Or again, "When you prayed for me, I felt His power, like heat, in my body." We should expect both incarnational and transcendent manifestations of His glory.

This is how we will fill His earth with His glory.

This glory will be demonstrated in women's and men's lives being restored to the Creator's purpose. It will be revealed as families are rebuilt, and become healthy, safe places to raise children. It will be manifest in neighborhoods, towns and cities, in businesses, offices, hospitals, schools and universities, in pubs and cafes, as the culture of the kingdom becomes the dominant culture of these places. God's glory will fill the earth as we, His glory-bearers, multiply and fill our places, influencing and impacting those around us with the good news of God's kingdom.

Does this mean that Jesus will return to a near perfect world? Clearly not. Scripture is unequivocal that there will be much darkness and persecution before Christ returns (Matthew 24), but even in those places where darkness seems to have taken the greatest root, I believe Jesus' people will shine the more brightly. Their glory will be the greater by contrast to the darkness around.

Church, let's be the people God intended us to be. Let's be "the church that Jesus died for and is coming back for". Let's become the bride that is "without

REIMAGINE CHURCH | 251

stain or wrinkle or any other blemish" (Ephesians 5:27). Let's commit ourselves to completing the great commission wherever we are, and become that spotless bride. Let's get ourselves in a place of mentoring, apprenticeship, accountability and personal development as missionary disciples. Let's find or create missional households and communities to be part of. Let's aspire to become multipliers and movement builders wherever the Father sends us –across the road, or across the world. Let's be his glory bearers!

## SIMPLE. STICKY. REPRODUCIBLE.

- Christ is our hope of glory in heaven, and we are His hope of glory on earth

## KAIROS CONNEXION

There are many applications of the tools, vehicles and practices outlined in this book. For further information about training, coaching, consultancy, local Kairos Connexion hubs, or leaders' gatherings, contact us at:

admin@kairosconnexion.org

Or visit our website:

www.kairosconnexion.org

# APPENDIX 1

## Discovery Bible Study - Overview (for christians and non-christians)

DBS' are intended to provide a basic discipleship platform for everyone in communities to grow as disciples of Jesus i.e. to become like him in character, conduct and competency. It provides a point of intersection between the Word of God (that is being studied), the Spirit of God (who is speaking through it), and the people of God (who are mouthpieces of God to each other). It is lightweight and low maintenance. It is simple, reproducible, and sustainable. And it provides a peer-led, accountability-based, group context for discipleship to happen.

## WHEN USING WITH CHRISTIANS

When doing a Discovery Bible Study with Christians, I suggest the following: (remember that a DBS is aiming for application and accountability, not just information and inspiration).

**Pick** a Bible story or passage, between 10-15 verses (stories are easier).

**Read** it together round the room, taking a few verses each.

**Listen** to it, while one person reads it to the others, without them reading along.

**Re-tell** it from memory. Use the group members to recall all the bits they can remember.

Then discuss the following questions:

1.  What does this passage tell us about God, Jesus, people and life?

2.  Does it give us any promises, principles, commands or warnings?

3.  What is God saying to me through this, and what am I going to do about it?

4.  Who can I tell about what I have learned here, within the next week?

Other suggestions:

- Pray before starting for God to speak.

- Aim to take about half your time on questions 1 and 2, which are the general unpacking questions, and the other half on questions 3 and 4.

- Be careful not to give the answers but to draw out the truth from what others are saying. God will be speaking to people as they hear each other's comments, as well as directly through the text. You are not meant to be the "expert" in the room, simply another learner. The Holy Spirit is the discipler in this process; all you are doing is providing a culture and context for the discipleship to happen in. If you have to be the "expert", then it is no longer reproducible.

- Pause between question 2 and 3, and ask them to listen to what the Holy Spirit is saying to them from the passage. If they're not sure how to hear God, encourage them to take note of thoughts that come to mind, or to simply imagine what God might be saying.

- Be prepared to lead by example at this point about what God is saying to you, and what you are going to do about it. Be vulnerable and real. Make a note of what others share they are going to do about what God is saying. One way of maximizing the accountability is to ask them what question they would like to be asked next time you meet, to show they have taken action on what God was saying to them.

- Question 4 is helping them begin to be a disciple-maker, not just a disciple. This is the ultimate aim of the process.

- After question 4, get them to pray in pairs for each other, praying into their kairos/key takeaways.

- Be prepared to ask next time you meet how everyone got on putting in to practice what God was saying. Once again, you go first. This accountability it vital to their growth.

## WHEN USING WITH NON-CHRISTIANS

Neil Cole recommends using the 7 signs in John's gospel as the passages to study.

I find that giving a John's gospel is useful so everyone is using the same version and can carry it around and read it at their leisure (e.g. the Love is the Bridge booklet published by Bridge Builders https://www.bridge-builders.net/booklets/). It's good practice to ask them to read the passage for the coming session every day in the build up to it. This familiarizes them with the passage and kick-starts the process of God speaking to them.

The 7 passages are:

1.  The turning of water into wine (John 2:1-12)

2.  The healing of the royal official's son (John 4:46-54)

3.  The healing of the paralytic at the Bethesda pool (John 5:1-17)

4.  The feeding of the five thousand (John 6:1-14)

5.  The walking on water (John 6:15-25)

6.  The healing of the man born blind (John 9:1-41)

7.  The raising of Lazarus (John 11:1-46)

8. /9. I have added an extra week or two on the death and resurrection of Jesus (John 19:1-18, and John 20:1-18)

And the four question variation for use in this context is:

1.  What does this story say to you about people?

2.  What does this story say to you about, Jesus, the Father or the Holy Spirit?

3. What does this story have to say about you?

4. Who needs to hear this story?

My suggestions to help group dynamics here are:

- In relation to question number 1 ("What does this say about people?"), to help them get into the process, get them to think of the story like a play, film or drama. Look at the individual characters that make up the story and get them to imagine what is going on. What are they thinking? How are they reacting? Why are they saying or doing what they are doing?

- Question 2 is getting people to think about the nature of God. What is he like? These thoughts will directly relate to some of the identity issues that will underpin a fresh understanding of what is now true of us in the light of who He is. This alone can be life changing.

- When you get to question 3 ("What does this story say about you?"), get them to imagine themselves in the drama. How would they be feeling? Which character do they most identify with? How would they have reacted etc.? This helps them to start making personal applications without realizing it.

- With regards to question 4 ("Who do you want to tell this story to?"), it's good to encourage them to think about what they are taking away, what they have learned and who might benefit from their insights? This is the question that gets them thinking as a disciple-maker before they are even a disciple themselves.

Although I recommend the 7 signs passages in John, I have also had non-Christians in a regular DBS, and they have been able to join in without any problems, whatever the passage.

Having watched the Holy Spirit drawing the participants to the Father, you will need at some point to ask them if they are ready to become a Christ-follower. It's good to ask the question confidently but not coercively. It may be useful to use a resource like Why Jesus? by Nicky Gumbel at this point.

# APPENDIX 2

## Accountability Questions

## FRONTLINE CHURCH VALUES CARD

### Disipleship

The process of being transformed by grace to become more like Jesus.

We've found the following questions about our four values to be helpful:

What is God saying to me?

What am I going to do about it?

What question do I need to be asked next time?

### Authentic Devotion

How am I pursuing intimacy with Jesus each day?

Do I love God's word and feed on it?

How am I living in the power of the Spirit?

What is stopping me connecting with God?

Is there anything I need to surrender to God?

### Extended Family

Am I commited to loving and spending time with others in Community?

Do others in Community know my needs and goals?

Is there anyone I need to forgive or ask forgiveness from?

Does my life have a sense of being a family on mission?

### Confident Witness

What challenges am I facing in discipling others?

Do I know and look to share God's story?

How often do I pray for a connection with my people of peace?

What stories can I share of God using me in the day-to-day?

### Kingdom Impact

How do I see my life as part of God's bigger story?

What passions/dreams has God

laced in me? What or who could help me with this?

What would the kingdom of God look like in my mission field?

What new opportunity is God opening for me to bring his Kingdom?

How am I being generous?

### Transformed

Let God transform you into a new person.
Romans 12:2

# PERSONAL DEVELOPMENT QUESTIONS

**Character – UP [relationship with God]**

How is my prayer life growing? Am I connecting and contending?

How am I expressing my praise and worship to God?

How much of my day is being led by the Holy Spirit. Am I walking in obedience?

How secure am I in God's love for me. Do I feel it?

Do I feel the pleasure of God, and know his joy?

Am I living in a state of inner peace, or are my thoughts or actions rooted in fear?

Which fruits of the spirit are growing in my life, and which am I struggling with?

How much of my life is self-motivated and how much is service orientated?

Do I love God's word and feed on it?

Which areas of my thoughts, words and actions are not glorifying God? What sin do I need to repent of?

**Character – IN [relationship with each other]**

How do I love the people in my community/small group?

Is my service motivated by love for others, or the need to be recognised / approved of?

Am I resting / exercising enough? How is my work life balance? Am I sleeping / eating well?

How are my relationships with my friends? Are they real and authentic? Do I feel connected / supported? Am I able to give and receive in them?

Do I keep my promises?

Is it easy for me to trust /be vulnerable to others?

Am I discipling others?

How well is my accountability relationship working?

Is my family happy?

Am I making my best contribution / do I know my strengths and gifts?

**Character – OUT (relationship with the world)**

Do I have a heart for the lost?

Am I praying for non-Christian friends?

How often do I share my faith?

Do I leave time for relationships with non-Christians?

Am I taking my opportunities with non-Christians?

Does my life carry a sense of mission?

Do I see work as a mission field?

Am I proud of the gospel or ashamed?

Do I find it easy to recognise those who are open to the gospel? Who are my people of peace?

Do I take risks in relationships?

Am I inviting people to Sunday services and to my community?

Am I confident to lead someone to Christ?

**Skills – UP**

How easy do I find it to help my Missional Community connect with God in some form of worship or prayer?

How easy do I find it to receive guidance for the next step in the life of my group?

How well can I talk to / teach a whole group "from the front"?

How well do I inspire a love for God's word?

Does my group share the vision God has given me for the Missional Community?

Do I feel relaxed about leading times of "Holy Spirit" led ministry?

How confident am I to lead a time of group prayer?

Is there an increasing sense of Christ-centredness in my group?

Is Jesus a normal part of our conversation?

How often do we break bread?

Are those I am leading growing in their discipleship?

**Skills - IN**

How well would others say I connect with people in my community / small group?

How do I know that members of my group feel cared for?

Are food and fun a regular part of our MC?

Am I modelling a generous heart in the sharing of resources? Are others following my example?

Am I effective at resolving conflict / handling confrontation?

Are new Christians being effectively followed up?

How is my group living as a community?

Have I defined my own boundaries well?

Am I flexible, coping with the unexpected?

Are there any difficulties in my relationships with co-leaders / assistant leaders?

Do I cope with over-dependant / difficult people?

Am I building a strong leadership team?

Am I too controlling as a leader?

**Skills - OUT**

Is my group growing in size and is it with existing Christians or new believers?

How welcoming is my group to new people?

Can all group members identify at least one person of peace they see as open to the gospel?

Do I have a vision for multiplication (budding off new groups)?

How am I developing and deploying and the gifts and abilities of my group members?

Are those I am discipling turning into effective disciple-makers?

Is my group effective in regularly doing 'out' activity, and how many different ways do we have of creating opportunities to meet unchurched people?

Does my group have a clear mission focus and do the members own it?

How often do we pray for the lost?

**Other books by Nic Harding:**

- Manifesto: A Blueprint for Missional Church (River Publishing & Media Ltd, 2012)

- Living On The Frontline: A Beginners Guide to Spiritual Warfare (CreateSpace Independent Publishing Platform; Second Edition, 2017)

**Books by Mike Breen** (all published by 3DM Publishing)

- Covenant and Kingdom (2010)

- Building a Discipling Culture (3rd ed., 2017)

- Multiplying Missional Leaders (2014)

- Leading Missional Communities (2014)

- Leading Kingdom Movements (2015)

- Huddle Leader Guide (2017)

- Family on Mission (co-authored with Sally Breen)(2015)

- Oikonomics (co-authored with Ben Sternke) (2015)

**Alan Hirsch:** The Forgotten Ways (Brazos Press, 2nd ed., 2016)

**Books by Caesar Kalinowski:**

- Transformed: A New Way of Being Christian (Zondervan, 2014)

- Small Is Big, Slow Is Fast: Living and Leading Your Family and Community on God's Mission (Zondervan 2014)

- Bigger Gospel: Learning to Speak, Live and Enjoy The Good News in

Every Area of Life (Missio Publishing, 2017)

- The Gospel Primer (workbook) (Missio Publishing, 2013)

**Books by Bob Rognlien:**

- Empowering Missional Disciples (3DM Publishing, 2016) [For leaders]

- A Jesus-Shaped life: Discipleship and Mission for Everyday People (3DM Publishing, 2016) [For members].

**Craig Millward, Disciplemaker** (3DM Publishing, 2015)

**Lynn Alexander,** Families, Children and God (Evangelista Media, 2012)

# ENDNOTES

1. The church that Jenny and I started in Liverpool in our front room in 1991. http://www.frontline.org.uk

2. https://www.premierchristianity.com/Past-Issues/2018/May-2018/I-visited-six-US-megachurches.-Here-s-what-I-learned

3. www.kairosconnexion.org

4. *Building a Discipling Culture* by Mike Breen, 3dm publishing 2011.

5. *Covenant and Kingdom* by Mike Breen, 3dm publishing 2010.

6. *The Rise of Christianity* by Rodney Stark

7. *Victory over the Darkness: Realize The Power of Your Identity in Christ* by Neil Anderson, 2nd edition, Bethany House Publishers, 2000.

*Steps to Freedom in Christ* by Neil Anderson, Monarch Books, 2003.

8. *You Can Change: God's Transforming Power for Our Sinful Behavior and Negative Emotions*, by Tim Chester, Chapter 5 p88. IVP, 2008.

9. *Bigger Gospel: Learning to Speak, Live and Enjoy the Good News in Every Area of Life* by Caesar Kalinowski, Missio Publishing, 2017.

10. *Multiplying Missional Leaders* by Mike Breen, p34 3dm publishing 2012.

11. *Bigger Gospel: Learning to Speak, Live and Enjoy the Good News in Every Area of Life* by Caesar Kalinowski, Missio Publishing, 2017.

12. *John Wesley: A Biography* by Stephen Tomkins, Lion Books; First Edition, 2003.

13. *Destined For the Throne* by Paul E Billheimer, Bethany House Publishers, 2005.

14. Generals International, *The Seven Mountains of Societal Influence*. https://www.generals.org/rpn/the-seven-mountains/

15. *Living on the Frontline* by Nic Harding, CreateSpace Independent Publishing Platform; Second Edition, 2017.

16. *The Hidden Power of Speaking in Tongues* by Mahesh Chavda, Destiny Image Publishers, 2013.

17. *Living on the Frontline* by Nic Harding, CreateSpace Independent Publishing Platform; Second Edition, 2017.

18. The account of Elijah's prayers can be found in 1 Kings 17 and 18.

19. One thing that will help mitigate this is if we are secure in our ambassador identity, as referred to in Chapter 1.

20. 'The4Points'. http://www.the4points.com/uk/

21. https://www.telegraph.co.uk/news/2017/09/14/church-england-christians-never-read-bible-survey-finds/

22. *Cracking Your Church's Culture Code: Seven Keys to Unleashing Vision and Inspiration* by Sam Chand, Jossey–Bass, 2010).

23. *Multiplying Missional Leaders* by Mike Breen, p83, 3dm publishing 2012

24. *Building a Discipleship Culture* by Mike Breen, ch. 6, 3dm publishing 2011

25. *Bigger Gospel* by Caesar Kalinowski, p115. (Missio Publishing 2017)

26. *You Can Change: God's Transforming Power for Our Sinful Behavior and Negative Emotions* by Tim Chester, IVP, 2008.

27. My rule of thumb is to count them "in" as disciples until they vote with their feet to let us know they are "out". For example, a young man was part of one of our in-home Alpha courses. He was very receptive to our input and seemed to be growing in his understanding of what it meant to follow Christ. After a while he backed away and stopped communicating with us. Eventually, we had to accept that he was no long wanting to pursue the life of a disciple, and whilst continuing to pray for him we had to "let go". We had counted him as in on the discipleship journey until he counted himself out.

28. *Bigger Gospel* by Caesar Kalinowski, p11 Missio Publishing 2017

29. *Building a Discipling Culture* by Mike Breen and Steve Cockram, Ch 2 3dm publishing 2011

30. *Building a Discipling Culture* by Mike Breen, p19. (3dm publishing 2011)

31. *Building a Discipling Culture* by Mike Breen, p79. 3dm publishing 2011

32. https://www.compellingtruth.org/law-of-first-mention.html
Some Bible students use the law of first mention as a guideline of study in which they find the first time a word, idea, or doctrine is introduced in Scripture to better understand the other references. The idea is that the first time it is mentioned will be the simplest, most understandable reference from which the others build.

33. *Transformed: A New Way of Being Christian* by Caesar Kalinowski, p 20. Zondervan.

34. http://www.moravian.org

35. *Building a Discipling Culture* by Mike Breen and Steve Cockram. Ch 11. 3dm publishing

36. *See The 59 One Anothers of the Bible* by Andrew Mason. http://www. smallgroupchurches.com/the-59-one-anothers-of-the-bible/ .

37. Some communities, extended families of believers, are not geographically based, and more network than neighborhood focused, i.e. focused on reaching out to a network or demographic of particular kind of people. The geographical proximity issue is less relevant in this situation.

38. http://www.the4points.com

39. The resources for this can be found at https://www.caesarkalinowski.com/ story-of-god-resources/

40. Alpha, https://alpha.org
Christianity Explored, https://christianityexplored.org
Story of God https://www.caesarkalinowski.com/story-of-god-resources/
Journeys videos http://www.disciplekit.org/resource/journeys-exploring-faith-in-the-21st-century/
Seven Signs of John, https://www.cmaresources.org/files/SevenSigns-Church3.0.pdf

41. I learned these three life-changing words, and this simple process of walking in step with the Holy Spirit, from Caesar Kalinowski

42. *Family on Mission* by Mike and Sally Breen, 3dm publishing

43. Ibid. Ch 1

44. *Family on Mission* by Mike and Sally Breen. p51., 3dm publishing.

45. www.moravian.org/todays-daily-text

46. *Small Is Big, Slow Is Fast: Living and Leading Your Family and Community on God's Mission* by Caesar Kalinowski, Zondervan, 2014.

47. The five love languages are: receiving gifts, quality time, words of

affirmation, acts of service, and physical touch. See *The Five Love Languages: The Secret to Love that Lasts* by Gary Chapman, Moody Press, 2009.

48. Caesar unpacks these six rhythms more fully in his book Transformed: A New Way of Being Christian, Zondervan, 2014. Caesar unpacks these six rhythms more fully in his book *Transformed: A New Way of Being Christian*, Zondervan, 2014.

49. Maslow's hierarchy of needs is a theory in psychology proposed by Abraham Maslow in his 1943 paper *A Theory of Human Motivation* in Psychological Review

50. *What's Gone Wrong With the Harvest?: A Communication Strategy for the Church and World Evangelism* by James Engel, Zondervan 1975.

51. http://www.hopetogether.org.uk

52. *Building a Discipling Culture* by Mike Breen and Steve Cockram, Ch 8. 3dm publishing 2011

53. *Movements that Change the World* by Steve Addison, IVP, 2011.

54. *Miraculous Movements* by Jerry Trousdale, Thomas Nelson publishing, 2012.

55. *Building a Discipling Culture* by Mike Breen and Steve Cockram, Ch 9  3dm publishing 2011

56. *Huddle Leader Guide: a path for your first year of leading huddle* by Mike Breen, 3DM Publishing, 2015.

57. *The Forgotten Ways* by Alan Hirsch, Ch 7. (Brazos press 2006, 2016)

58. Note that within a MC, an MC leader can afford to be much more open about who they take into their leadership development coaching huddle. This is in contrast to the 'invitation only' approach that is more appropriate at higher

levels of leadership. Within my MC, in the huddle I run, I open it to anyone who wants to learn to be a disciple-maker.

59. *Action-Centered Leadership* by John Adair, Gower Publishing 1979

60. A SWOT analysis is a study undertaken by an organization to identify its internal strengths and weaknesses, as well as its external opportunities and threats.

61. *The One Minute Manager* by KenBlanchard (William Morrow 2003)

62. https://www.form-uk.org

63. Although aimed at under 30 year olds, it has also had some much older people on it.

64. *The 7 Habits of Highly Effective People* by Steven R. Covey, (Simon & Schuster UK; Export edition, 2004).

65. Apostle, Prophet, Evangelist, Shepherd or Teacher.

66. *Gospel of the Kingdom: Scriptural Studies in the Kingdom of God* by George Eldon Ladd, Eerdmans; Later Printing edition, 1990.

67. And here I part from the Reconstructionist postmillennial views of Rushdoony and others from that camp from the 1980s, which continue to influence some of the 'kingdom now' theology that floats about some Charismatic churches.

68. *Prophet, Priest, and King: The Roles of Christ in the Bible and Our Roles Today* by Richard P Belcher, P & R Publishing Co Presbyterian & Reformed 30 Sept. 2016

69. 'Cinnamon Faith Action Audit 2016', http://www.cinnamonnetwork.co.uk/cinnamon-faith-action-audit/ .

70. 'Has Everyone Heard?' https://joshuaproject.net/resources/articles/has_everyone_heard

71. "The Story So Far", Gather. http://www.gather.global/about/

72. http://www.neighborhoodprayer.net

# Resources from Missio Publishing

### The Tangible Kingdom Primer

The *Tangible Kingdom Primer* is designed to help Christians, churches, and small groups get on the pathway of spiritual formation and missional engagement. This primer creates opportunities to experience authentic missional community step-by-step. It leads participants on a challenging 8-week journey toward an incarnational lifestyle and moves far beyond the typical small group experience. The *Tangible Kingdom Primer* is a great starting point when trying to transition existing small groups toward more incarnational and missional rhythms.

### The Gospel Primer

Many in our churches have spent years listening to sermons, studying theology and reading the Word of God, yet still feel intimidated or unable to naturally express the good news of the Gospel into normal life, conversations, and circumstances.

In community, over 8 weeks, the *Gospel Primer* will help you creatively learn: What is the Gospel? We'll look at the Story of God that illustrates the gospel throughout all of scripture. You'll learn how to form and tell your personal 'My Gospel Story' in a natural, yet powerful way. We'll also look at how the Gospel has actually given us a new identity in Christ and how to live out the truth of this gospel identity in the normal rhythms of everyday life. We know of no other resource that can help you gain such a useable understanding and practice of the Gospel in such a short period of time.

### The Justice Primer

Everyone's talking about social action and justice in the world. And for the first time in a long while, the Western church is looking for something designed to collectively point people outward and to give them a platform to do so together in community.

The *Justice Primer* is designed to be your guide on the journey of "learning to do right." It leads participants on a practical 8-week journey to put mission back into your small group or faith community. It's designed to help existing groups and churches begin or continue their journey toward being missional. If you desire to relearn the posture required to become missionaries in your context, and to equip others to engage culture through engaging the needs around them, the *Justice Primer* is your pilot.

# Additional Resources For Your Journey

In addition to our primer series, we recommend these other books from Missio Publishing and our authors.

### The Permanent Revolution Playbook

There is clear guidance from Scripture itself as to how the church can be the fullness of Christ in the world. A vital part of the answer to a renewed ministry matching the challenges we face, is found in Eph.4:1-16. The **Permanent Revolution Playbook** by Alan Hirsch and Tim Catchim is designed to introduce individual disciples or teams to their own, Jesus-given, vocational profile.

### BIVO: A Modern-Day Guide for Bi-Vocational Saints

The Gospel came to us through fully paid, barely paid, and mostly non-paid saints. The future of Kingdom life and ministry depends on God's people to finding creative pathways for leveraging all of life into one calling. **BiVO** by Hugh Halter is a story and a framework to help you find this leverage point whether you are a marketplace leader or ministry leader.

### Bigger Gospel: Learning To Speak, Live and Enjoy the Good News in Every Area of Life

Have you wished you could share your Christian faith with others in a natural way without feeling awkward or preachy? Have you ever longed for a faith that touched down more than just Sunday-to-Sunday leading up to one long afterlife?

**Bigger Gospel** will help you develop the confidence and grace to speak the truth in love—first to your self—and then with others in a way that is truly good news. Evangelism will no longer be a weird or stressful sales pitch and your discipleship and conversations will be supercharged with good news.

Missio Publishing is committed to resourcing the church with practical tools to help it engage more effectively in missional and incarnational ministry. To purchase the Primers and other resources, along with bulk discounts for churches, visit **missiopublishing.com**

CPSIA information can be obtained
at www.ICGtesting.com
Printed in the USA
BVHW031837140620
581350BV00003BA/191